SIR PHILIP SIDNEY
The Shepherd Knight

SIR PHILIP SIDNEY
The Shepherd Knight

ROGER HOWELL

LITTLE, BROWN AND COMPANY   BOSTON   TORONTO

LIBRARY OF CONGRESS CATALOG CARD NO. 68-24236

FIRST AMERICAN EDITION

Published simultaneously in Canada
by Little, Brown & Company (Canada) Limited

PRINTED IN THE UNITED STATES OF AMERICA

For my wife

ACKNOWLEDGEMENTS

Sir Philip Sidney has attracted the study of many scholars of the English Renaissance, and there exists a vast body of literature on him. There has not been, however, an attempt in recent years to write either a full biography of him or a study of his political career. This book is consciously the work of a historian, rather than a specialist in English literature, and the discussions of Sidney as a writer draw heavily on the research and ideas of others. But Sidney's importance to the Elizabethan world was felt in many areas besides literature and there has been a real need to place him in his political context.

One incurs many debts in writing a book, and it would be tedious to list all those who have at one time or another contributed to the author's thinking about his subject. But some do deserve special mention. The research for this book was begun while I was a Junior Research Fellow at St. John's College, Oxford; I am grateful to the President and Fellows for the many opportunities provided me. Continuation of the research was facilitated by grants from the Faculty Research Fund of Bowdoin College. To the librarians and staffs of the various libraries I used, particularly the Bodleian, the British Museum, and the Bowdoin College Library, I owe a great debt. In early stages of my research two former colleagues, now alas dead, helped with specific points: J. B. Leishman of St. John's College with Sidney's literary career, G. D. Bearce of Bowdoin College with overseas expansion. Keith Thomas of St. John's College and Charles Mitchell of Bryn Mawr College suggested possible lines of research. David Lander of Bowdoin, then the holder of a Research Fellowship at the College, helped me untangle some of the diplomatic history of the Elizabethan age. A. L. Rowse read portions of the manuscript and saved me from many errors. I should acknowledge a special debt to the work of M. W. Wallace, whose biography of Sidney has remained for years the standard account; without it, no student of Sidney could get far. Alan

Williams and Michael Sissons suggested the topic to me; I can only hope that the final product lives up to their expectations. For those errors and infelicities which remain, I am, of course, totally responsible.

I am grateful to the following authors and publishers for permission to quote from copyrighted material: The Clarendon Press, Oxford for C. Read, *Mr. Secretary Walsingham*; W. Ringler, ed., *The Poems of Sir Philip Sidney*; and N. Smith, ed., *Greville's Life of Sidney*; the Oxford University Press, London for J. A. van Dorsten, *Poets, Patrons, and Professors*; the Oxford University Press, New York for J. Purcell, *Sidney's Stella*; the Cambridge University Press for A. Feuillerat, ed., *Complete Prose Works of Sir Philip Sidney* and M. W. Wallace, *The Life of Sir Philip Sidney*; F. A. Yates for *John Florio*; Thomas Nelson and Sons, Ltd. for G. Shepherd, ed., *Apology for Poetry*; the Huntington Library, San Marino, California for T. Moffett, *Nobilis*; Rupert Hart-Davis, Ltd. for M. Wilson, *Sir Philip Sidney*; Routledge and Kegan Paul and the University of Chicago Press for F. A. Yates, *Giordano Bruno and the Hermetic Tradition*; Macmillan & Co., Ltd., the Macmillan Company of Canada, and St. Martin's Press for J. Buxton, *Sir Philip Sidney and the English Renaissance* and J. Buxton, *Elizabethan Taste*; the *New Statesman* for H. R. Trevor-Roper, 'The Last Magician'; Chatto and Windus, Ltd. for J. Bromley and E. Kossman, *Britain and the Netherlands* (article by R. B. Wernham, 'English Policy and the Revolt of the Netherlands'); and Martin Secker & Warburg, Ltd. for O. L. Dick, ed., *Aubrey's Brief Lives*.

The spelling has been modernised throughout with the exception of Sidney's poems which are printed in the authoritative version of W. Ringler.

ROGER HOWELL

Brunswick, Maine

CONTENTS

⤬

The Funeral of Philisides
the Shepherd Knight

PROLOGUE

Fellow in arms he was in their flowr'ing days
With that great shepherd, good Philisides;
And in sad sable did I see him dight,
Moaning the miss of Pallas' peerless knight.
With him he served, and watch'd, and waited late
To keep the grim wolf from Eliza's gate.

George Peele, *An Eglogue Gratulatorie to*
Robert, Earle of Essex (1589)

ൟ

'Farewell the worthiest knight that lived ... farewell the friend, beloved of all, that had'st no foe but chance.' So it is said the multitudes who crowded the streets to witness the funeral of the young Sir Philip Sidney cried as the procession wound its slow way past them. The great men of Elizabethan England lived in spectacular and ostentatious surroundings, and they took their leave of the world in a manner fully compatible with the style of their life. Yet few were buried with such pageantry, few were mourned with such genuine affection. In grandeur and ceremony his funeral rivalled those of peers of the realm, men far above his own social station. It was the measure of the importance which his death in a minor skirmish in the Netherlands had assumed in the minds of his countrymen.

Sidney's father-in-law, Sir Francis Walsingham, had 'spared not any cost to have this funeral well performed'.[1] When the great occasion was held on 16 February 1587, in grandeur it matched all that Walsingham could have desired for it. Walsingham himself had borne the great brunt of the expense because he was determined that his son-in-law and the idol of the Protestant party should be buried with honour commensurate with his position. As the procession wound its way through the streets from the Minories to St Paul's, the populace of London had their chance to show their respect. The 'streets all along were so thronged with people that the mourners had scarcely room to pass; the houses likewise were as full as they might be, of which great

[1] Superior figures refer to end-of-text notes.

multitude there were few or none that shed not some tears as the corpse passed them by'.[2] The official procession was large and impressive.[3] It was led by two conductors and gentlemen of the Inns of Court. Behind them came two conductors to the poor followed by thirty-two poor men to symbolise the years of Sidney's short life. The second group in the procession was symbolic of his military activity and martial death and represented the officers of his foot soldiers in the Low Countries. At the head were two sergeants of the band, their halberts trailing on the ground behind them. Following them were fifers and drummers, playing softly, and a youth trailing an ensign. Officers of his horse were also represented, two corporals, trumpeteers, the lieutenant of the horse Edward Crispe, and William Bulstrode trailing the guidon. Then came yeoman conductors and Richard Gwyne bearing aloft Sidney's standard with its motto *Vix ea Nostro Voco*, behind them servants of Sir Philip to the number of sixty clad in long black cloaks. A surgeon William Kelley and the physician Dr James who had attended him on his death-bed walked next in a pair. The loyal servant Griffin Madox, who had travelled with Sidney on his Grand Tour, acted as steward to the members of his house, leading some sixty esquires and twelve knights in dark gowns. Among the knights were companions in arms of Sidney and men famous in the story of Elizabethan England: Sir Francis Drake, Sir Henry Unton, Sir Thomas Perrott. Following them came the preacher and two chaplains. Proudly aloft was the pennon of Sidney's arms borne by James Skidmore. Sidney's horse for the field, led by a footman, was ridden by a page trailing a broken lance. The boy was Henry Danvers, once page to Sir Philip and later to become the Earl of Danby. A second horse followed, also led by a footman, 'the barbed horse whose caparison was with cloth of gold'; the page Daniel Batchiler carried a battle-axe with the head downward. After him came heralds displaying the symbols of Sidney's knighthood: the great banner, his spurs, gauntlets, helm and crest, his sword and targe, and his coat of arms. Then came Robert Cooke, Clarenceux King at Arms, who had drawn up the order of the procession, and Henry Lynley, the usher. Immediately behind them was borne the coffin itself. At the corners of the coffin, carrying banners, walked four of his near kindred: Henry and William Sidney, Edmund Pakenham, and Edmund Walsingham, while holding the corners of the pall were his 'dear

loving friends' Edward Wotton and Thomas Dudley in company
with the two surviving members of what Sidney had called the 'happy
blessed Trinity', Edward Dyer and Fulke Greville. Fourteen yeomen
bore the coffin which was covered with velvet and emblazoned with
Sidney's arms. His brother Robert Sidney walked immediately in the
train of the coffin as chief mourner, followed by assistants who were
knights and kinsmen, including his youngest brother Thomas, then
only nine years of age. Led by two gentlemen ushers there next came
representatives of the nobility of England: Huntingdon, Leicester,
Pembroke, Essex, Willoughby, and North, and behind them representatives of the States of Holland then resident in England. 'And to
solemnise the same there followed next unto the mourners the Lord
Mayor, Aldermen, and Sheriff of the City of London, riding in purple,
after them the Company of Grocers of which he was free, and lastly
certain young men of the city marching by three and three in black
cassocks with their shot, pikes, halberts, and ensigns trailing on the
ground to the number of three hundred.' The total size of the procession reached near to seven hundred; 'of the mourners every gentleman had a man, every knight two, some noblemen twelve, some more,
some less, as also sundry English captains of the Low Country with
divers other gentlemen that came voluntary'.

As the procession made its way to St Paul's the multitude watched
and cried out their lamentations. At the great west door of St Paul's,
where the mourners entered, the yeomen of the guard kept an honour
watch. The cenotaph and hearse stood in the main aisle, the pillars
along the aisle draped in black cloth bearing Sidney's arms. Following
the sermon and service and the burial of the body in the crypt, 'the
soldiers in the churchyard did by a double volley give unto his famous
life and death a martial *vale*'.

With Sir Philip buried, the crowds drifted away. For many, it had
been a spectacle, no more. But for some, and their number would
greatly increase in the succeeding years, it had been an event of the
greatest importance. For once dead, Sidney took on a fame far wider
than he had enjoyed in life. The central event of his career had been
his death; his arguments for England's policy had been listened to only
haltingly while he was alive, but they would inspire now that he was
dead. The great and the near great competed to honour his name;
verses in celebration of what he was taken to stand for were published

both in England and abroad.[4] Few are of lasting poetic value but they
are indicative of the feeling of loss. And with their publication the
legend of Sidney as the perfect hero knight of militant Christianity
grew and prospered. He was 'the noblest plant that might from East
to West be found',[5] and with his passing many came to feel that something vital had been lifted from their lives.[6]

> Knowledge her light hath lost; Valor hath slain her Knight:
> Sidney is dead! Dead is my friend! Dead is the world's delight.

Forgotten was the Sidney of quick temper, forgotten the fact that his
career contained more of promise than it had of result. Remembered
was the shepherd knight, the hero of England who had kept Eliza's
foes at bay even while she pursued a policy of greater caution and
would not face them outright.

Symbolic truth is often more potent than the actuality it has been
designed to illustrate. So it is with the life of Sir Philip Sidney. The
picture which we have of Sidney is a convention, a figure of symbolic
truth illustrating a moral of which we are no longer completely aware
but which we honour just the same. For who was Philip Sidney? He
was the shepherd knight, the perfect Protestant hero, the author of
poetry which set Elizabethan lyricism a-song, the gallant who, mortally
wounded, offered his cup of water to one with a greater necessity than
his own. Was he in actuality all these things—or was he both more and
less? The major part of the biographical fascination of Sidney lies in
the attempt to answer that question.

To his contemporaries there was no doubt about the matter,
although we should also remember that for them his death was something greater than his life. Sidney had done some notable things, but
he had not startled the world like a Drake, nor even been a quietly
successful administrator like his own father. Related by blood and by
political inclination to many of the great men of the realm, his own
political career is a very negligible affair indeed compared with theirs.
One could not write a political narrative of Elizabethan England and
leave out his uncle, the Earl of Leicester, or his father-in-law, Sir
Francis Walsingham, but one could, without too many qualms, write
that history and leave out Philip, or perhaps relegate him to a footnote.

What, then, did his contemporaries see in him that made him at his death the subject of such mourning and regret? Clearly it was not the passing of a proven statesman (he was only thirty-two) or of a proved warrior (he was killed in his first campaign). Equally clearly it was not the passing of the great writer which many now consider him to have been, for the works by which he is best known had not appeared in print at the time of his death. Scholars have pointed out that among the large group of Latin poems written to Philip Sidney or in his memory the concern was almost uniformly with the man, not with his literary works. The only exceptions were some incidental remarks about his multilingual ability, an oblique reference to *Arcadia* in one poem, and a more direct reference in a second.[7] What his contemporaries mourned was what Sir Philip seemed to be or might have been. They mourned the perfect hero of Protestant chivalry, the knight in spotless armour, or, even more directly, the knight in the guise of the gentle shepherd. Sidney had been, even in his own lifetime, displayed and heralded as the Shepherd Knight. There is perhaps an almost direct reference to this in his work *Arcadia*. There at an annual tournament appeared an Iberian knight Philisides.[8]

Against him came forth an Iberian whose manner of entering was with bagpipes instead of trumpets, a shepherd boy before him for a page, and by him a dozen apparalled like shepherds for the fashion, though rich in stuff, who carried his lances, which though strong to give a lancely blow indeed, yet so were they coloured with hooks near the mourn, that they prettily represented sheephooks. His own furniture was dressed over with wool, so enriched with jewels artificially placed, that one would have thought it a marriage between the lowest and the highest. His impresa was a sheep marked with pitch, with this word, Spotted to be known. And because I may tell you out his conceit (though that were not done till the running for that time was ended) before the ladies departed from the windows, among them there was one (they say) that was the Star whereby his course was only directed.

The echoes of Philip Sidney in this passage are overwhelming. The name Philisides itself is an obvious case in point. Spenser had used it to refer to Sidney in *Ruins of Time*; his one-time companion-traveller Ludovic Bryskett had likewise used it in a similar context in a volume of elegies on Sidney's death.[9] The motto 'Spotted to be known' was one that was clearly associated with Sidney himself; a gloss on it, 'No blemish is found on the peerless body: there is and can be no place for spots', points out its message.[10] And there is the reference to the lady who was his Star; this may be purely conventional language, but it is also remarkably evocative of Stella, whom Sidney in the guise of Astrophel honoured in his famous sonnet sequence.[11]

The character of Philisides the Shepherd Knight was one which seemed to suit Philip Sidney particularly well. It conformed to his own aspirations to play the role of the Protestant activist hero; it coincided equally well with the aspiration of his friends and relatives. As early as 1579 this identification was being established. In that year Spenser dedicated *The Shepheardes Calender* to him and in the text used extensively the shepherd formula to convey a distinctly Protestant theological moral. Within two years after this the annual Accession Day tilts had become an established feature of Elizabethan life. These yearly ceremonials seem to have been to a large degree the idea and invention of Sir Henry Lee, who appeared in them up till 1590 as the Queen's Champion. A very definite part of his purpose and plan for the celebrations had been the use of imagery and ceremonial that would build up in the terms of chivalrous romance the political and theological position of Protestant England. There can be little doubt that the emergence of Sidney as the Shepherd Knight was more than mere show or literary convention. Sidney was as aware as Lee that serious meanings could be conveyed through the imagery of chivalry and that it was indeed possible to translate the Catholic chivalry of the Middle Ages into a Protestant device in the sixteenth century. Of a fictional tournament, he was to comment that it was 'such as carried riches of knowledge upon the stream of delight',[12] and it is certain that in the world of the imagery of the tilts he was seeking to give visual representation to what he and his colleagues felt would be the best policy for his country.

It is precisely in this respect that his death became important. He was a young man of great promise, of seeming perfection, but one who was cut off before that promise could be fully realised, before that perfection could be completed. He was one of the very few Elizabethans of gentle birth who died in battle, and he died as a hero for the international Protestant cause, resisting its greatest enemy, Spain. Because of this he became a symbol, and his life and exploits were recalled to memory in subsequent Accession Day celebrations. At the first

Accession Day tournament after his death, a brief but solemn remembrance of him was held,[13] to illustrate dramatically the loss of England's Shepherd Knight who had so bravely defended his Queen, his religion, and his country both by deed and writing. Four years later, at one of the most spectacular tilts of the reign, the one at which the ageing Sir Henry Lee resigned his post as Queen's Champion to the Earl of Cumberland, there were further and significant echoes of the Sidney theme. Among some manuscript material relating to that tilt is a volume which contains copies of some of the verses from Sidney's *Old Arcadia*. On the cover is the inscription 'Sir Henry Lee delivered being champion to the Queen delivered to my Lord Cumberland deli by William Simons'.[14] It is possible that the inscription has nothing to do with the present contents of the volume. It is just as possible, however, that Lee, the Queen's Champion, intended to pass on to his successor Cumberland these copies of Sidney's own verses as a representation of the 'scriptures' of the Shepherd Knight, for it is known that books were sometimes given at the tilts.[15] In any case, there was a far more direct echo of Sidney at the 1590 celebrations. At Sidney's death his mantle as the the hero knight was conspicuously passed on to the young Earl of Essex. Sidney himself had helped to establish that identification when he bequeathed 'my beloved and much honoured Lord, the Earl of Essex, my best sword'.[16]

This sort of symbolism was much in evidence at the 1590 tilt. Essex appeared dressed in black armour and was accompanied by an all-black pageant of followers. It was a public demonstration of the mourning for the hero now dead for over four years. One writer described Essex and his company in the following terms:[17]

> Young Essex, that thrice honourable earl
> Y-clad in mighty arms of mourners dye,
> And plume as black as is the raven's wing
> That from his armour borrowed such a light
> As boughs of yew receive from shady stream:
> His staves were such, or of such hue at least,
> As are those banner staves that mourners bear,
> And all his company in funeral black,
> As if he mourn'd to think of him he miss'd,
> Sweet Sidney, fairest shepherd of our green,
> Well-letter'd warrior, whose successor he
> In love and arms had ever vow'd to be.

It would be foolish to dismiss all this as something completely super-ficial. What Sidney stood for was an ideal very real to the Protestant activists of his age. Although it may be true that he was not a 'great' man by concrete tests of achievement, he was very plainly the *beau ideal* of his age.

It is perfectly true, of course, that this passion for the trappings of chivalry and for the ceremonial aspects of what had once been a very different thing was not a development confined to the Protestant circle nor even to England. It has been accurately said that something like an imaginative re-feudalisation of culture was going on at this time all over Europe; Ariosto's *Orlando Furioso* is a perfectly clear Italian manifestation of precisely the same sort of thing. Feudalism as a working mechanism for the organisation of society was dead in all but its completely misleading Marxist sense, but its forms were still very much alive, and they were the source of and vehicle for genuine emotional feeling and expression. In countries like France and England, where new powerful monarchies were making their marks, this chivalrous ceremonial was carefully wedded to the task of focusing what amounted to religious loyalty on the national monarch. Queen Elizabeth was being carefully built up as a sort of vestal virgin of the reformed religion.[18] In short, the chivalric revival in which Sidney played such a part suited the world of Elizabethan England almost perfectly. It emphasised the majesty of the monarch, it glorified the knights who sought to serve her, and it reflected the hierarchical view of society which prevailed.

It was all this in the case of Sidney, and it was more, for in dealing with Sidney's chivalric role we are dealing with a whole outlook and way of life. Sidney was not just a chivalrous hero; he was to many the archetype of the hero, and he sought in his own life and works to give as serious a representation of this ideal as his friends sought to provide one in and through his image after his death. What Sidney and his circle added to the tradition of chivalry was the element of active Protestantism. And here the shepherd was no doubt a useful symbol. It had religious overtones with its echoes of the Good Shepherd. He was gentle, he was beneficent, and he tended faithfully to his master's business, preserving his charges against any dangerous and popish wolf, risking his life for any helpless ones who strayed. And, too, he represented the potential purity of the country against the possible corruption of the court. The shepherd would set true duty and honour above the Machiavellian statecraft and fawning sycophancy of the court; he would feel that his greatest honour lay in the preservation of his faith, that which was most dear to him, and in his empire of England as the bastion of that faith.

Sidney seemed to his contemporaries all that was required of such a figure; at least he became all with his death. But even before he had died his friends and relations were pushing him forward into this prominent position. To Edmund Spenser he was 'the president of noblesse and of chivalry'.[19] His own father expressed a very similar emotion when he recorded of his eldest son that 'he is a rare ornament of this age, the very formula that all well-disposed young gentlemen of our court do form also their manner and life by . . . he hath the most rare virtues that ever I found in any man'.[20] When his companion Fulke Greville came to write a memoir of him it was in this way that he too saw him: it was as Philisides, the Protestant knight, the shepherd, the statesman, the scholar. And we should respect that picture, for it is an important one. Though we now look on Sidney primarily as a poet, in doing so we miss what to him and his friends had been the whole point of his life, even if we do see the value of his work. Sidney has been called a typical or representative Elizabethan. He was not. No ideal can ever be typical, and Sidney was a consciously created ideal. He was, of course, not perfect; his own character had its faults, particularly a quick temper; his policy, while daring, bordered on the simple-minded in its ignorance of the facts of political life. But he stood for the goal at which many of the greatest Englishmen of one of England's greatest ages aimed. How did he achieve this prominence? The answer is not a simple one.

It was suggested earlier that the political history of Elizabethan England might be written without the mention of Philip Sidney. In a conventional sense this is true, but if we are to understand what the great Elizabethans like Leicester and Walsingham really sought we find ourselves turning back on the symbol of their policy, Philip the Shepherd Knight, and we find that we must take him far more seriously than we have been inclined to do. Fulke Greville commented that he hoped his memoir of Sidney would be a beacon to the policy-makers of his age.[21] 'I am delighted in repeating old news of the ages past, and will therefore stir up my drooping memory touching this man's worth, power, ways, and designs. to the end that in the tribute I owe him, our nation may see a sea-mark, rais'd upon their native coast, above the level of any private Pharos abroad, and so by a right meridian line of their own, learn to sail through the straits of true virtue, into a calm and spacious ocean of humane honour.'

Like Greville, we too must try to approach him in this manner and try to see him as an historical personage, not simply as a shadowy figure composing fine poetry.

PART ONE

The Courtier-Diplomat

INTRODUCTION:
DUDLEY, SIDNEY, AND THE POLITICS OF
TUDOR ENGLAND

Remember, my son, the noble blood you are
descended of by your mother's side and think
that only by virtuous life and good action
you may be an ornament to that illustrious
family.   Henry Sidney to Philip Sidney (1566)

The decade that witnessed the birth of Philip Sidney was one of the
most disturbed in the history of sixteenth-century England, indeed in
the entire history of the realm. Against a background of recurrent
financial difficulties and tensions, influenced by a high degree of
mobility within the social structure, politics became a sordid battle
between conflicting factions. Over all hovered the uncertainty of the
religious situation. England had broken with Rome in the reign of
Henry VIII, moved towards radical Protestantism in the reign of his
son Edward VI, reverted to Catholicism under his daughter Mary.
Issues of foreign policy and the backbiting of political factions were
closely intertwined with the religious manœvrings. The emergence of
Spain as the champion of resurgent Catholicism posed a considerable
threat to England's precarious claim to be an empire, a self-governing
political unit in its own right.[1] Philip of Spain had shared the crown
of England with his wife Mary Tudor and he was unlikely to let it slip
without protest back to Protestantism. Increasing tensions in the
Netherlands added yet another ingredient to the problems facing
statesmen and politicians; in England there was a realisation how much
the nation's commercial interests depended on trade with the Low
Countries.[2] To many countries the threat of the Counter-Reformation
in the form of Spanish military power was genuine. The Protestant
revolt had shaken Catholicism but not broken it, and already there
was talk of the necessity of forming a general Protestant League to pull

together the diverse elements of the Reformation in a common cause of defence against the Catholic menace.

The family into which Philip Sidney was born was intimately connected with many of these tumultuous developments. On his mother's side he was a Dudley. Years later Sidney was to write: 'I am a Dudley in blood that Duke's daughter's son and do acknowledge though in all truth I may justly affirm that I am by my father's side of ancient and always well-esteemed and well-matched gentry yet I do acknowledge I say that my chiefest honour is to be a Dudley.'[3] At the time of his birth at quarter past five in the morning of St Andrew's Day, 1554,[4] to have been a Dudley must have seemed something of a mixed blessing. While the name of Dudley was written prominently across the records of sixteenth-century England, misfortune had seemed to be its inevitable companion. In the reign of Henry VII Edmund Dudley had risen to a high level in the King's service by exploiting his talents as a ruthless uncoverer of royal rights. Perhaps his reputation for avarice has been exaggerated, perhaps he did truly have the best interests of the commonwealth at heart, but he had none the less gone to the block after his royal master's death, an offering of peace to an enraged nation by the young King Henry VIII who was busily repudiating the rapacity of his father's reign.[5]

The career of Edmund Dudley was a salutary example of the vicissitudes of fortune in court service. The career of Philip's grandfather John Dudley, the Duke of Northumberland, was more spectacular, but equally salutary.[6] Rising to power and influence during the reign of the boy King Edward VI, Northumberland was able to gain virtual control of the country for a short time. But his rise to the top illustrated clearly the dangers of the internecine struggle by the governing classes of England. His rule was nothing but factious magnate rule, and when his slippery hold on power was threatened by the death of the boy king he staked all on the desperate expedient of attempting to bypass the established succession in his own family's favour. He persuaded the dying youth Edward VI to set aside the will of his father Henry VIII, to declare both of his sisters, Mary and Elizabeth, bastards, and to pass the throne on to the daughter of the Duke of Suffolk, Lady Jane Grey. Lady Jane was married to Dudley's son Guilford. When the King died, Lady Jane was duly proclaimed. A talented and sprightly young lady, her reign was too short to leave any impression but pathos. As she was proclaimed ruler of England, Mary Tudor was proclaimed in Norfolk to which she had fled for support. The popular backing for the Tudor line was far stronger than Dudley had gambled on, and his flirtation with altering the succession ended in swift tragedy. Along with the innocent victim of his plotting, Lady Jane, whose only wish was to go home once the pathetic charade had come to an end, Dudley and the rest of the conspirators were led to the Tower as enemies of the realm, and Mary Tudor was acknowledged to be Queen.

John Dudley is not only to be associated with this political catastrophe; he is also linked to the troublesome religious differences of the period. Opposition to the Henrician Reformation had been surprisingly slight. By the reign of Edward VI, however, the political revolution had become a religious movement, fostered by ardent Protestants in positions of power but in the main running out of government control in that almost certain fashion in which revolutions always outrun those who think they can control them. The *furor* created by religion cut two ways. It is clear that as the Edwardian Reformation became more openly and radically Protestant it became less uniformly accepted.[7] But religious ferment and the emergence of Protestantism in England worked in another way as well. While there were martyrs to the old faith, there were also converts to the new. The winds of Protestantism were blowing in England, and this was of great importance to the background of Philip Sidney, for his family was associated with the Protestant tide, at least on the Dudley side. It was one of the measures of Sidney's affection for his Dudley connection that he would emerge as a more out-spoken advocate of the reformed religion than many of his contemporaries.

With the failure of Lady Jane Grey, however, both the Protestant cause and the Dudley fortunes suffered a severe setback. On 18 August 1553 John Dudley, Duke of Northumberland, and his eldest son appeared before a jury to confess that they were guilty of treason. Four days later he went the same way to the scaffold which his father had gone some forty-three years before. The eldest son, John, was also condemned, but lived on at the pleasure of the new Queen. Dudley's wife and the rest of his children suffered too. The Duchess was soon released, but her fortune was much reduced and her prospects almost obliterated. The youngest son, Henry, followed her into freedom, apparently because of his age. Several others of the family remained in prison, and her son Guilford was executed the following February after Wyatt's attempted rebellion against Mary had nearly succeeded and then failed. Two remaining sons, Ambrose and Robert, the later Earl of Leicester, continued in confinement. They and their brother John were finally released in October 1554, still standing attainted of high treason; John was to survive only three days after his release. On leaving the Tower with his scarce three days of life remaining to him, John had gone directly to Penshurst, the home of Sir Henry Sidney, and there he died five weeks before Philip Sidney was born. His choice of Penshurst was an obvious one, for there, for the moment, lay the hopes of the Dudley family. Of thirteen children from this generation of Dudleys, only five now survived: three sons, Robert, Ambrose, and Henry, and two daughters. Of the daughters, the eldest was Mary, the wife of Sir Henry Sidney and soon to be mother of Philip.

On his father's side Sidney's family background was less spectacular, but it was not inconsiderable; more to the point at the moment, it was a family which managed to adjust to the changes in government with less pain than the Dudleys. The families were quite similar in background. Just as the Dudleys were recent arrivals at the top of the governing class, so were the Sidneys. The very newness of their status is best confirmed by the passion with which they attempted to conceal it.[8] If one were to trust the genealogies of the family as they were prepared for Sir Henry Sidney he would find the family descended from respectably old stock. According to these documents, the founder of the Sidney family in England was one William de Sidne, a knight who is represented as having been in the service of Henry II before he became King. There is, in fact, no real evidence that William de Sidne ever existed. When Sir Henry Sidney, anxious to provide his family with a suitably elevated heritage, paid £6 in 1568 to 'the Heralds at London for my Lord's Petigrewe'[9] he received ample for his expenditure in the form of a spurious genealogy and forged documents to support it. The deception was eminently successful; although Sir Henry was doubtless aware of the nature of the documents, Philip believed firmly in the truth of his French ancestry. The later stages of the genealogy were more accurate. It would not have been overly difficult, in fact, to trace in the family deeds the real origins of the

Sidney family. No chamberlain of Henry II would then appear as the founder, but instead a John de Sydenie, who was a Surrey yeoman in the reign of Edward I. Yeoman status was not negligible, but the fortunes of the family before the fifteenth century were not such as to suit the elevated ideas of the later Sidneys. Following the middle of the fifteenth century, their position began steadily to improve. A fortunate marriage was made between Nicholas Sidney and Anne Brandon, aunt of a later brother-in-law to Henry VIII. Their son William was the real architect of the family fortune. He proved to be a distinguished warrior both on land and sea during the reign of Henry VIII and was knighted for his services to his monarch on Flodden Field in 1513 following the English defeat of the Scots. Like many of the new men of the age, he profited from the spoilation of the Church which occurred in Henry VIII's time. Moreover, he was rising rapidly in royal favour. At the birth of Edward VI he was appointed tutor, chamberlain, and steward to the heir apparent, and after his young protégé became King he received additional grants of land, including Penshurst, which was to become the family's main seat.

William Sidney had only one son, but Henry proved to be an exceptional man and developed into one of the most selfless and able servants of the Tudor state. Early in life, he was introduced into the court service; no doubt as a result of his father's position as tutor and steward to Edward VI, Henry Sidney was selected as a companion for him.[10] His prospects seemed very bright indeed, and they were crowned by his marriage to Mary Dudley, daughter of the Duke of Northumberland. There can be little doubt that the marriage was, like so many marriages among the important people of the period, an arranged match, but it seems as well to have been a match which well fitted the two; the marriage was a happy one.

Shortly before the death of Edward VI, then, the prospects of the Sidneys, like those of the Dudleys, looked considerable. We have seen how the death of the young King brought temporary ruin on the heads of the Dudleys; how did it affect the Sidneys? The answer is that it left them surprisingly unscathed. Despite the fact that Henry Sidney had been so high in the boy King's favour, despite the fact that as one who recognised the validity of the succession of Lady Jane Grey he stood as technically guilty of treason as the Dudleys, despite all this Henry Sidney was among the first who received pardon at the hands of the new Queen. This can be attributed to several things. Probably political acumen is one; Sir Henry Sidney did not actively take part in the conspiracy over Lady Jane Grey. More directly influential, perhaps, were his family connections. While he had acted as companion to Edward VI, another member of his family, his niece Jane Dormer, had been present as well, and she provided an active friend at court, for she was Queen Mary's favourite lady-in-waiting.[11] Moreover, two of Sir Henry's sisters, Mabel and Elizabeth Sidney, had died while in the service of Mary, and they had much commended themselves to the new Queen, not only on account of their loyalty to her person but also because they were faithful members of the Catholic Church.

So it was that Mary was willing to overlook the close link between the Sidneys and the Dudleys, overlook the fact that Mary Sidney had been the one to tell Lady Jane of her accession to the throne, overlook all and welcome the Sidneys, if not into the royal pleasure at the fullest at least out of the circle of the damned. Sir Henry responded well to this, at least from the point of view of the government. His loyalty to the state was always greater than the fixity of his religious inclinations, and during the Catholic reaction under Mary, Sir Henry displayed complete conformity in civil and religious matters. In 1554 Sir Henry was high enough in royal favour to be part of the embassy which went to Spain to fetch Philip, Mary's fiancé, and several months later his offices under the crown and several grants of land were confirmed.

Such was the situation when Philip Sidney was born in November 1554. Yet his christening was to show that the Dudley link, far from forgotten by the family, was preserved even in the days of their service to Catholic Mary and her Spanish husband. The godparents at the christening ceremony were an ill-assorted trio. 'The great King, Phillipe of Spayne' was chosen as one of the godfathers. His presence indicated something of the Sidney acquiescence in the new order, and the naming of the infant heir after him indicates even more. It was an ironic coupling. The dour, powerful, industrious Philip of Spain was to be for much of Philip Sidney's life *the* great enemy, the scourge of Protestant Christendom, the oppressor of the true faith. Certainly Sidney could have learned little from this godparent; their direct contact was of the slightest, their personalities almost completely opposed. Yet it should not be thought that this odd coupling was without its repercussions. The black grandeur of Philip II was not untouched by nor ignorant of the path that his godson followed. In the years that passed, many references to the glittering career of the youth crossed the busy desk of the Spanish King and increasingly he became aware of his own godson as one of those who were most devoted to thwarting the plans which Philip of Spain himself held most dear. And yet when Sidney died even Spain paused to wonder at what had been taken from them. Mendoza, the Spanish ambassador who was expelled from England for plotting against the Queen, mourned the loss that all Christendom had suffered in the passing of such a hero,[12] and across the dispatch which brought him the news of Sidney's death the great Philip of Spain scribbled the laconic note, 'He was my godson'.[13] For a man apparently so untouched by everyday emotion Philip II said a great deal in those brief words. Both anger and pride are mingled in them, and it has been truly said that they constitute a far greater tribute to Philip Sidney than all the fine words, eulogies, and lamentations heaped on him by his friends and supporters.[14]

These days were in the future; at the present moment of the christening, however, some foreshadowing of them can perhaps already be discerned in the other godparents. The second godfather was the Earl of Bedford; like Sir Henry Sidney, he was a man with Dudley connections who survived the changes introduced by Mary and the catastrophe which had attended the Dudley family. He was an old man with but few months to live; behind him lay a long and distinguished career of public service. He had been high in the favour of Henry VIII and had held the office of Lord Privy Seal in the reigns of both Edward VI and Mary. Like Sir Henry, he had aided in the negotiations which resulted in the marriage of Mary and Philip, but also like Sir Henry, he had remained a close friend of the Dudleys. The godmother was a bolder and even more indicative choice—Jane, the Duchess of Northumberland. Although only forty-six years old, she was prematurely aged and in fact had only weeks to live, but what was of the greatest significance about her was that she was not only the widow of an executed traitor but had been one of his most active abettors in the desperate game of advancing the Dudley fortunes. Thus it was that Philip was christened with the old, the new, and the yet to come represented around him. From his godfather of Spain he would inherit little save his name. From his godfather of England he could learn of a tradition of service to the monarchy; while from his god-mother he inherited a taste for the Dudleys.

The months that followed Sidney's birth were not entirely easy ones for the family, despite the fact that Sir Henry was apparently safely installed in the service of the state. Even in the warmth of favour, Sir Henry seems to have been ill-at-ease. 'Neither liking nor liked as I had been, I fancied to live in Ireland and to serve as Treasurer',[15] and to Ireland he went. In April 1556 he was appointed Vice-Treasurer and General Governor of all the King's and Queen's revenues in the kingdom of Ireland. In the strenuous business of governing that nation he was able to pass away the latter and more disastrous half of Mary's brief reign.

When Sir Henry finally returned to England for more than a fleeting visit his son and heir was nearly five years old and a new Queen had been on the throne for almost a year. The accession of Queen Elizabeth marked a notable change for the families of Dudley and Sidney. The Dudleys, especially Robert, a boyhood friend of the Queen, were in high favour once again, and the temporary setback to their ambitions which the reign of Philip and Mary had caused was very definitely a thing of the past. Mary Sidney, as a Dudley, was also in great favour and was called to the court; for himself, Sir Henry was able to make the same easy adjustment to the new conditions that he had made earlier when Mary came to the throne.

The very glory of the Elizabethan age tends to blind modern readers to the precariousness of the position in which England stood at the commencement of the reign. England was far indeed from being a great power, especially when compared with Spain and France. The hold of Elizabeth on the affections of her nation was certainly strong, but her effective grasp on government was less certain. We tend to forget how ramshackle the Tudor state was. Elizabeth inherited all the contradictions which plagued Henry VIII and Edward VI. The finances of the realm were in severe disorder, and only a cautious foreign policy involving the avoidance of a major war was a possibility. The foreign situation itself was, however, not entirely satisfactory. In 1559 the French and the Spanish declared peace and ended the hostilities between them, and both of the Catholic powers sheltered potential rivals for the crown. Philip II of Spain was anxious to preserve the hold on England which he had established through marriage with

Mary Tudor, while in France Mary Queen of Scots, who had married into the powerful Guise family, was not unambitious for the throne either. Nor was the internal settlement of England, especially in the matter of religion, a completely happy one. Nowadays it is common to talk of the *via media* of the Anglican Church, of the comprehensiveness which enabled it to draw to its fold a wide perspective of religious opinion, and somehow to attribute all of this to the splendid common sense of the English people. How different from this were the realities of the case. England was driven to the Protestant position from political motives. The Elizabethan church settlement was something far less than a splendid compromise; it would be a long time before the Church of England would obtain real prestige. For the moment it was a Church which failed to attract any dominant loyalty and was harassed from one side by the Catholics, from the other by the Puritans.[16]

If one looked elsewhere one could see other tensions. It was no peaceful, secure, and happy England that Philip Sidney grew up in. The youthful hope of the Dudley faction, Sidney knew that his proper role was to be a courtier and a servant to his Queen and country. It was a lesson impressed on him from his earliest schooling. Yet he knew, too, both from the perusal of the past history of his family and from a glance at the situation of Europe, that such a role was not an easy one to play. In the last stage of his formal education, his Grand Tour, he had come under the tutelage of a Protestant statesman, Hubert Languet.[17] Languet's hopes were built on the religious and family tradition inherited by Philip. He inspired Philip's sense of duty to country and religion; he fostered in him a loyalty to the conception of a Protestant League. When Sidney was ready to fulfil family ambition by entering the life of the court he had much to draw on, but he was soon to find that this heritage of family, religion, and service to sovereign contained elements that were not always compatible.

Chapter 1

THE YOUNG COURTIER

For wherever he travelled not so much the
name as the authority of Sidney seemed to go.
Moffett, *Nobilis* (1594)

What excellency of understanding and what
staidness was in him at those years.
Bryskett, *A Discourse of Civill Life* (1606)

When Sidney had left on his continental tour in 1572 he had been
described as 'young and raw' by the Earl of Leicester, who knew him
well and cherished great hopes for him. That description would no
longer suffice to characterise the young man, still short of his twenty-
first birthday, who had returned on the ship from Antwerp. There can
be little doubt that Sidney aroused high hopes on the part of his
friends, and especially of the Leicester circle. In the year in which
Sidney returned to England Thomas Drant addressed a poem to
Leicester and in it he expressed the aspirations for Sidney which many
now felt:[1]

> Sic redeat toto laudatus ab orbe Philippus,
> Spes generis tanti, praestans Sydneia proles

In fact, the youth had already taken on many of the attributes which
would single him out as the embodiment of the Protestant cause. The
power of his personality is obvious from all that can be read about
him, yet it is now difficult, even impossible, to recapture what it was in
Sidney that enabled him to move with ease and to elicit respect from
the most influential men of his time, even when he was young and so
obviously lacking in experience. Perhaps the answer is that he made
up for what he lacked in experience by the power of his intellect, that
the natural grace and open charm of his person compensated for his
lack of experience of court life, and that we exaggerate his youth,

adopting modern standards where they are not applicable. We might remember that twenty-one would not seem so young to a promising Elizabethan courtier, especially one who could refer to his sovereign, then not yet forty-two, as 'somewhat advanced in years'.[2]

Philip came to court life well armed with advice from Languet. One of the last letters that Languet wrote to Sidney before he sailed for home had advised him on both his friends and his demeanour:[3]

When you reach England, see to it that you cultivate the good-will of Cecil, who is friendly to you and who can smooth your path in every way. In no way will you be able to secure his favour more certainly than by your affection for his children, or at least by pretending that you love them. But remember that an astute old man who has been made wise by his long experience in affairs of state will easily see through the pretences of youth. It will also be to your advantage to cultivate the friendship of Mr Walsingham. . . . Men are wont to feel warmly towards youths who, they see, are seeking out the society of the wise. . . . To sum up, it is necessary that he who wishes to live above contempt in the courts of powerful Kings should moderate his pretensions, digest many injuries, avoid with the utmost care every occasion for quarrelling, and cultivate the good-will of those in whose hands rests his fortune. But I shall cease to weary you further, for you understand all these things better than I.

Sidney, it should be admitted, did not follow this advice to the full. It is one of the problems which confront his biographer that a youth of admitted and admired talent should so long have hung on the fringes rather than gaining posts of major importance. The reason was not that the Queen or Burghley were alone blind to the abilities so widely recognised by others. More precisely, it was just those abilities—including his basic honesty and devotion to principle—which would on the whole keep him on the fringe. The more that Sidney was to emerge as a spokesman for the Protestant cause, the more he was to advocate its importance to foreign relations, the less a cautious Queen and circumspect minister, who together played a delicate game of international balancing from the less than impressive stronghold of desperate government finance, were likely to welcome either him or his ideas. Nor could Philip, any more than his father, flatter and cajole when matters of principle were involved. When Philip felt strongly about matters he tended to speak on them, a characteristic little endearing to a Queen who was less than receptive to unsolicited advice about her policy, although it was a trait which commended Sidney increasingly to the Protestant activists of the country.

When Sidney rejoined his family in England it cannot be said that their fortunes were at their highest. Shortly before he returned, his sister Ambrosia had died at Ludlow Castle and had been buried in the parish church of the town. Moreover, the financial plight of the family appears to have been near desperate. There are a number of letters from Lady Sidney in this period which reflect both her poor health and her monetary problems. Leicester, whom we might assume would have been a source of aid, appears to have taken little interest in the problems of the parents of the young man who was expected to be his heir. Lady Sidney seems to have been increasingly of a complaining and petulant nature in these days; doubtless, part of the blame for this was due to her own faults, but she also appears to have been the victim of petty maliciousness stemming from court rivalry. The Lord Chamberlain Sussex seems to have been particularly at fault. She complained to him bitterly about her rooms at the court: 'The chamber the Gentleman Usher saith your Lordship hath appointed me, truly, my Lord, was never yet but the place for my servants: neither is it fit for the coldness and wideness of it for one of my weakness and sickliness.'[4] But Sussex was no friend to his brother-in-law Sir Henry Sidney, and was, moreover, a bitter opponent of Leicester, and there is more than a suspicion that he was taking out this animosity on Lady Sidney.

A third factor also very much influenced the affairs of the Sidney family in this year: Sir Henry, long recognised by many as the man who knew most about the affairs of the troublesome Irish, was recalled again to serve his country in that graveyard of English reputations. Since he had left Ireland four years earlier, Sir Henry had busied himself with a careful and capable administration of the Presidency of the Council in the Marches, and there can be little doubt that he personally had no desire to return once again to what he called the 'thankless charge'[5] of Ireland. Yet the chaos of Irish affairs was such that there was little to do but recall him. The Tudor experience of governing Ireland was far from imposing, but in the period between 1571 and 1575 the barrenness of the English approach had been revealed at its most sordid level. The Deputy, Fitzwilliam, and the Earl of Essex were at constant loggerheads over policy; perhaps all that they could agree on was that the Queen needed to spend more money in Ireland, something which she was not inclined to do in the first place and virtually incapable of doing in the second. The reputation of Essex was badly damaged after his failure to pacify Munster, and his desperate expedient of massacre was hardly the way (though it frequently appeared so to the English commanders) to effect any sort of meaningful settlement. Fitzwilliam, moreover, had demanded and finally succeeded in obtaining his recall. So it was that Sir Henry was at the end of July sworn a member of the Privy Council and then at the beginning of August appointed Lord Deputy of Ireland. By the beginning of the following month he was once more in the island.

During the interval Philip had not been without amusement. Languet had written him shortly after his return to warn him against the seduction of the court life to which he was called. 'I know it is almost absurd to beg of you that amid the turmoil of a court and so many temptations to waste time, you will not altogether give up the practice of the Latin language.'[6] It is doubtful, though, whether Sidney followed the advice, for it arrived in his hands just at the moment when the most celebrated spectacle of Elizabethan pageantry, Leicester's entertainment of the Queen at Kenilworth, was about to begin. The Queen's progress of this summer was one of the most spectacular and sumptuous of the reign, and the stay at Kenilworth was the chief reason for this. Accounts of the entertainment have been widely circulated, both at the time and in later ages, and the details of it need not be retold yet again.[7] The days were passed in sporting and entertainment: hunting, bear-baiting, morris dancing, masques, and the performance of an historical show featuring the celebrated Captain Cox of Coventry. The resources of Leicester were poured out to provide suitable honour for his Queen, and the words spoken to the Queen by the Lady of the Lake in the opening pageant were truthful:[8]

> Pass on, madam, you need no longer stand:
> The lake, the lodge, the Lord are yours for to command.

The showy magnificence of Elizabethan pageantry is still infectious, and given the fact that this particular entertainment had such a lively and enthusiastic reporter as Thomas Laneham, there is little wonder that it is so well remembered. The adulation of the Queen even by those who sought to stir her to more active policies was an integral part of the neo-chivalric tradition of Elizabethan England, and the enthusiasm for this sort of heroical pageantry was not confined to the upper classes. As one writer noted: 'When the Queen paraded through a country town, almost every Pageant was a Pantheon; even the pastry-cooks were expert mythologists: at dinner select transformations of Ovid's *Metamorphoses* were exhibited in confectionery, and the splendid icing of an immense historic plumb-cake was embossed with a delicious bass-relievo of the destruction of Troy.'[9]

The celebration at Kenilworth provided the second occasion on which young Sidney was present at the elaborate ceremonial involving the Queen, the first being a visitation of the Queen to Oxford which he had witnessed as a schoolboy. Both times Sidney had been in the company of his uncle and virtual sponsor, the Earl of Leicester. The ceremonial aspects of court life were to play an increasingly important part in the history of Elizabethan England and in the life of Sidney as he came to be the symbol himself of a policy on behalf of the Protestants. The present celebrations at Kenilworth were too much concerned with the affairs of Leicester to have a surpassing national importance, yet it might not be too dangerous to speculate that, even here, the idealisation of the Queen was a part of policy. The Queen was respected, admired, and clung to even by those whose policy differed from hers, and the symbolic glorification of their earthly mistress could be an effective way of healing over the breaches occasioned in real life by differences in policy. There is no reason to doubt, every reason to respect the truth of the sentiments so fulsomely elaborated at Kenil-worth and elsewhere to hail their glorious Gloriana:[10]

> O Queen without compare, you must not think it strange
> That here, amid the wilderness, your glory doth so range.
> The winds resound your worth, the rocks record your name,
> These hills, these dales, these woods, these waves, these fields
>   pronounce your fame.

From Kenilworth the royal entourage removed first to Lichfield and then to Chartley, the home of the Earl of Essex. Biographers of Sidney have, in the past, pointed to the visit to Chartley as the occasion on which Sidney first met the daughter of the Earl of Essex, Penelope Devereux, the Stella of his sonnets. As we shall see later, this probably was not the case, yet the visit to Chartley was not without importance for Sidney since it afforded him a good opportunity to strengthen his acquaintance with Essex and confirm in that nobleman's mind the good impressions he had already engendered. The friendship and respect between the two was to be manifested further in Ireland where Philip, in the company of his father, was to engage in his first service for the realm.

Sidney accompanied his father as far as Shrewsbury and probably to the point of embarkation; at least he excused a long silence to Languet with the plea that his time had been occupied with court ceremonial and with seeing his father off.[11] Sir Henry arrived in Ireland at the beginning of September, but Philip was still in London almost a year later. The interval was an important one for him, for not only did he continue to grace the court and gain appointment as Cup-Bearer to the Queen, but he commenced an education in the practical aspects of his nation's politics. Obviously, he would have had an interest in and some knowledge of Irish affairs because of the position held by his father. Of more significance for his development was his growing interest in the cause of the Netherlands, for which he was eventually to give his life. The revolt in the Netherlands became something of a touchstone for the Protestant activists. They tended to see the struggle very much in black and white as the godly Protestants resisting not merely Catholicism but Catholicism's greatest arm, Sidney's own godfather, Philip of Spain. It is clear from references in his letters to Languet that Sidney had already joined the ranks of the activists, that he was already warning his countrymen of the Spanish danger; Languet commented at one point that if Sidney's exhortations did not persuade his countrymen to be on guard against Spain it would be vain for any man to try to persuade them.[12] This rather overstates the case; Sidney's was not the voice to which men turned as an oracle in 1575. At the same time that he cried up the Spanish danger, Sidney was turning increasingly towards ideas of a general Protestant union to resist the Catholic tide. His interest here was heightened by the arrival of commissioners from the Netherlands in the autumn of 1575; they had been sent from William of Orange to press Queen Elizabeth to take a more active role in the protection of the Dutch, indeed to urge on her that she accept the sovereignty of the rebel nation.

Such a policy decision was never seriously contemplated by the Queen. To understand the increasing frustration of Sidney and the other activists in the face of the Queen's refusal to commit England deeply in the war, it is necessary to understand not only their relatively straightforward and bellicose policy on behalf of their co-religionists, but also to appreciate the thinking that lay behind the cautious official policy of the Queen.[13] And to appreciate that policy it is essential not only to remember that England had its most extensive trading interests in the Netherlands but also that, in a strategic sense, the possession of the Netherlands was a matter of vital concern to the English nation; as Lord Burghley himself put it, they were the counterscarp of Protestant England.[14] England, in international affairs, was poised precariously between the two great powers of her age, France and Spain. As Elizabeth and her most congenial advisers saw the situation, it was very definitely in their interests to maintain the relative independence of the Netherlands, lest England's counterscarp should fall too definitely under the control of either of these great powers. And events in the preceding years had suggested that either of these possibilities might occur. In August 1567 the Duke of Alva had arrived with the Spanish army in Brussels determined to crush 'these men of butter', as he termed the Dutch opposition. In 1571–2 the French had begun intervention in the Netherlands at the instigation of the Huguenot leader Admiral Coligny. In many ways, as Elizabeth saw it, this new French threat was an even greater one than the Spanish. They had obviously more compact lines of communication, they were England's traditional enemy, and on top of this they had a connection with England's northern neighbour Scotland. In such a situation English official policy was sharply defined by national interests and security. 'Its aim, put quite simply, was to get the Spanish army out of the Netherlands without letting the French in. . . . This could best be ensured by restoring to the Netherlands their ancient liberties and the considerable measure of at least negative control over their own government that they had possessed under Charles V.'[15] English official policy, then, aimed at restoring the liberties of the Netherlands, not at their independence; the sovereignty of Spain was to remain. And it aimed at a religious compromise, not the dominance of the Calvinists.

With such considerations forming the backbone of English policy, it is not surprising that the Dutch commissioners were disappointed in their mission to the Queen. Nor is it surprising to find Sidney disappointed as well. Although his ideas were not yet fully formed, the outlines of the Protestant activist policy were clearly in his head, and he does not seem to have had undue worry about the French element, so long as they were Protestant. In fact. he seems to have contemplated a visit to Alençon whom he considered as head of the French Protestants, and Alençon did write him, urging him to visit France.

While these interests in continental affairs were widening his grasp of politics, Sidney also found himself being drawn back into the Irish affairs which so concerned his father. Philip had been acquainted long before this time with the Earl of Essex, but during this same winter, he became a close friend, or at least as close a friend as a young courtier can become to an established political figure.[16] Essex had been and still was closely involved in Irish affairs; on 9 March he was appointed Earl Marshal of Ireland and late in July he departed once again for that turbulent island. It is very likely that the young Sidney accompanied him on the trip and was thus reunited with his father. Certainly, he was with his father well before mid-August, for at that time Sir Henry indicated in a letter that Philip had been with him for some time.[17] Although Sir Henry had been far from idle in the year he had been in Ireland, and even though his hopes were quite high that some sort of a settlement could be reached, the truth of the matter was that the solution to the Irish problem was as much a will of the wisp as it had ever been. Complicating all and in the end reducing all to confusion and defeat was the ever-present problem of Elizabethan administration —the want of money. To raise sufficient funds to carry out his work of establishing English authority Sir Henry was forced to rely on a tax on the landholders, the cess, and it was, naturally enough, far from popular. What, if anything, young Philip contributed to his father's efforts during a short stay in Ireland is not readily apparent. Probably he did some military service; a contemporary memoir of him refers to 'his service in Ireland',[18] but it is also probably true that he was there too short a time to learn more than an appreciation of his father's difficulties. Even the suggestion that he learned from the Irish his reverence for poets through personal experience at this time seems a bit far-fetched.[19]

In any case, Sidney's stay in Ireland came to a sudden and unexpected end. The Earl of Essex, with whom Sidney had come, suddenly entered on an 'extreme and hopeless sickness', and 'most lovingly and earnestly' expressed a desire to see the young Sidney.[20]

Philip was not able to reach the Earl before he died, but he soon, apparently, was busy with the preparations for Essex's burial. Philip's relatives (and also the dying Essex, who expressed strong hopes on the matter) were busy planning, as they often did, his matrimonial affairs, this time with the Earl's daughter, Penelope. Many no doubt felt that the match was as good as made. Edward Waterhouse wrote to Sir Henry that 'all these Lords that wish well to the children and, I suppose, all the best sort of the English lords besides, do expect what will become of the treaty between Mr Philip and my Lady Penelope'.[21] And Waterhouse went on to comment that if the match were to be broken off by default on the part of either Philip or Sir Henry it would 'turn to more dishonour than can be repaired with any other marriage in England'.[22] We shall have occasion to return to this projected marriage later when discussing Sidney's sonnet sequence *Astrophel and Stella*, for many feel that the Stella of these poems was Penelope Devereux, the true love of Sidney. Suffice it to say at this point that the scheme did not materialise and that there is no evidence that Philip was particularly attracted by Penelope at this time in his life. Most of the evidence suggests, on the contrary, that what happened was simply one of a number of cases of Philip's future life being discussed by the ambitious matchmakers of his family.[23]

Philip apparently had little interest even in the moderate amount of domesticity that an Elizabethan marriage alliance would have afforded. The young courtier had his eyes more clearly on a life of action and service than he did on married life. He had returned to England very shortly after the Earl of Essex's death, and even though, as Languet suggested, he might have been expected to enjoy the 'delightful ease of the court',[24] especially in contrast to the perils and rigours of the Irish campaign he had just completed, this was not to be the case, nor was it what Sidney himself desired. In fact, he was about to embark on his first real engagement for the commonwealth. His plans seem not to have been revealed at this point to his father, for Sir Henry wrote to Leicester from Ireland at just about this time: 'Good my Lord, send Philip to me; there was never father had more need of his son than I have of him. Once again, good my Lord, let me have him.'[25] A month later than this Sir Henry was still apparently ignorant of his son's plans, for he wrote to Philip asking him to look after an Irish chief who was shortly to visit London.[26]

Philip's concerns were very much elsewhere, however, for he was preparing to represent his country on a diplomatic mission. As his instructions from the Queen defined his task,[27] he was to go as an ambassador of the Queen to the Emperor Rudolph to 'condole the death' of the late Emperor; while on the mission he was also to visit the Counts Palatine Louis and Casimir to express regret at the death of their father. Behind the seeming formality of the mission lay a far deeper and more meaningful purpose: Philip was plainly commissioned to inform himself and his realm on the state of religious opinion and loyalties on the continent. There was no commission here to investigate the possibilities of an actual Protestant League, but, for the activists, there was at least the chance of sensible diplomatic exploration, and it is worthy of note that the Earl of Leicester, who was to become increasingly important among the activists, provided Sidney with a letter of introduction to Count Casimir.[28]

The embassy was a distinguished one. Philip was accompanied not only by his friends Fulke Greville and Edward Dyer but also by a host of others. The young Sidney was plainly conscious of his own dignity as he advanced on his tour. Perhaps with a touch that was too self-consciously ostentatious he set up wherever he lodged on the journey a tablet bearing the Sidney coat of arms and an inscription describing himself as the 'most illustrious and generous' Philip Sidney, son of the Deputy of Ireland, nephew of the Earls of Warwick and Leicester, and ambassador of the great English Queen to the Emperor. It was all true, but it is perhaps the sign of a young man that he felt compelled to display it so conspicuously, even if he were not the only Elizabethan diplomat to act in this fashion.[29]

It is interesting to note, however, that Sidney's meetings with continental statesmen were not confined either to the Emperor or to Protestant leaders. One of the first men he had an interview with was the natural son of Charles V, Don John of Austria, the hero of Lepanto. The two could have had little in common: the ambitious Don John was in the Netherlands acting as the Spanish governor and as such represented the policy Sidney was coming to hate so fiercely. The account we have of their meeting, penned by Fulke Greville, may not be entirely trustworthy, but if it is taken to have a semblance of truth it provides yet another case of the powers of Sidney's charms and his talents to woo even his enemies:[30]

That gallant prince Don John de Austria, viceroy in the Low Countries for Spain, when this gentleman in his embassage to the Emperor came to kiss his hand, though at the first, in his Spanish hauteur, he gave him access as by descent to a youth, of grace as to a stranger, and in particular competition (as he conceived) to an enemy; yet after a while that he had taken his just altitude, he found himself so stricken with this extraordinary planet, that the beholders wondered to see what ingenuous tribute that brave and high-minded Prince paid to his worth, giving more honour and respect to this hopeful young gentleman than to the ambassadors of mighty princes.

The meeting with Don John had taken place in Louvain. From there, Sidney moved on to Heidelberg to consult with the rulers of the Palatinate. He reported the details of that visit to Walsingham by letter at the end of March 1577.[31] He had been unable to see both the Dukes, the Elector being at a town in the upper Palatinate, and so he had to confine his mission to Casimir. This circumstance was not without appeal to Sidney. Of the two rulers in the Palatinate, Casimir was the one to whom he would naturally incline, for not only was Casimir a sincere and devoted Calvinist but he was also one of the prime movers behind the idea of a Protestant League. It is noteworthy in this respect that Greville commented that the idea of the Protestant Union was foremost in Sidney's own mind as the reason behind his embassy; Greville noted that Sidney felt his instructions 'gave him scope (as he passed) to salute such German princes as were interested in the cause of our religion or their own native liberty'.[32]

Sidney's report to Walsingham was a model diplomatic newsletter, mainly concerned with the problems of forming a Protestant League, an idea as dear to Walsingham's own heart as it was to Sidney's, but making observations as well on the other aspects which the Queen had asked him to investigate. Sidney unfortunately found the prospects for the league to be rather bleak. There was religious difference between Casimir and his brother Louis who had established Lutheranism in the upper Palatinate and contemplated further religious alterations. The greatest hope that he could see was that Louis was 'of a soft nature, led to these things only through conscience, and Prince Casimir wise, that can temper well with the other's weakness'.[33] For the rest, matters were scarcely favourable. Sidney's impression, and it was accurate enough, was that the other princes of Germany were little inclined to stir on the matter; 'the other Princes of Germany have no care but how to grow rich and to please their senses; the Duke of Saxony so carried away with the ubiquity that he grows bitter to the true Lutherans. The rest are of the same mould, thinking they should be safe though all the world were on fire about them, except it be the Landgrave William and his brethren and this Prince Casimir'.[34] There were no forces being prepared publicly for the proposed league.

Sidney left Heidelberg on this unfavourable note, failed to meet the Elector as planned in the upper Palatinate, and then journeyed on to Prague where he accomplished his purpose in the mission. The period in Prague has often been misinterpreted, both on the nature of his formal embassy and also on the meaning of his meetings with the Catholic exile Edmund Campion there. The first matter is easily resolved; some biographers of Sidney with more zeal than sense have credited their Protestant hero with a violently anti-Catholic speech before the Emperor, urging him to regard the menace of both France and Spain.[35] The confusion apparently results from a misreading of Greville's account of the audience, and it is, of course, unrealistic to think that an ambassador, even an inexperienced one like Sidney, would have indulged in such a foolish and fruitless action on such an occasion when he was supposed to be bearing the condolences of his Queen to the Emperor. Sidney's own account of the interview should dispel any feeling that he performed his task with anything other than tact. In formal audience with the Emperor on Easter Monday he made 'known unto him how greatly her Majesty was grieved with the loss of so worthy a [friend as (?)] the Emperor his father was'.[36] He further expressed briefly the 'good hope' which Elizabeth had of the new Emperor, expecting 'that he would second his father in his virtues and the manner of his government'. Lastly, he explained the actions that England had so far taken in regard to the Netherlands. The imperial reception of this was brief but favourable; 'he answered me in Latin with very few words', but though they were rather general, Sidney felt them to be friendly. The following day he had an interview with the Empress, 'with the singular signification of her Majesty's great good will unto her', and again Sidney handled the situation with both skill and tact.[37]

Of the Emperor deceased I used but few words, because in truth I saw it bred some trouble unto her to hear him mentioned in that kind. She answered me with many courteous speeches and great acknowledging of her own beholdingness to her Majesty. And for her son she said she hoped he

would do well, but that for her own part she said she had given herself
from the world and would not greatly stir from thence forward in it. Then
did I deliver the Queen of France's letter, she standing by the Empress,
using such speeches as I thought were fit for her double sorrow, and her
Majesty's good will unto her, confirmed by her wise and noble governing
of herself in the time of her being in France. Her answer was full of humble-
ness, but she spake so low that I could not understand many of her words.

For the rest of the time at the imperial court Sidney informed himself
as well as he was able of the state of affairs in Germany. What he
discovered was not entirely favourable. The Emperor was 'wholly by
his inclination given to the wars, few of words, sullen of disposition,
very secret and resolute, nothing the manner his father had in winning
men in his behaviour'.[38] His brother Ernest was 'much like him in
disposition', but more frank and forward. Both of them were 'extremely Spaniolated'.[39] The advice the Emperor sought was not such
as was likely to be of aid to the cause Sidney was interested in; he was
greatly influenced by the Master of his house who 'bears the red cross
of Spain and [is] a professed servant to that crown and the inquisitor's
government' and by the papal nuncio, 'so that what counsels such
authors give may be easily imagined'.[40]

There can be little doubt that Sidney took small comfort in the
Catholic–Spanish inclinations of the imperial court. Yet to imagine
that he lectured the Emperor on this is ridiculous. What Greville
asserted he actually did was to bring the matter to the attention of
those German princes who might be inclinable to the proposed
Protestant League.[41] There is a great deal of difference between the
ceremonially correct procedure of Sidney at the imperial court,
performing that solemn but hardly significant task the Queen had
allotted to him, and the more outspoken, persuasive Sidney, performing the task of Protestant diplomacy which he interpreted to be his
real function. When the occasion permitted, Sidney was strong in his
warnings against the machinations of the Catholic powers; 'though to
negotiate with that long-breathed nation proves commonly a work in
steel, where many strokes leave hardly any print, yet did this master
genius quickly stir up their cautious and slow judgments to be sensible
of the danger which threatened them hourly by this fatal conjuction of
Rome's undermining superstitions with the commanding forces of
Spain'.[42] Sidney was making these warnings in the face of the obvious

success of the Counter-Reformation, and his interpretation of its methods are not without interest.[43] As he saw it, the Catholics first infiltrated through the power of mysterious religion; 'the manner of this conjunction was not like the ancient undertakers who made open war by proclamation, but craftily (from the infusion of Rome) to enter first by invisible traffic of souls, filling people's minds with apparitions of holiness, specious rites, saints, miracles, institutions of new orders, reformations of old, blessings of Catholics, cursings of heretics, thunderbolts of excommunication under the authority of their mother church'. Once by means of 'these shadows' the Church had taken possession of the weak, discouraged the strong, divided the doubtful, and lulled men asleep, the spiritual reformation was followed by more definitely political moves; 'then . . . follow on with the Spanish less spiritual, but more forcible engines, *viz*. practice, confederacy, faction, money, treaties, leagues of traffic, alliance by marriages, charge of rebellion, war, and all other acts of advantagious power'. The answer to such a threat, Sidney felt, was very obviously a league.

Lastly he recalled to their memories how by this brotherhood in evil (like Simeon and Levi) Rome and Spain had spilled so much blood as they were justly become the terror of all governments and could now be withstood or balanced by no other means than by a general league in religion, constantly and truly affirming that to associate by a uniform bond of conscience for the protection . . . of religion and liberty would prove a more solid union and symbolise far better against their tyrannies than any factious combination in policy, league of state, or other traffic of civil or martial humours possibly could do.

These words were for those who would or could hear, but the imperial court itself neither could nor would, and Sidney did not ply his diplomatic trade there.

The other incident occurring while Sidney was in Prague that has given rise to much ill-founded speculation was his contact with Edmund Campion. In some respects his apparent intimacy with the Catholic refugee should not occasion too much surprise. The two had been resident in Oxford at the same time and probably knew each other even then; certainly Campion knew the Sidney family in more than a passing way, since he had been protected by Sir Henry in Ireland after he had been forced to leave England. When Campion had in turn left Ireland he went to Douai and then in 1572 to Rome, where he became a Jesuit, a member of that company which formed the most effective and disciplined arm of the Counter-Reformation Church. In September 1574 he had come to the Jesuit College in Prague as Professor of Rhetoric and had remained there since, actively engaged in the educational work which made the Jesuits so successful.

Accounts of the meeting of the two are highly coloured. It is related how Sidney found much difficulty in meeting with Campion because of the necessity of avoiding spies set about him by the English Council, but that none the less he managed a number of secret meetings with him.[44] Some have gone so far as to suggest that Campion succeeded in converting the young Protestant here; others, only slightly less incautiously, coupling this incident with the reports of Sidney's Catholic friends on his Grand Tour and his later moderate actions towards Catholic recusants in England, have tried to argue that, if not a practising Catholic, Sidney was at least sympathetic to the religion and hence cannot be seen as the true Protestant or Puritan hero.[45] How true these flights of fancy are may be judged from Campion's own letter relating the experience:[46]

A few months ago Philip Sidney came from England to Prague as ambassador, magnificently provided. He had much conversation with me— I hope not in vain, for to all appearances he was most eager. I commend him to your sacrifices, for he asked the prayers of all good men, and at the same time put into my hands some alms to be distributed to the poor for him, which I have done. Tell this to Doctor Nicholas Sanders, because if any one of the labourers sent into the vineyard from Douai seminary has an opportunity of watering this plant, he may watch the occasion for helping a poor wavering soul. If this young man, so wonderfully beloved and admired by his countrymen, chances to be converted, he will astonish his noble father, the Deputy of Ireland, his uncles the Dudleys, and all the young courtiers, and Cecil himself. Let it be kept secret.

The one further bit of evidence that might be added to this (albeit of a hearsay variety) is that, according to a letter of Father Thomas Fitzherbert in 1628 (fifty-one years after the event), Sidney had had the courage to confess in England that 'one of the most memorable things he had witnessed abroad was a sermon by Campion at which he had assisted with the Emperor in Prague'.[47]

What are we to conclude from this? Certainly not that Sidney was converted, for Campion specifically states that he was not at this time. Campion's high hopes for a conversion were totally ill-founded, and perhaps he himself really knew they were, as his list of those who would be 'astonished' suggests. It is reasonable to conclude that Sidney was drawn to Campion on grounds other than religious ones. Whether this was simply due to an old acquaintance or a family connection is impossible to say. It is equally probable that Sidney was interested in seeing Campion because of the undoubted powers of his intellect. Sidney made a point of seeking out men of intelligence and learning, and in doing so he paid scant attention to their religion (with the exception of one Pibrac whose relation to the Massacre of St Bartholomew overweighed in Sidney's mind anything else about him). And Campion had no such blot on his career. We should not find the incident so unusual. It is perfectly consistent with the behaviour of a Protestant intellectual, even in those darkest days of political and religious tension. Here indeed Sidney was doing little else than follow the path set by his mentor Languet. It was, in addition, an action perfectly compatible with Sidney's own religious outlook so far as we can perceive it. Sidney was a firm Protestant more in a political sense than in a theological one. His objection to Rome was not a clerical one, but one very much bound up with the political implications of a resurgent Catholicism and the expansionist ambitions of Philip of Spain. It was an attitude he shared in common with Leicester and Walsingham and with his father, the men who, in conjunction with Languet, shaped his political orientation. Many people try to force the Elizabethans into rigid frames in which they will not fit. It was perfectly conceivable and far from abnormal for an Elizabethan to be a firm Protestant and yet be on terms of friendship or at least on terms of tolerance with individual Catholics. Their reaction to Catholicism was measured not so much in terms of individuals as it was in terms of international politics.

His assessment of the situation completed, his messages of condolence delivered, Sidney's mission to the imperial court was concluded. But he did not yet return to England; imbued still with aspirations for a Protestant League, he returned to Heidelberg to seek out the Elector Palatine whom he had not yet encountered. There, on 30 April, he had an audience with him. While the audience was friendly, it was hardly satisfactory. After delivering his formal message of condolence,

Sidney pressed the Elector 'to have merciful consideration of the Church of the religion, so notably established by his father as in all Germany there is not such a number of excellent learned men, and truly would rue any man to see the desolation of them'.[48] The Elector made tokens of his favourable inclinations to Elizabeth and England, but he evaded any direct answers on matters like a Protestant League, arguing that events forced him to act as other rulers in the Empire did. Sidney desired to discuss the matter further with the Landgrave of Hesse and Prince Casimir, in whom he had found the most favourable response, but he admitted in a letter to Walsingham that prospects for any sort of an effective union became less favourable the more he discovered of the attitudes and reactions of the German princes; 'I see their proceedings such that my hope doth every day grow less and less'.[49]

On 4 May Sidney set out for Kaiserlauten to discuss affairs with the Landgrave. On the way there he was intercepted by a letter from the Queen stating that for 'weighty reasons' she was recalling him at once.[50] What those weighty reasons were was not stated, but it is perhaps not idle to suggest that they may have been connected with Sidney's activities in pressing for a league among the German princes. The Queen was no activist in foreign affairs, and it is at least possible that she feared her young diplomat intended to commit England to a policy she and Burghley could not approve of. This interpretation of the event is strengthened by the subsequent actions of Sidney's mission.

At some point on this continental trip Sidney had been joined by Languet, and they were together at Cologne when the missive from the Queen arrived. Languet noted that Sidney was 'burning to be presented to Orange and form an acquaintance with him',[51] in other words to see the most prominent and successful of the Protestant leaders on the continent, no doubt to discuss further these diplomatic plans. Sidney appears to have contemplated a visit to Orange despite his recall to England, but Languet urged him to obey his instructions precisely. It is probable that Sidney's low spirits, on which Languet remarked, were not entirely occasioned by their parting but also by the evident failure of what Sidney considered to be the most important part of his mission. Within a few days of the first message, however, a second arrived directing Sidney to visit William of Orange, a task which he accepted with considerable enthusiasm.[52] He finally joined Orange and his Princess at Gertruidenberg.

The opportunity was one of the greatest of Sidney's life, and he took advantage of it. It gave him a chance to converse with the man whom, Greville tells us, he admired above all other politicians, the man 'who never divided the consideration of estate from the cause of religion, nor gave that sound party occasion to be jealous or distracted upon any appearance of safety whatsoever, prudently resolving that to temporise with the enemies of our faith was but (as among seagulls) a strife not to keep upright but aloft upon the top of every billow'[53]. In addition, it allowed Sidney to make the acquaintance of Orange's shrewd wife, Charlotte de Bourbon, and once again to come into the presence of St Aldegonde, the commissioner who earlier had arrived in England to offer the sovereignty of the Netherlands to Elizabeth. That the respect was not one-sided is abundantly documented. Sidney became the godfather to Charlotte's second child, who was named Elizabeth in honour of the English Queen. Moreover, when he left, Sidney was presented with a chain of gold and a jewel, and two years later Orange was to recall to Greville the extent to which he had been impressed by the bearing and intelligence of Sidney. 'He protested unto me . . . that if he could judge, her Majesty had one of the ripest and greatest counsellors of estate in Sir Philip Sidney that at this day lived in Europe'.[54] Even more to the point in assessing the value Orange put on Sidney was that the Dutchman entrusted the young man with an important diplomatic mission of a sort that Sidney most enthusiastically approved; he was commissioned on behalf of Orange to offer to Elizabeth the virtual union of Holland and Zealand with the crown of England. This would have been a notable first step towards the formation of the Protestant League. No doubt the conversation between Orange and Sidney, of which we have no record, was very much concerned with this point, and it reveals the extent to which the Queen probably was justified in her earlier recall of Sidney, for Philip was going well beyond the terms of his employment and indulging in a type of diplomatic conversation that could only be displeasing to the Queen even if Sidney was conducting it in what he firmly believed to be her best interests. Given the attitude of the English Queen to such a scheme, it is hardly surprising to find that it came to nothing. The Queen merely dispatched another ambassador to Orange to discuss matters further.

Early in June, Sidney left Orange to return to England. Although the

Protestant League had not been formed, Sidney's service both in the formal and informal parts of his mission was highly commended. Walsingham wrote enthusiastically to Sir Henry about the success of the trip:[55]

> Now touching your Lordship's particular, I am to impart unto you the return of the young gentleman, Mr Sidney, your son, whose message very sufficiently performed, and the relating thereof, is no less gratefully received and well liked of her Majesty, than the honourable opinion he hath left behind him with all the Princes with whom he had to negotiate hath left a most sweet savour and grateful remembrance of his name in those parts. The gentleman hath given no small arguments of great hope, the fruits whereof I doubt not but your Lordship shall reap, as the benefit of the good parts which are in him, and whereof he hath given some taste in this voyage, is to redound to more than your Lordship and himself. There hath not been any gentleman I am sure these many years that hath gone through so honourable a charge with as great commendation as he. In consideration whereof I could not but communicate this part of my joy with your Lordship, being no less a refreshing unto me in these my troublesome business than the soil is to the chafed stag.

Perhaps the most striking feature of the letter is the extent to which Walsingham now saw Sidney, if he had not fully done so before, as a man of promise.

There may be two ways to judge this embassy. In one sense, it was of clear importance to Sidney in his development as a hero-figure for the Protestant cause. From the time of the embassy, the thoughts he had about the cause had hardened into the principles on which he would base his political action. No longer unclear abstractions in his mind, they were his foremost thought and to the realisation of them he would devote his active career. So, in this sense, the embassy can be seen as both the first fruits and the culmination of the education of the Protestant statesman. But the embassy must also be viewed in another way; it was Sidney's major effort in the diplomatic sphere and in the course of it he had turned a relatively meaningless ceremonial occasion into a concerted, if unsuccessful attempt to organise the Protestant powers or at least to sound them out on the chances of such an organisation. His efforts were praised and respected, admittedly most loudly and enthusiastically by those who shared his fervour for the Protestant cause. The Queen's reaction was at least outwardly gracious; she could not deny that he had performed his formal functions well and with a grace that belied his young years and lack of experience, even if she were less enthusiastic about his actual diplomacy. Yet the fact that the Queen would not trust him with such a mission again in some ways reveals her recognition of the extent to which he had accomplished something. More striking than this praise and reserve, which was to be expected from these particular quarters, was the treatment afforded Sidney by Alberico Gentili when he wrote a textbook on proper diplomatic behaviour. Gentili was one of the age's great experts on international law, and his opinions are to be respected. Not only did he dedicate the work to Sidney, but when he came to the model of the perfect ambassador, none other came to his mind than Philip Sidney. To be sure, Gentili may be dismissed as a special friend, for he knew Sidney personally and the family had treated him well when he came to England from Italy to escape the Inquisition: 'You treated me, not only in correspondence but also in frequent personal interviews, with such consideration that I am now of the opinion that nothing more opportune ever reached my ears than this fame of yours.'[56] But even with this allowance made there is a notable tribute which cannot be ignored in the closing lines of Gentili's *De Legationibus Libri Tres* which he published in 1585:[57]

I have endeavoured to transmit, so far as lay in my power, a pattern of the excellent ambassador, either specifically described or outlined in discussion of greater sweep, and after that I have made an effort to include my representation within the compass of this smaller picture, not however without the addition of some embellishments. But I shall not dismiss you without showing you what Socrates considered to be a still greater source of pleasure: a living image and example of the perfect ambassador. Nor do I think that I shall have need of the skill of Zeuxis or any artist of that kind. For I am sure that this excellent pattern can be found and demonstrated in one man only—a man who has all the qualities which are needed to make this consummate ambassador of ours, and has them indeed in greater abundance and on a more generous scale than is required. That man is Philip Sidney.

While many like Gentili would praise the young Sidney for his noble work, the reaction of the Queen, as has been noted, was less enthusiastic. And her enthusiasm was lessened further still by the rumours that a Sidney marriage would soon provide a crucial link in the forming of the Protestant League. Philip was often at the mercy of the matchmakers among his friends and relatives, and the year 1577 was no exception, for now they postulated a marriage alliance between Sidney and the House of Orange. Rumours of this alliance were reported by the Spanish ambassador Mendoza to the King of Spain in April of 1578: 'There is much talk here of a marriage between Sidney, Leicester's nephew, the heir of Henry Sidney, of the Earl of Warwick, and of Leicester's property, and a sister of Orange, who enters very willingly into the suggestion, and promises as a dowry to make him lord of Holland and Zealand, by this means and other gifts gaining over Leicester, who has now turned his back upon France, to which he was formerly so much attached.'[58] There are also numerous references to the same matter in the correspondence of Sidney and Languet during the previous summer. It is interesting to see Languet emerge here as one of the matchmakers for the young English courtier; up to this point proposed marriage alliances had been suggested by relatives, but now Languet, with a more than fatherly interest and one eye fixed very definitely on the Protestant cause, emerged as a person most concerned with seeing Sidney married. Actually, Languet had alluded to the desirability of marriage in earlier letters to Philip. In one letter apparently Sidney made some slightly joking comments about taking a wife; to Languet this was no joking matter, and in his answering letter he attempted to discuss the proposition on a more serious plane.[59] He urged Sidney not to be too confident in his firmness and confessed that he would actually be glad if Sidney were caught by a wife, for then he would be able to give his country sons like himself. Languet pointed to the marriage of Sidney's friend Edward Wotton and suggested that 'his boldness seems to convict you of cowardice'.[60] Apparently, however, these early discussions of marriage between Sidney and Languet had no reference to any specific proposal. While he had been on his Grand Tour there had been some talk of matching him with a daughter of Lord Berkeley, but nothing came of these negotiations and there is little reason to suppose they were still being discussed when Languet wrote Sidney in 1575.[61]

Fifteen seventy-seven was, however, a very different matter, and the tone of Philip's letters at this time was also very different from his earlier, jesting references. There is every suggestion that he not only took this proposal to marry into the House of Orange seriously but also that for the first time in the marriage negotiations which went on around his name he was interested himself directly in the outcome. The references to this new negotiation for a marriage are somewhat cryptic, but with the aid of Mendoza's notice we can be sure that they do refer to a proposed marriage between Sidney and the sister of the Prince of Orange. Languet had raised the possibility when he was with Sidney at the end of his diplomatic tour, and in his very first letter to Philip after the two had parted he wrote: 'See that you do not forget what I said to you at the mouth of the Maine, and write about it as soon as you can, as you have more than once promised me.'[62] It is apparent that Sidney, though interested, was from the beginning of the negotiations doubtful whether they could be brought to a successful conclusion. Languet commented: 'You have written me from Bruges that there are reasons which almost make you despair of the possibility of a successful issue, and you have asked me as far as I can to discourage the hopes of the other parties.'[63] Languet urged Sidney to consider the matter further; he also stressed the point that, while he had advanced the scheme, he was not the author of it: 'I simply made a proposal to you which others had ordered me to make, nor if you remember rightly did I use any persuasion; I simply referred the whole matter to your consideration.'[64] Sidney had suggested (with accuracy) that he was not his own master in this; Languet had urged him to sound out his friends in England on the subject, but Sidney was already aware of a factor which Languet persistently overlooked: it was not the opinion of friends in England that mattered; it was the attitude of the Queen, and Sidney had no illusions that she would look on the marriage, which had such diplomatic overtones, with much favour.

Languet did not despair, but he was critical of the cautious attitude Sidney displayed towards the negotiations. 'Your reputation and my own have begun to suffer with our friends here. They are persuaded that you changed your mind in Holland and that you preferred another proposal to that which was agreed upon between us.'[65] Languet also had fears that the marriage would work out in another way, and in the course of stressing this to Sidney he pointed out that Orange's sister was in favour of marriage with Philip and would be most disappointed to learn that he was cold to the scheme: 'The Elector of Brandenburg is said to be looking eagerly in that direction, but the other's constancy has not yet yielded to his rank and greatness, so strong are the hopes which she has conceived. So now she will sigh when she discovers the uselessness of her constancy and the frustration of her hopes.'[66] Languet also seems to have been aware that he was perhaps pushing Sidney too hard on this matter: 'I beseech you to pardon me if I have perchance been too insistent in importuning an answer to the matters we agreed upon.'[67] And by January 1578 he was openly aware that Sidney was resolute on the matter. 'I greatly wonder that you, whom all the world pronounces to have been reared in the lap of the graces, should have been able to preserve your freedom so long. Perhaps you have determined to follow the example of your Minerva.'[68]

It is rather difficult to reconstruct Sidney's attitude through all these negotiations. He wrote no letters (or none have survived) between October and March, at a time when Languet's letters to him are filled with comments on the marriage. By March, Sidney seemingly had made a firm resolve to reject the proposals. His letter to Languet at the beginning of March revealed him in a despondent mood, critical both of his own idleness and of the very nature of the age in which he lived. 'The use of the pen, as you may perceive, has plainly fallen from me and my mind itself, if it was ever active in anything, is now beginning, by reason of my indolent ease, imperceptibly to lose its strength, and to relax without any reluctance. For to what purpose should our thoughts be directed to various kinds of knowledge, unless room be afforded for putting it into practice, so that public advantages may be the result, which in a corrupt age we cannot hope for?'[69] As far as the proposed marriage, his answer was curt and negative: 'regarding her of whom I readily acknowledge how unworthy I am, I have written you my reasons long since, briefly indeed, but yet as well as I was able'.[70]

Languet would long cherish this fleeting hope of allying England's Protestant courtier with the House of Orange; he was still alluding to the Orange marriage as late as March 1580. But Sidney was by now looking in other directions. On 10 March 1578 he wrote to Languet: 'For my own part, unless God powerfully counteract it, I seem to myself to see our cause withering away, and I am now meditating with myself some Indian project.'[71] Sidney was, in his mind and in his actions, separating the marriage alliance which affected him personally, from the hopes for a Protestant League, which he saw as a matter of international moment. The hopes for the Protestant League were fading fast as well, and for many of the same reasons that Sidney's proposed marriage was abandoned. They, like the marriage, ran counter to the policy of England, and though the Queen could occasionally display some interest in such a scheme, it was only in the long run the prelude to her abandoning it. Sidney, for his part, may have turned away from the Orange marriage proposals because he believed them an impossibility; he did not turn away from the concern of the Netherlands, because he considered that a necessity. His personal activity in the course of the year was very much bound up with desires to promote the formation of the Protestant League and to lead the Queen to intervene directly in the tangled web of the Dutch revolt. He corresponded with those who might be of aid, Prince Casimir and Orange himself, and at one point it did appear that his policy was gaining favour with the Queen when she sent Daniel Rogers and later Robert Beale (both acquaintances of Sidney) to the continent to discuss the Protestant cause. But even at this point, hopes were built on the flimsiest of foundations, and the shrewd Languet guessed correctly that they would come to naught; 'those who are only moderately versed in the affairs of Germany know that it is not an easy task to bring about that which Master Rogers attempted in the first instance with a few princes and Beale afterwards with more'.[72] Languet admitted that such tentative negotiations did enhance the reputation of the English Queen in Germany, but they did little more than this, for only a few of the German princes like Casimir were prepared to commit themselves in such a struggle. Hopes of aiding the Netherlands directly at this point were equally vain. Orange himself wanted very much to see Leicester appointed to a command of English troops in Flanders with Sidney as his deputy. Again, there were some signs of token encouragement from the Queen, but once more such action ran counter to the cautious foreign policy of balance she and Burghley were pursuing, and there was no hope that real action would be taken. It is little wonder that Philip Sidney, anxious to aid the Protestant cause and already emerging as a gallant spokesman of the Protestant interest, should have felt in March 1578 that he was living in a corrupt age.

Chapter 2

LEICESTER, WALSINGHAM AND THE
FRENCH MARRIAGE

> Thus sat she as an heroical princess and
> umpire betwixt the Spaniards, the French, and
> the Estates, so as she might well have usurped
> that saying of her father . . . to whom I adhere
> getteth the upper hand, and true it was which
> one hath written, that France and Spain are as it
> were the scales in the balance of Europe and
> England the tongue, or the holder of the
> balance.   Camden, *Annals* (1635 edn.)

Sidney was beginning to find his existence at the court unappealing, not so much because of the life itself as because he yearned to play a vital role in the affairs of his nation and found himself being isolated from this since his views were somewhat removed from the sort of policy which the nation was pursuing. If in grander and broader schemes he was thus cut off from employment he found ample opportunity for exercising his talents on behalf of his father and in defence of Sir Henry's policy in Ireland. Sir Henry faced great difficulties in Ireland, not the least of which stemmed from the landed families of the Pale, who might, at quick glance, be thought to have been natural supporters of the English government. We have already noticed, however, that even before Philip had gone on his embassy to Germany the great landholders of the Pale were beginning to stir restlessly under the imposition of taxes which Sir Henry found it necessary to impose on them in order to finance the costs of his government. The situation had much worsened in the interval. Despite various efforts to make the tax palatable, Sir Henry had been unable to ward off sharp criticism, and finally, when some of the landed gentlemen refused to pay, Sir Henry had them incarcerated in Dublin Castle. His treatment of them in Ireland differed little from their reception in England; members of a deputation on behalf of the landowners to England were locked up in the Fleet.[1]

Yet this hardly represented an end of Sir Henry's problems, since his administration of the tax was very much complicated by the presence of the Earl of Ormonde, a favourite of the Queen. Elizabeth wished her favourite to be exempted from the tax, and this placed Sir Henry in an awkward position. To do so would perhaps gain him the favour of the Queen and Ormonde, but it certainly would have added to his difficulties with the lesser landowners who could justifiably complain of partiality. Sir Henry preferred the other course of levying the tax on all impartially, even though in doing so he added to his long continued enmity with Ormonde and endangered his relations with the crown. The latter were, in any case, tense, for the Queen objected to the level of expenditure in Ireland. When Sir Henry had to raise the money to meet a threatened invasion of the island he had some difficulty persuading the Queen to cooperate. As his agent in England Waterhouse reported it to him: 'Her Majesty, angry at first when money was demanded, said that Sir Henry did always seek to put her to charge',[2] but in the long run Sir Henry was able to gain his point and the necessary funds with the aid of Leicester and Walsingham.

These affairs came to concern Philip directly, for he was supervising the activities of Waterhouse in England. Philip found that he was called to a considerable task to defend his father's conduct in Ireland, for Ormonde was spreading rumours against Sir Henry. The disgruntled Earl suggested that Sir Henry was about to be recalled basically on the grounds of corruption, that he was enriching himself and was stirring up sedition in the island. Relations between Ormonde and the Sidney family became extremely strained, and this was especially so between Philip and the Earl at the court. Waterhouse reported to Sir Henry in September:[3]

Some little occasions of discourtesies have passed between the Earl of Ormonde and Mr Philip Sidney, because the Earl lately spake unto him and he answered not, but was in dead silence of purpose, because he imputeth to the Earl some practices as have been made to alienate her Majesty's mind from your Lordship. . . . The Earl of Ormonde saith he will accept no quarrels from a gentleman that is bound by nature to defend his father's causes, and who is otherwise furnished with so many virtues as he knows Mr Philip to be; and on the other side Mr Philip hath gone so far, and showed as much magnanimity as is convenient, unless he could charge him with any particularities, which I perceive he yet cannot.

Though on this occasion Philip had decided to maintain silence to press his point home, he also took to the pen to defend his father's administration. At the end of the month Waterhouse reported to Sir Henry that Philip had collected the various objections to Sir Henry and had composed an answer to them in the form of a discourse. 'Let no man compare with Mr Philip's pen. I know he will send it to your Lordship, and when you read it you shall have more cause to pray God for him than to impute affection to me in this my opinion of him.'[4]

The *Discourse on Irish Affairs*, which contains some of the first formal statements on politics by Sidney, has not completely survived, only the last four of his seven points being preserved in the manuscript in the British Museum. Since it was mainly conceived as a defence of his father's actions, primarily in connection with the levying of the cess, it contains little in the way of general comment, although there are several observations of interest which should not be overlooked. There is a suggestion, for example, that Sidney had some concern for the lot of the poor, the most pressing social problem of the century; he criticised his father's adversaries sharply for oppressing the lower classes. 'This toucheth the privileges forsooth, and privileged persons be all the rich men of the Pale, the burden only lying upon the poor, who may groan, for their cry cannot be heard. And Lord to see how shamefully they will speak for their country, that be indeed the tyrannous oppressors of their country.'[5] This concern for the plight of the poor should not be read in too democratic, too modern, a sense. In the first place, of course, Sidney is here scoring only a debating point off his opponents. In the second place it is probable that Sidney's attitude towards the poor was more conditioned by thoughts of social and political harmony than it was by any conception of a democratic or altruistic character.[6] Sidney advocated an impartial treatment of the Irish, the policy which he felt his father was following, but impartiality was not in his mind to be confused with leniency. Sidney knew that his father's government in Ireland was strict and ruthless, but he was as prepared to defend this as any English spokesman on Irish affairs in the reign of Elizabeth. To his way of thinking, a conquered people

were a people to be dealt with severely, and he felt that he had all
historical precedent behind such a view. Considering the question
whether leniency was better than severe means, he commented in the
following terms:[7]

> Truly, the general nature of all countries not fully conquered is plainly
> against it. For until by time they find the sweetness of due subjection, it is
> impossible that any gentle means should put out the fresh remembrance of
> their lost liberty. And that the Irishman is that way as obstinate as any
> nation, with whom no other passion can prevail but fear, besides their story
> which plainly paint it out, their manner of life wherein they choose rather
> all filthiness than any law, and their own conscience who best know their
> own natures, give sufficient proof of. For under the sun there is not a nation
> which live more tyrannously than they do over the other. . . . For little is
> leniency to prevail, in minds so possessed with revengeful hate to all English
> as to their only conquerors, and that, which is most of all, with so ignorant
> obstinacy in papistry, that they do in their souls detest the present
> government.

No one would claim that the *Discourse on Irish Affairs* was one of the
major products of Sidney's pen. It is limited in its scope, not overly
imaginative in its argument. To this point, the judgment of Waterhouse
on the quality of Sidney's pen may seem a little overstated. But even in
a political defence of this sort, Sidney showed he had a forceful, if
not yet a fully graceful style, and he was already capable of composing
a memorable line: 'There is no so great injustice as that which puts on
the colour of demanding justice.'[8] Nor would anyone claim that this
spirited defence of his father as 'an honest servant, full of zeal in his
prince's service and not without well grounded hopes of good success'[9]
had much effect on the policy of the Queen. The Queen had already
some inkling that Philip was a potentially troublesome young man;
moreover, she made up her mind on such matters on different grounds,
and with the pressure mounting for the recall of Sir Henry from Ireland,
it was inevitable that sooner or later he would be summoned home. As
Walsingham reported to Sir Henry in January, the Queen had been
somewhat appeased, yet she still contemplated his recall, admittedly
under pretext of a conference on reducing the cost of administering
Ireland.[10] In February he was in fact summoned to the royal presence,
but since he did not want to leave the island without reducing it to the
best order possible, he did not return until the middle of September.

His reception at court was openly friendly, but hardly reflected the debt owed to a hard-working administrator, and Sir Henry was himself conscious of this. 'When I came to the Court to know how I was entertained, I confess well, but not so well as I thought and in conscience felt I had deserved. . . . Notwithstanding all these my painful services I was accounted *servus inutilis* for that I had exceeded a supposed commission . . . and although somewhat I had exceeded in spending her Majesty's treasure, I had too far exceeded in spoiling my own patrimony.'[11] The Queen was not often too generous to her servants, but Sir Henry seems to have fared rather worse than most.

This concern with his father's affairs served to some extent to fill Sidney's time, but his impatience at being denied some greater opportunity was growing. He had written to Languet suggesting that he was contemplating some 'Indian project' and he also toyed with the idea of leaving England to join the forces of Orange or Casimir. For a year or so he swayed between these two projects.

Sidney, like many of the Protestant activists, had been interested in overseas exploration and expansion for some time, and as early as 1576 he had invested in a voyage of Frobisher;[12] he did so again in the following two years, each time subscribing a larger amount. His enthusiasm grew to the extent that Languet felt he detected a desire on Sidney's part actually to partake in one of the explorer's voyages. In October 1577 Sidney wrote to Languet with great enthusiasm about the results of Frobisher's most recent voyage.[13] He was convinced that Frobisher and his men had discovered gold. On the first voyage in 1576 one of the men had brought back an ore sample which had been pronounced confidently to be 'the purest gold and without any intermixture of other metal'. On the second voyage Frobisher had returned to the same spot and brought back some two hundred tons of ore. Moreover, the explorer announced that it was his opinion that the island where he had mined this was 'so productive in metals as to seem very far to surpass the country of Peru'; in addition there were six neighbouring islands apparently equally rich in the precious metals. Sidney was greatly elated at the prospect of this source of mineral wealth and the influence it might have on his country and the Protestant cause. He enquired of Languet his opinion on the best ways of working ores and also on the best way to protect the source of supply from marauders of other nations like the Spanish. He added that unless

Languet forbade it he would show his answer to the Queen. It seems reasonably certain that Sidney saw in this a new chance to interest the Queen actively in the Protestant cause. If her cautious policy had been due, at least in part, to restricted financial resources, then here was an answer to that problem. 'The thing is truly of great importance', he noted to Languet, 'and one which may probably, some time or other, be of use to the professors of the true religion'.[14]

Languet's response did not express the great enthusiasm that Sidney had expected. Languet was prepared to believe that Frobisher had discovered gold and to admit that if all Sidney said of him was true, then 'he will doubtless eclipse the reputation not only of Magellan, but even of Christopher Colombus himself'.[15] But even if this were so, the discovery of gold was, in Languet's opinion, a mixed blessing. 'Who could have expected that the extreme North would at last supply us with so great incitement to evil.' Gold, Languet said, was the gift of nature, 'of all others the most fatal and hurtful to mankind, which nevertheless nearly all men desire with so insane a longing that it is the most powerful of all motives to bring them to incur the risk'.[16] Languet feared that gold-fever would have evil effects both on England as a nation and on Sidney as an individual. He pointed to one of the constant sources of complaint in the sixteenth century, depopulation of the countryside due to the enclosing of land for pasture, and suggested that it had been foolish of the crown to allow this because an abundant population was the surest strength of a country; now he feared that the process of depopulation begun by enclosing would be completed by a rush of Englishmen to the New World in a mad search for gold. Languet's reasoning here, perhaps correct in its moralistic aspects, was less sound in its grasp of the problems of the English economy and in any case ran counter to the general enthusiasm which the Protestant activists like Sidney had for overseas exploration. His fears for the effects of this on Sidney's own character were likewise somewhat misplaced. 'If the vain hope of finding a passage which Frobisher entertained had power then to tempt your mind so greatly, what will not these golden mountains effect, or rather these islands all of gold which I dare to say stand before your mind's eye day and night? Beware, I entreat you, and do not let the cursed hunger after gold which the Poet speaks of creep over that spirit of yours, into which nothing has hitherto been admitted but the love of goodness and the desire of earning the good will of all men.'[17] Sidney's interest, however, was not for himself; it was for the possible financing of the Protestant cause.

Fear and hopes were both removed when the assayers discovered that this 'purest' gold was totally worthless. The setback in this may have dampened Sidney's enthusiasm for New World projects for a while though he was to return to them later with renewed vigour. Or perhaps it was because his financial position bordered on the impossible that his interest in the voyages of Frobisher seemed for the moment to decline. Whatever the cause, as late as April 1579 Philip's name is among those who had not paid up their subscriptions undertaken on behalf of the explorer's voyages.[18] Perhaps too the not so gentle chiding of Languet that he could spend his time in ways far more useful both to himself and his nation influenced Sidney to concentrate on other things, especially affairs on the continent. As Languet put it, if the gold and the new world islands had fixed themselves deeply in Sidney's mind he should turn them out before they overcame him and kept him from serving his friends and country in a better way, and if his desire for fame and glory made his present court life seem irksome he should follow older examples of service to the state rather than pin vague hopes on the gold of North America; in such a way he could secure greater glory than by obtaining all the wealth which Spain had brought over from the New World.[19]

There was a large measure of good sense in what Languet wrote, and Sidney was led to see this. Probably Languet's was not the only influence working on him at this time. There is evidence that Philip was in the close confidence of his uncle the Earl of Leicester and was drawn with him into the affairs of the Netherlands. His closeness with Leicester is strikingly revealed by his knowledge of his uncle's secret marriage with Essex's widow. The Queen apparently did not learn of the marriage until the late summer of 1579; even the bride's family were ignorant of the clandestine marriage for the better part of a year and did not insist on a more formal ceremony until September 1578. But in December 1577 Philip concluded a letter to his uncle with the words: 'I will no further trouble your Lordship but with the remembrance of my duty to your Lordship and my Lady and aunt, and so I humbly leave you both to the Eternal, who always prosper you.'[20] The only plausible construction to be put on these words is that Leicester was already married; his nephew must have been one of the few people in England who knew.

Sidney's desires to do something on the continent were fostered not only by his closeness to Leicester and Languet. In large part they grew from within himself; he was not a man who could remain inactive for any length of time, and if the New World ventures were fruitless and if the Queen was not disposed to take advantage of his services in England, then his thoughts turned naturally to the Netherlands. He continued to see much of continental Protestant leaders when they were in England, notably the Frenchman du Plessis Mornay. The latter's wife remarked that her husband's closest friends during the eighteen months he spent in London on a mission from the King of Navarre were Sidney and Leicester; of Sidney she commented that he was 'the most accomplished gentlemen in England',[21] and the admiration was echoed in the fact that Sidney became the godfather to Mornay's daughter. Sidney also saw much of Butrech, whom Languet referred to as 'our Equestrian Doctor'[22] and who appears to have been in the suite of Prince Casimir. It seems likely that Butrech came to Sidney with some sort of proposal about the German states and the Protestant League, but what its exact nature was is not clear. Moreover, Sidney maintained a scholarly interest as well as a practical one in German affairs, and he received books from Languet and from Frankfort booksellers on the state of affairs.

His yearnings to do something active began to take more definite shape in the form of military service for the Protestant forces on the continent. Already Orange had sought the services of Philip and his uncle; now Casimir in 1578 sought to have him appointed as a sort of joint commander with himself. The rumours steadily grew that Sidney was on the verge of departing to the continent in some capacity. In April a correspondent writing to Walsingham assumed that Philip's departure was imminent;[23] rumours reached Languet on the continent that Elizabeth had decided to send troops to the Netherlands under the command of the Earl of Leicester,[24] and the Spanish ambassador reported that Sidney was to be Vice-Admiral of a fleet destined for Flanders.[25] There was little substance in the rumours, but it is important to see here a segment of the leadership of the Protestant activists clearly revealed, Leicester, Sidney, and behind the scenes Sir Francis Walsingham; Mendoza castigated the latter as 'such a devilish heretic that he constantly favours those like himself and persecutes the Catholics in order to pledge the Queen more deeply to his way of thinking'.[26] There were various manœuvrings to secure permission for Leicester and Sidney to embark on this continental adventure, but in the last analysis, permission rested with the Queen, and the Queen's attitude was not favourable. She would not permit Leicester to go at all; Sidney she would allow to take part in these adventures only in a private capacity. If this was all that could be extracted from a grudging Queen, it was better than nothing, or so Leicester thought when he wrote to Sir Christopher Hatton in July; since it was not to be his fortune to go on 'so honourable a voyage' he was 'most glad' that Philip was being allowed to go to serve with Casimir, 'and if he may not as from her Majesty, yet after the other sort you say her Majesty could like of [*i.e.* in a private capacity] I beseech you further it, and I shall be most glad it may be obtained'.[27]

But even this promising opening was to be closed. Sidney did get his permission to go to serve Casimir, but he got it in such a way as to make it useless for him to go; the Queen insisted that Sidney carry a message to Casimir effectually cutting off any hope of English aid. Apparently the Queen was alarmed at rumours that Sidney was going to Casimir in some official capacity, for she knew that such rumours could be extremely dangerous to her cautious balancing policy; at least this is the impression that one gets from Leicester's account of the matter:[28]

When my nephew Philip was to take his leave and receive his dispatch, among other small comforts he should have brought to the Prince, he was specially commanded by her Majesty to tell Duke Casimir that she marvelled not a little, and was offended with him for giving out that his coming was by her means, and that she misliked any such speeches, and prayed her name might not be so abused, since she did not command him to come, but the States had entertained him and they should maintain his coming; with such other small encouragements to that prince, whose cause of coming you and I and almost all men know. Yet this earnestly has she commanded Philip to say to him, writing . . . a letter besides of cold comfort.

Leicester, when he heard of the Queen's attitude and the letter she was asking Sidney to take to Casimir, did all he could to stay Philip at home, 'seeing I know not what he should do there but bring discouragement to all her best friends. For my part, I had rather he perished in the sea than that he should be the instrument of it'.[29] Leicester was not the only person to press Philip to remain at home; his father did so too, though he was, as he expressed it in a letter to Leicester, willing to let him go rather than 'hinder his determination in a matter wherein he is to purchase himself so much honour and credit'.[30] Sir Henry explained his attitude to Philip by saying that he was striving between honour and necessity; he knew that Philip could gain the former by such an expedition, yet he thought that perhaps family necessity was such that it could hold his son at home.

The necessity of which he was thinking was the continuing furore over his Irish administration and his conflict with Ormonde. The matter had been far from settled by the recall of Sir Henry in February 1578. We have seen how Sir Henry remained in Ireland during the summer of that year, and in this time Philip continued to be busy in his interests. That the situation seemed serious and tense is well illustrated by one of the more spectacular of Sidney's outbursts of temper; beneath the surface of the polished young courtier there lurked a temper that could be bitter, blunt, and brutish when provoked. Sidney began to suspect in May 1578 that someone was communicating the contents of his correspondence with his father to Ormonde and his faction. Without any real proof he decided that his father's secretary Molyneux was the guilty party, and he addressed to him a short but savage note:[31]

Mr Molyneux: Few words are best. My letters to my father have come to the eyes of some. Neither can I condemn any but you for it. If it be so, you have played the very knave with me, and so I will make you know if I have good proof of it. But that for so much as is past. For that is to come, I assure you before God, that if ever I know you do so much as read any letter I write to my father without his commandment or my consent, I will thrust my dagger into you. And trust to it, for I speak it in earnest. In the meantime, farewell.

The matter was quickly smoothed over; Molyneux wrote in his own defence,[32] and it seems clear from the content of the later letters that good relations between the two were restored.[33] Biographers of Sidney have long been embarrassed by this temperamental outburst against an apparently faithful servant. Yet it is perfectly in keeping with what we know about Sidney's character. He was no saint; he was impulsive and, like most Elizabethans, he did not scorn violence when he thought that it would serve his purposes. In addition, there can be little doubt that Sidney was, at this time, in a depressed mood which could make idle suspicion seem like certain treachery. He was much concerned over the treatment of his father which reflects so little credit on England's Queen; he was personally frustrated by the Queen's refusal to follow those schemes which he felt to be in the best interests of the nation, and he was beginning to feel somewhat bitter towards his age as a whole. It seemed to offer him so many courses of action and so few opportunities for fulfilling any of them.

Among the things which served to retrieve Sidney from this mood of bitter depression was the arrival in England of two of his most loyal and admired friends, Prince Casimir and Languet himself. The reasons for Casimir's arrival in England were obvious; he wanted to see if he could somehow rationalise his relationship with the Queen, whose favour blew alternately hot and cold towards him. He did not understand that this was precisely the way Elizabeth wanted her relationship to the continental Protestants to remain, so that she could take advantage of their successes when they had any and could repudiate any responsibility when they suffered setbacks. Languet's visit was also easy to explain, though rather more unexpected. Two days before departing, Languet had apparently not made up his mind to come,[34] but then, with the opportunity at hand, and the prospect of failing health before him, he decided to take advantage of what might be his last chance to see his promising student.

Casimir's and Languet's visit to England between January and February 1579 was a series of dazzling spectacles and receptions. Philip and his father were commissioned to meet him and they accompanied him to London where on 22 January Casimir and his company were 'by divers noblemen and others honourably received and conveyed by cresset light and torch light to Sir Thomas Gresham's house in Bishopsgate Street where [they] were received with sounding of trumpets, drums, fifes, and other instruments of music and there lodged and feasted till Sunday next'.[35] Casimir was summoned to talk with the Queen, and for a while he lodged in Somerset House and hunted at Hampton Court. At the beginning of February he watched tilting and jousting at Westminster and the following day watched men fighting at the barriers with swords on horseback. He dined with the Duchess of Suffolk and with the Lord Mayor of London, and the Queen made him a Knight of the Garter, although he was not at this time formally invested. In the course of his visit he was, naturally enough, frequently in the company of the Protestant activists, especially Sidney and Leicester, the latter of whom took him to visit Wanstead.

In like manner was Languet entertained and introduced to the circle of friends who had gathered about Sidney. Two of them he took particularly to his heart: Edward Dyer, 'a precious gem added to my store',[36] and Fulke Greville. They were probably Sidney's closest friends as Sidney himself noted in a poem.[37]

> My two and I be met;
> A happy blessed Trinitie;
> As three most joyntly set,
> In firmest band of Unitie.
> > Joyne hearts and hands, so let it be,
> > Make but one Minde in Bodies three.
>
> Welcome my two to me,   E.D. F.G. P.S.
> The number best beloved,
> Within my heart you be
> In friendship unremoved
>
> Like Lovers do their Love,
> So joy I, in you seeing;
> Let nothing mee remove
> From always with you beeing.
>
> Now joyned be our hands,
> Let them be ne'r a sunder,
> But linkt in binding bands
> By metamorphoz'd wonder.
> > So should our sever'd bodies three
> > As one for ever joyned bee.

The visit was brief, but it was immensely cheering to Sidney. There was no time for a lingering farewell at the end of the visit; Casimir left so hurriedly that Languet in fact never said good-bye to Sidney and Dyer. He wrote to Philip from Flushing to apologise for this, 'though in truth I had nothing for you but tears and sighs'.[38] Languet's comment on the haste of the departure provides a revealing footnote on Casimir's visit to the Queen. Though she showed him considerable favour by making him a Knight of the Garter, and even though the city of London had displayed a solidarity with his cause, Casimir had gone away without that which he had hoped for in the way of tightening up his relations with the English crown. 'Our party were hastening away as if they were taking leave of enemies, not of friends, and I should have given great offence if I alone had behaved with common sense instead of being mad with the rest.'[39]

Philip was not unmindful either at this time of family matters. His younger brother Robert had begun his tour of education on the continent. Robert shared little of the scholarly attainment which Philip had; his record at Oxford had been far from inspiring, but Philip (with some obvious encouragement from his father) took a lively interest nonetheless in attempting to further the education of his brother and to widen his horizons. Perhaps Robert chafed somewhat under the constantly presented example of his elder brother, but it was the example that was most consistently held up to him. 'Follow the direction of your most loving brother who in loving you is comparable with me or exceedeth me. Imitate his virtue, exercises, studies, and actions; he is a rare ornament to this age'.[40] Philip appears to have taken this relationship with his brother seriously. He wrote him long letters advising him on the manner of his life, what to see, who to meet. At times a very human streak shows through the long-winded letters of advice; at the end of one such letter, conscious of having gone on at inordinate length, Philip wrote: 'Lord, how I have babbled'.[41] At another time it appears the petulance Philip felt at being inactive in such stirring times had been communicated to his brother by urging him that if he heard of any 'good wars' he should go off to them.[42] In the main, however, the importance of the relationship for Robert was the opening to him of the same doors that Philip himself had opened on his Grand Tour. After Languet returned to the continent he began to look after the younger brother with much the same affection that he had displayed towards the elder. Lobetius, Sturm, Orange, La Noue, all took an interest in young Robert, mainly because he was Philip's brother, and behind all the interest and courtesy was the arranging hand of Languet: 'I have taken care that he should make the acquaintance and prepare a way to the friendship of such persons here as I consider eminent for their character. The Prince of Orange and La Noue especially welcomed him, and La Noue, who is full of courtesy, showed him every attention yesterday as long as we were in the citadel.'[43] Languet even arranged for a tutor for Robert, a man named Peter Hubner, and there is a curious echo of Languet's inability to get Philip to pursue the study of German with sufficient diligence in his careful instructions to Hubner to see that Robert learns to speak the language.[44]

Sidney's interests could scarcely be satisfied by advising his brother. On several occasions his anger and annoyance at being deprived of meaningful occupation and his fear that English policy was not bent enough to favour the Protestant cause had been openly expressed. Languet had criticised him somewhat unfairly for his part in court life:[45]

The habits of your court seemed to me somewhat less manly than I could have wished, and most of your noblemen appeared to me to seek for a reputation more by a kind of affected courtesy than by those virtues which are wholesome to the state, and which are most becoming to generous spirits and to men of high birth. I was sorry therefore, and so were other friends of yours, to see you wasting the flower of your life on such things, and I feared lest that noble nature of yours should be dulled, and lest from habit you should be brought to take pleasure in pursuits which only enervate the mind.

But what Languet was here pointing out was just what Sidney himself felt, and even though he knew the path to favour and employment lay along these lines, he could not fully reconcile himself to them.

These uneasy feelings, both about his own future and about his country's policy, came to a head in the complicated negotiations in 1579 for a marriage between his sovereign and the Frenchman Alençon. The proposal that there should be a marriage negotiation with France was not a new feature of Elizabeth's diplomatic courtships, and it seems certain that this affair too was well within the realm of diplomacy and far removed from the realm of passion. The revival of interest in Alençon was closely related to the problems of Elizabethan diplomacy in the Netherlands. It has been noted how the English policy aimed at keeping a balance in the area with the least expense conceivable to itself. It was felt that Alençon might well accomplish the military side of this for England. It became, as a result, part of the Elizabethan policy to maintain Alençon and his force in the Netherlands as a resistance to Spain, while at the same time doing whatever was possible to see that he did not overpower the area himself. 'Her main business . . . was to place him in a position in which he could be depended upon to subserve her interests.'[46]

This consideration had much to do with the seeming attractiveness of Alençon's renewed proposal of marriage in the summer of 1578. Alençon for his part was equally well playing a diplomatic game; he was after an advantageous alliance, and, as Walsingham expressed it, Elizabeth was the best marriage in her parish and provided a kingdom for a dowry.[47] The kingdom and the chief advisors in it were not, however, by any means united in favour of the proposed marriage. The Puritan activist faction was wholeheartedly opposed. Walsingham saw that the negotiations for the marriage, which were bound to be involved and protracted, would constitute a major stumbling block to his aggressive policy. Leicester agreed with this view, and the younger member of their circle, Philip Sidney, also concurred. On the other side Sussex and Oxford stood out firmly for the match, while the crucial Burghley carefully weighed the pros and cons and then found that he too was in favour. The makings of a serious political split were at hand, and with the Queen seemingly inclined towards the match and certainly favourable to opening the negotiations, the position of the activists was less than comfortable. Walsingham, who returned to England from the Low Countries in October 1578, found that he was quite definitely out of favour with the Queen. 'I find her Majesty altered from that I left her touching those causes, so that I am out of hope of any good resolution, for the which I am very sorry, knowing that upon this resolution dependeth either the conservation or alienation of the Low Countries people's hearts from her Majesty'.[48] Shortly afterwards Walsingham retired from the court for a fortnight.

It must be admitted that there were apparently sound diplomatic grounds for reopening the marriage negotiations with France. Elizabeth's policy of balance demanded close attention to affairs in Scotland, Spain, and the Netherlands as well as France, and as the diplomatic relations developed between 1578 and 1580, the situation seemed to argue more and more for a French tie. It was to be hoped that the marriage would lead to close ties between the countries; this would not only help control Alençon's actions in the Netherlands in such a fashion that they would be useful to England but also could counterbalance any potential danger from Scotland. Since 1573 the latter kingdom had seemed safe to England; with the crushing of the Marian faction there, the Regent Morton had governed the country and his inclinations towards the English were favourable. While he was in power Elizabeth could breathe easily as far as danger from the North. But in the spring of 1578 a coalition of opposition groups forced Morton out. He did succeed later in the year in reinstating himself into the confidence of the young King James, but the situation was further complicated by the arrival in Scotland during September of Esmé Stuart, Sieur d'Aubigny. The latter quickly rose in the King's favour, and what was dangerous about him was that he represented the French Guise policy and seemed to be working towards a renewal of the old policy of Scottish–French alliance aimed at England. The Guise party in France were known to be advocates of such a policy and they constantly attempted to persuade the French King of its worth. The chances of their doing so seemed to be increased at this point by the outbreak of civil war within the French kingdom, a war which set the Protestants at odds with their sovereign and led him towards an alliance with the Catholic Guise family.

At almost the same time the turn of affairs in Portugal added further impetus to the desires for a French alliance. In August 1578 the King of Portugal, Don Sebastian, was killed in the battle of Alcazar Kebir. He was childless and the succession passed to his great-uncle, a cardinal of the Church; like Don Sebastian, his uncle Henry was also childless and in addition was over sixty years old. It was obvious that there would be a dispute over the succession at his death and that his death would come soon. There were many claimants for the title, including the French Queen Catherine de Medici, the bastard nephew of the King Don Antonio, the Prior of Crato, and Catherine of Braganza, the King's niece. But the clearest and best title plainly was that of the King of Spain, Philip II, hammer of the Protestants and foe of England. Initially, there appears to have been some speculation in England that the passing of the Portuguese title to Philip of Spain might not be a bad thing; it might serve to divert him from the Netherlands.[49] But more serious heads soon saw the danger, so clearly pointed out by the Portuguese ambassador to London; were Philip to absorb into his dominions the vast possessions of the Portuguese empire, the delicate European balance would be violently upset. Both France and England stood to lose much by this; even though the rumours that Elizabeth had offered troops to the rival claimant Don Antonio were certainly false, it is true that Elizabeth and her councillors knew that the Portuguese situation was crucial to any diplomatic undertakings. It was true too that Catherine de Medici was determined not to see the prize go to Spain, although she probably entertained few serious thoughts about the efficacy of her own claims.

Finally, there were the pressing events in the Netherlands, and again the developing situation seemed to call for a meaningful rapprochement between France and England. The foreign intervention so far attempted on behalf of the rebels had proved of little benefit. Casimir's efforts were to as little effect as Alençon's, and in Casimir's case at least a substantial part of the trouble stemmed from the lack of consistent English financial support. Moreover, the Pacification of Ghent, which had for the moment produced a peace in the Low Countries, was no more than a truce, and in January 1579, when two unions were formed (the Catholic Union of Arras and the Protestant Union of Utrecht), the Pacification was a dead letter despite the protestations of loyalty to it by both unions. Five months afterwards the Union of Arras had reconciled itself to Spain, and conflict was again in the open. Nor did the prospects for the Protestant provinces appear any too good; the new Spanish commander, Parma, rapidly demonstrated why he was considered one of the military geniuses of the age, and the Dutch rebels were soon very much on the defensive. In looking abroad for aid, the Dutch did turn to the English, but Queen Elizabeth was not receptive and in May 1579 she recalled Davison, her agent at Antwerp, and sent no successor. Consequently William of Orange and the Dutch began to look more favourably towards Alençon and his tentatives of aid, while Alençon for his part began to evidence a lively interest in the affairs of the Dutch. This raised again the spectre of a French ascendancy in the Low Countries, and a marriage, it was urged, might be the means to control the situation.

The scene was thus a confusing one for the councillors like Walsingham who were opposed to the match on general and religious grounds but who knew that the international situation contained in it factors which argued for just such an alliance. Events seemed to move rapidly towards a realisation of the project. A formal proposal of marriage was made to Elizabeth in the summer of 1578. Her reply, characteristically committing her not a bit, was still open enough to excite French interest. Among the conditions she stated was the provision that she would not marry anyone whom she had not first seen. The result of this declaration was the mission of Jean de Simier, Alençon's master of the wardrobe, and later a visit of Alençon himself. Simier, who had his first audience with the Queen on 11 January 1579, was 'a most choice courtier, exquisitely skilled in love toys, pleasant conceits, and court dalliances'.[50] He quickly ingratiated himself with the Queen and earned the nickname of 'her ape'. But when it came to practical decisions the Queen was still evasive and Simier found himself dealing with a Council that was badly divided against itself on this matter; he was instructed to deal with Burghley, Sussex, Leicester, and Walsingham, and he seemed to make little progress.

Opinion in England was none the less persuaded that Alençon would come to the Queen, and many suspected that he would achieve success with his proposal. The Privy Council found itself spending much time on the project. As Gilbert Talbot wrote from the court on 4 April: 'These five days past, Privy Council has sat from eight a.m. till dinner time and presently after dinner, and an hour's conference with her Majesty, to council again and so till supper time. And all this, as far as I can learn, is about the matter of Monseigneur's coming here, his entertainment here, and what demands are to be made to him in the treaty of marriage.'[51] It is apparent that Elizabeth was withholding a decision on the main matter of the marriage and referring the discussion of details to her council. At the end of the month, however, she put the major question to them directly and apparently in doing so expressed herself very strongly in favour of the marriage. The Council emerged, as might be expected, with Burghley favouring the match and Walsingham opposing it. Since Walsingham was in the position at this point to be the major spokesman of the opposition activist policy, his opinions are worth noting carefully; they were closely related to those which Philip Sidney was soon to utter. Walsingham divided his analysis of 'the diseased state of the realm' into inward and outward perils.[52] He saw the inward diseases as being linked to the problems of the succession, the establishment of a uniform religion, and the treatment of Mary Queen of Scots. Outward diseases included the natural enmity of France and Spain, the situation in

Scotland, and the fear that Alençon, if rebuffed in England, might make a Spanish marriage alliance. It is clear all through Walsingham's recitation of the problem that he distrusted the French and their motives, but beyond this he raised the question whether the match could be considered expedient even if Alençon were sincere in his protestations. He felt that there were 'incommodities' to the marriage: the wide gap in age between Elizabeth and Alençon, the dangers of childbirth, and above all the question of religion, 'a matter principally to be weighed by Christian counsellors in giving advice to a Christian prince, seeing the prosperity or adversity of kingdoms dependeth of God's goodness who is so long to extend his protection as we shall depend of his providence and shall not seek our safety (carried away by human policy) contrary to his word'.[53]

Walsingham was a shrewd statesman and diplomat; he knew that there appeared to be compelling arguments on the level of international relations for the marriage, yet even here he introduced a note of questioning and criticism; he feared that whatever the ostensible gains in foreign relations might be, they would be offset by the incitement the marriage would give to discontent at home. The people wished to see their Queen married, but, he noted, they would not want this if the price were a Catholic husband. In general he offered instead of the policy of alliance his own and the Protestant activists' view of the proper conduct of foreign affairs: avoid alliance with Catholic powers and attempt to offset them by encouraging Protestant rebels. The vision of the Protestant League was offered anew, with the firm faith that the bond of common religion was the strongest which could unite countries; the hand of God would be on the Protestant side. It has been said with justice that Walsingham here spoke with the true voice of Elizabethan England, judging its temper and its aspirations far better than the Queen or Burghley.[54]

This view received support in the country at large. In March a preacher at the Royal Chapel commented to the Queen that the nation had no need of another foreign marriage; that of her sister Mary had been example enough.[55] In April the Bishop of Ely urged a similar point in attempting to persuade the Queen to abandon the marriage project.[56] Despite these indications and the pointed quality of Walsingham's remarks, the Council remained divided and rumours continued to be widespread that the marriage would take place. In August

Alençon himself arrived for a short visit. Attempts were made, with some success, to keep the visit a secret, and the negotiations seemed to proceed smoothly.

The Protestant activists were discouraged and somewhat desperate. Their cause was in official disrepute. Not only was the Queen openly annoyed at Walsingham for his continued opposition but she was even more displeased with their other titular leader Leicester, for Simier had revealed to the Queen the details of Leicester's secret marriage and the Earl was temporarily induced to leave the court. Mendoza, the Spanish ambassador, reported that Leicester 'retired to a house of his five miles away where the Queen has been to see him and where she remained two days because he feigned illness. She afterwards returned secretly to London. A sister of Leicester's [? Lady Sidney] of whom the Queen was very fond and to whom she had given apartments at court retired at the same time as her brother'.[57]

The Protestant activists seemed to be very much in retreat. With Walsingham's views hardly prevailing with the Queen and Leicester 'like a wise man under colour of taking physic'[58] retired to Greenwich Castle, from which, according to Camden, he was forbidden to venture by the Queen, there seemed need for more dramatic action. Chance for such action came in mid-August when Leicester was allowed to return to London. If the account of Mendoza is to be believed the activists met at the Earl of Pembroke's home, and at the meeting the presence of Philip Sidney was especially to be noted.[59] They discussed the affair of the marriage at considerable length contemplating the possibility of thwarting it in parliament and raising apparently the question of popular pressure as well; Mendoza commented that 'the people in general seem to threaten revolution about it'.[60] The latter point is certainly doubtful; Spanish commentators were prone to see the possibility of civil war in England when such possibility was, in fact, slight. In any case, it is not to be expected that a circle of aristocratic leaders would have looked with favour on any proposals for a genuine popular insurrection; the fear of the masses was too great a preoccupation with them. Nor is it likely that they expected very much from parliamentary pressure; the power of that body to force its way on the monarch was still very much circumscribed. It is possible, then, that a third course was discussed and eventually settled on: that a formal statement against the marriage be written and presented to the Queen. And who else should be the author but Philip Sidney? He was eminently qualified on most counts. He had already revealed that he had a power with words in his defence of his father's Irish policy; he was clearly committed to the Protestant cause; although not a statesman of stature or experience or a royal adviser, he had already achieved some eminence in the country, partly through his family relations, partly through his diplomatic mission. In addition, Sidney had already been pointed to as the Protestant hero knight by Spenser in the *Shepheardes Calendar* which had been dedicated to 'the noble and virtuous gentleman, most worthy of all titles both of learning and chivalry, Mr Philip Sidney'.[61] In short, Sidney was being put forward by the Protestant activists as their most respectable spokesman; Sidney confessed later to Languet that he had written his letter to the Queen on the subject of the French marriage at the command of those he felt obliged to obey;[62] there can be little doubt that they were Walsingham and Leicester.

Sidney's opposition to the proposed French marriage was well known by this time; shortly before the meeting at the Earl of Pembroke's house he had displayed his position and his slight patience with the favourers of the marriage in a celebrated incident. While Sidney was clearly among those opposed to the marriage, Burghley's son-in-law, the Earl of Oxford, was one of the most ostentatious supporters of the alliance. When the two encountered each other at the tennis court the scene rapidly turned into a violent argument:[63]

And in this freedom of heart being one day at tennis, a peer of this realm, born great, greater by alliance, and superlative in the prince's favour, abruptly came into the tennis court and speaking out of these three paramount authorities, he forgot to entreat that which he could not legally command. When by the encounter of a steady object, finding unrespectiveness in himself (though a great Lord) not respected by this princely spirit, he grew to expostulate more roughly. The returns of which style coming still from an understanding heart, that knew what was due to itself and what it ought to others, seemed (through the mists of my Lord's passions, swollen with the wind of his faction then reigning) to provoke in yielding. Whereby, the less amazement or confusion of thoughts he stirred up in Sir Philip, the more shadows this great Lord's own mind was possessed with, till at last with rage (which is ever ill-disciplined) he commands them to depart the court. To this Sir Philip temperately answers that if his Lordship had been pleased to express desire in milder characters, perchance he might have led out those that he should now find would not be driven out with any scourge of fury. This answer (like a bellows) blowing up the sparks of excess already kindled made my Lord scornfully call Sir Philip by the name of Puppy. In which progress of heat, as the tempest grew more and more vehement within, so did their hearts breathe out their perturbations in a more loud and shrill accent. The French Commissioners unfortunately had that day audience in those private galleries whose windows looked into the tennis court. They instantly drew all to this tumult, every sort of quarrels sorting well with their humours, especially this. Which Sir Philip perceiving and rising with inward strength by the prospect of a mighty faction against him, asked my Lord with a loud voice that which he heard clearly enough before. Who (like an echo that still multiplies by reflections) repeated this epithet of Puppy the second time. Sir Philip resolving in one answer to conclude both the attentive hearers and passionate actor, gave my Lord a lie, impossible (as he averred) to be retorted, in respect all the world knows puppies are gotten by dogs and children by men.

Hereupon those glorious inequalities of fortune in his Lordship were put to a kind of pause by a precious inequality of nature in this gentleman. So that they both stood silent a while, like a dumb show in a tragedy, till Sir Philip, sensible of his own wrong, the foreign and factious spirits that attended, and yet even in this question between him and his superior tender to his country's honour, with some words of sharp accent, led the way abruptly out of the tennis court, as if so unexpected an accident were not fit to be decided any farther in that place. Whereof the great Lord making another sense, continues his play, without any advantage of reputation, as by the standard of humours in those times it was conceived.

The incident with Oxford reflected little credit on either participant, and it is only illustrative of the extremely frayed tempers at the time. It has been suggested that Sidney did not challenge Oxford to a duel because of the disparity in their rank, but it is apparent that he was acting according to the strict code of the gentleman.[64] Many of his friends were badly upset by the incident, especially Languet who wrote to Sidney that news of the argument gave him great pain;[65] Languet admitted that it was a habit 'inveterate' in all Christendom that a noble would be disgraced if he did not resent such an insult, although he still thought it was unfortunate that Sidney had been drawn into it. Languet was, however, able to see some possible good in the interchange at the tennis court; it gave Sidney a chance to display to the world his constancy and courage and perhaps would be a goad to spur him from the inactive life of the court. In the last analysis, though, Languet cautioned Sidney: 'You want another stage for your character, and I wish you had chosen it in this part of the world.'[66] The Queen, needless to say, was even less pleased with the tennis court quarrel, and she took firm steps to see that no duel would take place. Sidney's own attitude was clear; he was thoroughly resolute in his opinion and saw the matter as a test of honour in which he could not give in without pressure being exerted on him from above. He expressed himself clearly on this in a letter to Sir Christopher Hatton: 'As for the matter depending between the Earl of Oxford and me, certainly, Sir, howsoever I might have forgiven him, I should never have forgiven myself if I had lain under so proud an injury as he would have laid upon me, neither can anything under the sun make me repent it: let him therefore, as he will, digest it: for my part, I think tying up makes some things seem fiercer than they would be.'[67]

With the tennis-court quarrel so obvious to all, the views that Sidney expressed on the French marriage in his letter to the Queen could hardly have come as a surprise to anyone. That Sidney's views echoed the sentiments and assessments expressed earlier in the Council by Walsingham was also not a fact to amaze anyone, least of all the Queen. The letter of Sidney was direct and to the point; while he did not neglect the customary flattering of Elizabeth, he pointed out with clarity the breadth of the opposition to the proposed marriage and the chief arguments against it from the Protestant side. 'Therefore carrying no other olive branches of intercession but the lying myself at your feet, nor no other insinuation either for attention or pardon but the true vowed sacrifice of unfeigned love, I will in simple and direct terms (as hoping they shall only come to your merciful eyes) set down the overflowing of my mind in this most important matter, importing, as I think, the continuance of your safety and as I know the joys of my life.'[68] He argued, much as Walsingham had done earlier, that the chief support of Elizabeth was her loyal Protestant population, and that the proposed course of action would certainly gall them, perhaps alienate them. Alençon was no suitable match, however attractive the diplomatic advantages might for the moment seem. He was nothing but 'a Frenchman and a papist, in whom howsoever fine wits may find either further danger or painted excuses, yet very common people will know this, that he is the son of that Jezebel of our age: that his brothers made oblation of their own sister's marriage to easier make massacres of all sexes, that he himself, contrary to his promise and against all gratefulness, having had his liberty and principle estate chiefly by the

Huguenot's means did sack La Charité and utterly spoiled Issoire with fire and sword'.[69] Sidney urged the Queen to listen to the feelings of her Protestant subjects; the others in the realm, papists or crypto-Catholics, were to his mind essentially disloyal. 'This double rank of people how their minds have stood, the Northern Rebellion and infinite other practices have well taught you.[70] And using the analogy of the nation as a sick person, which Walsingham had employed in the Council, Sidney went on to urge that any encouragement to the Catholic faction would infinitely worsen the state of the common-wealth. 'If then the affectionate have their affections weakened and the discontented have a gap to utter their discontent, I think it will seem an evil preparative for the patient (I mean your estate) to a greater sickness.'[71] There was even more to be objected to in Alençon; neither his will nor his power commended him:[72]

His will to be as full of light ambition as is possible, besides the French disposition and his own education, his inconstant attempts against his brother, his thrusting himself into the Low Country matters, he sometimes seeking the King of Spain's daughter, sometimes your Majesty are evident testimonies of a light mind carried with every wind of hope, taught to love greatness any way gotten and having the motioners and ministers of his mind only such young men as have showed (they think) evil contentments a sufficient ground of any rebellion, whose ages giveth them to have seen no commonwealth but in faction and divers of them which have defiled their hands with odious murders. With these fancies and such favourites is it to be hoped for that he will be contained in the limits of your conditions.

Sidney was not oblivious in his condemnation of the proposed marriage to the diplomatic advantages that were alleged to go with it. But he chose to be sceptical of these. The strength of the commonwealth was not to be added to by ties with a Catholic power; in fact, the true strength of England, as Sidney diagnosed the situation, lay precisely in the affections of those Protestant activists who were the most vociferous opponents of the marriage, and to pursue the alliance in the hope that it would settle the succession question would be to pursue an illusion. 'Virtue and justice are the only bonds of the people's love: and as for that point, many princes have lost their crowns, whose own children were manifest successors, and some that had their own children used as instruments of their ruin. Not that I deny the bliss of children, but only mean to show religion and equity to be of themselves sufficient stays.'[73] Sidney concluded his address to the Queen with an urgent request that she take up the cause advocated by the Protestant activists, that she turn England into a bastion of the Protestant faith, that she make her nation the source of succour for beleaguered fellow-religionists abroad. 'I do with most humble heart say unto your Majesty that (laying aside this dangerous help) for your standing alone you must take it as a singular honour God hath done you to be indeed the only protector of his church; and yet in wordly respect your kingdom very sufficient so to do; if you make that religion upon which you stand to carry the only strength and have abroad those who still maintain the same cause, who (as being as they may be kept from utter falling) your Majesty is sure enough from your mightiest enemies.'[74]

Sidney's letter was but one part of the onslaught on the marriage, and it would be idle to maintain that it was the only or indeed the crucial document in the proceedings. Walsingham had cast his net wider than this. At about the same time a pamphlet by John Stubbs, *The Discoverie of a Gaping Gulf whereinto England is Like to be Swallowed by another French marriage*, also appeared; it was far more outspoken than the letter of Sidney and was intended for a far wider audience. To Stubbs, Alençon was not merely a Frenchman and a papist, but the devil himself, 'the old serpent in shape of a man whose sting is in his mouth and who doth endeavour to seduce our Eve that she and we may lose this English Paradise'.[75] The marriage, he thought, would be a breach of God's law; it was a sin 'to couple a Christian lady, a member of Christ, to a Prince and good son of Rome, that anti-Christian mother city'.[76] Stubbs's main arguments, like those of Walsingham and Sidney, were religious and nationalistic: 'Can it be safe that a stranger and Frenchman should as owner possess our Queen, the chief officer in England, our most precious rich treasure, our Elizabeth',[77] and he stressed how the Queen's official position made it even more necessary for her than for her subjects to avoid falling into the Catholic trap if the true faith were to be maintained. 'It were more perilous to the overthrow of religion in this faithful household of England than if in one day were consummated the like marriages of a hundred thousand of her subjects, for the straightest and roundest going Prince shall with much ado keep his people upright, especially in religion, but let the Prince lack never so little and the people will halt right down'.[78] It was rumoured at Paris that Walsingham had had something to do with Stubbs's pamphlet,[79] just as he almost certainly had with Sidney's letter, and the Queen's angry denunciation of the Secretary as being a man only good for the protection of heretics possibly reflects her knowledge of what was going on.[80]

Stubbs paid for his advice to the Queen in the brutal fashion typical of the sixteenth century. In company with the bookseller Page, who had distributed his tract, he was tried and in November at Westminster 'their right hands were struck off with a cleaver driven through the wrist with a beetle'.[81] Sidney's action in making similar criticism was not well received by the Queen, but he merited no such drastic treatment. It was indicated to him that his presence at the court was unwelcome, and he withdrew under what Languet called 'a sort of cloud'.[82]

Had Sidney pushed the matter too far? Languet perhaps thought so and wrote him to be careful lest his opposition should completely cut him off from the circles of power where he belonged:[83]

I admire your courage in freely admonishing the Queen and your countrymen of that which is to the State's advantage. But you must take care not to go so far that the unpopularity of your conduct be more than you can bear. . . . I advise you to persevere as long as you can do anything that may benefit your country, but when you find that your opposition only draws on you dislike and aversion, and that neither your country, your friends, nor yourself derive any advantage from it, I advise you to give way to necessity and reserve yourself for better times; for time itself will bring you occasions and means of serving your country.

Sidney may have responded to this suggestion; he took no further active part in the negotiations over the French alliance which continued to occupy the minds of English statesmen for months after until the Queen herself finally set aside the whole scheme, just at the time when the arguments in its favour seemed most cogent. But mistaken or not, Sidney had done what he felt was the only thing a true Protestant could do, and his biographer Greville recorded what must be the proper judgment of his actions, that he was entitled, even obligated to take the stand he did in opposition to the known wishes of his sovereign and that in acting so he was in no way being disloyal to the monarch whom above all he sought to serve:[84]

I must answer that his worth, truth, favour, and sincerity of heart together with his real manner of proceeding in it were his privileges.

Because this gentleman's course in this great business was not by murmur among equals or inferiors to detract from Princes, or by a mutinous kind of bemoaning error to stir up ill affections in their minds, whose best thoughts could do him no good, but by a due address of his humble reasons to the Queen herself, to whom the appeal was proper. So that although he found a sweet stream of sovereign humours in that well-tempered Lady to run against him, yet found he safety in herself against the selfness which appeared to threaten him in her: For this happily born and bred Princess was not (subject-like) apt to construe things reverently done in the worst sense, but rather with the spirit of anointed greatness (as created to reign equally over frail and strong) more desirous to find ways to fashion her people then colours or causes to punish them.

Nor was the year that Sidney was to spend in the shadows a wasted one. While he no doubt pined for active service, his year in retirement was an important and happy one in his career. In retreat at Leicester House and Wilton he was to develop more fully the talents for writing that he had within himself and which so far he had displayed mainly in political pamphlets.

Chapter 3

SIDNEY AND THE STATE
1580–85

These are the signs preceding the end of the
world. . . . Satan is roaring like a lion, the
world is going mad, Anti-Christ is resorting
to every extreme, that he may with wolf-like
ferocity devour the sheep of Christ.
                                    Dr Humphrey

I fancy I see a picture of the age in which we
live: an age that resembles a bow too long
bent; it must be unstrung or it will break.
                    Sidney to Languet (1574)

∞✠∞

In the New Year, 1581, Sidney had made his reconciliation with the
Queen and his gift of a jewel-encrusted whip symbolised his submission to her will. For the next few years Sidney's life was very busy;
he participated (though surely not to the degree he hoped for) in
affairs of state, serving as a member of parliament and gaining a not
insignificant foothold on the ladder of Elizabethan administration. His
contacts with the Puritan activists remained firm, cemented by his
marriage with the daughter of Sir Francis Walsingham. He participated
fully and splendidly in the ceremonial life of the court, adding to his
reputation as a model courtier. At the same time his visions widened.
As his thoughts matured, his contacts with other nations, with men of
learning and affairs, and with literature deepened and became more
complex. Because of his multiform activity in these years it is useful to
look at his career more topically than chronologically. In the present
chapter his 'official career', that is his service in parliament, court, and
administration, will be discussed. In later chapters we shall turn to
look at the broadening of his interests and at the nature of his mature
thought.

The parliament that assembled in 1581 was the third and last session
of the longest lived of Elizabethan parliaments, a parliament that had

been prorogued no less than twenty-six times.[1] Sidney, who sat in this
last session, had probably gained election to a vacancy caused by the
death of some member. The session was called in perilous and tense
times, the Catholic threat to England seeming even greater than ever
and the Queen desperately in need of a further subsidy. How much of
a part Sidney actually played in the proceedings of the parliament is
open to question; he was probably, as Professor Neale has suggested,
'an ornament rather than a power in the House'.[2] Yet his name is not
absent from the list of those who were concerned with the great issues
of the parliament, especially the Catholic threat. Sir Walter Mildmay
had presented the government's set speech for supply, treating extensively the theme of present dangers and necessary remedies. Under the
heading of remedies, Mildmay drew attention to the fact that the
current reign had been one of clemency, especially compared with the
persecution under Queen Mary. But, he added, 'when by long proof
we find that this favourable and gentle manner of dealing . . . hath
done no good . . . it is time for us to look more narrowly and straitly
to them, lest . . . they prove dangerous members . . . in the entrails of
our commonwealth'.[3] What was needed, he urged, were severe laws
against the Catholics, laws that would force them at least into open
obedience to the practices of religion in England. At the conclusion of
Mildmay's address, another member, Norton, spoke, pursuing the
same theme; in the course of his comments, he moved for the creation
of a committee 'to consult of bills convenient to be framed' to ward off
the dangers that Mildmay had pointed to. The motion was a significant
one in parliamentary history. Norton, as leader of the non-official
members, was seeing to it that one of the main bills of the session would
be coming from a committee of the House rather than from the government, as had been the practice in earlier sessions.[4]

On the strength of Norton's motion, a large committee consisting
of all Privy Councillors and fifty-seven others, including Philip
Sidney,[5] was appointed. The committee, in which Norton was successful in seizing the leadership, produced a bill 'for obedience to the
Queen's Majesty against the see of Rome'. It was a very harsh measure,
but it was not the one which was eventually to become law. The parliamentary history of this recusancy bill is complex. A second
bill was introduced after a consultation with the House of Lords; it
was longer and amended the first form, but its main provisions and

penalties against the Catholics remained substantially the same. At the beginning of March a third and milder bill was introduced, pushed through quickly, and eventually received the royal assent. It is apparent that the Queen had intervened and had succeeded in reducing the severity of the original measure.

What part, if any, Philip Sidney played in these proceedings is impossible to tell. It is not even quite clear what his own attitude towards the various bills was. One clue does, however, exist, and it may suggest that Sidney was more favourable to the milder bill which eventually became law than he was to the first version. On 28 March, after the prorogation of parliament, Sidney wrote a letter to a Catholic, Lady Kitson, and in it mentioned to her that 'there is a present intention of a general mitigation to be used in respect of recusants. . . . There is meant a speedy easing of the greatness of your burden'.[6] Sidney's comment was not exactly accurate even in the context of the milder bill, though it did represent an easing of the burden imposed by the first bill. It is interesting to note, however, that one of the statesmanlike aspects of the third bill coincided fairly closely with Sidney's own attitude towards Catholics, which, as we have seen, was far from being a universal and blind hatred. The main provision of the bill declared 'that all persons whatsoever, which . . . shall by any ways or means put in practice to . . . withdraw any of the Queen's Majesty's subjects . . . from their natural obedience to her Majesty, or to withdraw them for that intent from the religion now by her Highness' authority established . . . to the Romish religion, or to move them to promise any obedience to any pretended authority of the See of Rome, or any other prince, state, or potentate, to be used within her dominions, or shall do any overt act to that intent or purpose . . . shall be adjudged to be traitors'.[7] The three words *for that intent* made all the difference. As one modern scholar has put it, 'the law refrains from plainly defining conversion to Catholicism as treason; it was rather conversion accompanied by withdrawal of allegiance which was condemned'.[8]

Sidney was also a member of another committee in this parliament, the committee to consider the bill against seditious words and rumours uttered against the Queen.[9] Again, it was a bill with a complicated parliamentary history.[10] It had been introduced in the House of Lords by Burghley and was intended to extend a similar act of Mary Tudor's time. Many in the House of Commons objected to the bill, largely it would seem because the bill's terms were not specifically confined to Catholics but would cover Puritan controversialists like John Stubbs as well.[11] The Commons, again under the leadership of Norton, sought to make amendments which would safeguard the position of the Puritans, and it was the bill with these additions that the committee of which Sidney was a member discussed. While the Commons were not able to win the battle entirely, the bill as it became statute was substantially the work of the lower house; it had been rephrased with only one reference to the Marian statute, and that mention repealed the older law. What Sidney's attitude towards this was is again something which is impossible to determine. Given his general inclination to the left-wing Protestant cause (and the fact that he and Stubbs had, in their very different ways, come to the same conclusion about the French marriage) it may not be rash to presume that he endorsed that attitude which the Commons adopted towards the bill.

The parliament was prorogued on 18 March. The Queen thanked the House for their work, although in her general thanks she did not include some members of the Commons who 'have this session dealt more rashly in some things than was fit for them to do'.[12] The reference was obviously to Norton and his followers. Though Sidney probably agreed with their views on the sedition bill, his part in this session of parliament was not such, apparently, as to merit either credit or blame. The parliament was to drag on its fitful life, kept alive by a whole series of prorogations, until April 1583, but it was not to hold another session.

When a new House of Commons was elected in 1584, Sidney was again returned as a member, probably sitting for the county of Kent.[13] In this House, he was joined by many of his friends and associates: Fulke Greville, Drake, Hawkins, Raleigh, Wotton, Henry Neville among others. If the times in which the previous parliament had met seemed perilous, how much more so did they seem in 1584. The revelation of the Throckmorton plot to assassinate the Queen and invade the country had brought home to many who had ignored the problem before the tiny thread of security on which the country depended; it was a line which seemed even less of a safeguard when the news reached England that the Prince of Orange had been assassinated. Moreover, the country was facing the full onslaught of the Jesuit mission. In anticipation of these problems, the Bond of Association, a document which was to be circulated throughout the country to organise a sworn group of avengers to protect the life of the Queen, had already been drawn up, and it is clear that parliament assembled in the spirit of the Bond, determined to protect their Queen, especially against the claims of any who, like Mary Queen of Scots, should express a title to the throne and thus seek 'to disturb her Majesty's possession during her life'. The tone of the parliament was set by the speeches of Sir Walter Mildmay and Sir Christopher Hatton on Saturday, 28 November. Mildmay stressed the Catholic threat. He drew particular attention to 'divers . . . malicious and secret practisers', especially the Jesuits and seminary priests, 'a rabble of vagrant runagates that creep . . . into sundry parts of the realm and are occupied to stir sedition . . . under pretence of reforming men's consciences'.[14] He pointed to the trial of Campion and his fellows; they had been prosecuted, Mildmay stated, 'not for the superstitious ceremonies of Rome but for most high and capital offences and conspiracies', the latter including 'the deposing of our most gracious Queen, advancing of another in her place, alteration and subversion of this whole state and government'.[15] Mildmay then suggested what were to be the two main measures proposed for the parliament: an act for the Queen's safety and an act against Jesuits and seminary priests.

Of the major legislation of the parliament, Sidney appears only to have been concerned with the act against the Jesuits. The act followed directly on from a suggestion in Mildmay's speech. 'Like as raging waters would destroy whole countries except they were kept in with strong banks, even so, lest these malicious, raging runagates, these Jesuits and priests, should overflow and overrun all the corners of this realm to the destruction of us all, let us provide strong and strait laws to keep them under . . . letting them find how dangerous it shall be for them to come here or once to put their foot on land within any her Majesty's dominions'.[16] The bill against the Jesuits and seminary priests passed through the Commons in mid-December. It was, however, amended slightly in the House of Lords when they considered it after the Christmas recess. There was some grumbling in the Commons about this, especially by those who felt that the original Commons' bill was not itself severe enough. In the long run, the Commons made a few minor changes in the amendments offered by the House of Lords, and these involved some consultation between the two houses, since there were some misgivings about amendments to amendments. It was at this point that Sidney played what role he did in the proceedings, acting on the committee for conferring with the Lords.[17] Like most parliaments, however, this one, though called for the specific business of protecting the Queen, concerned itself with many other matters, some very miscellaneous and of minor importance. It is interesting to see that Sidney appears to have played a relatively active role in this sort of work, for he sat on a reasonably large number of committees considering such items.[18] We find him, for example, on a committee which considered the preservation of timber in Sussex, on another which was involved with letters patent to Walter Raleigh for overseas discovery, on a third to look out for the preservation of the bridge at Rochester, a fourth again considering preservation of timber (this time in Kent), a fifth dealing with the curriers of London, and finally the committee for the subsidy. The parliament itself, like its predecessor, revealed a strong Puritan streak and was sharply critical of the episcopacy of the realm. What role Sidney had in this or even what his attitude towards it was is not now to be discovered.[19]

It was not only in parliament that Sidney sought to serve his nation. He also clamoured for some office under the crown, and in this he was seconded, though unsuccessfully, by his father. Partially his concern with office at this time was connected with his active desire to serve the state; in part, perhaps great part, it was due to pressing financial need. The life at court was an expensive one, especially if the courtier, like Sidney, indulged heartily in the elaborate ceremony of the revived Elizabethan chivalry. These two motives, gain and service, cross and mingle with one another in a letter from Sidney to Burghley in 1581.[20]

Yesterday her Majesty at my taking my leave said again that I came up again she would take some order for me. I told her Majesty I would beseech your Lordship to have care of me therein. Her Majesty seemed then to like better of present manner of relief than the expecting the office. Truly, Sir, so do I too but being wholly out of comfort, I rather chose to have some token that my friends might see I had not utterly lost my time. So then do I leave it to your Lordship's good favour towards me. My suit is for 100 *l* a year in impropriations, if not the one then the other, if neither, yet her Majesty's speedy answer will . . . be much better to me than delay.

In an attempt to procure some office Sidney also enlisted the aid of

Sir Christopher Hatton, who for a price was usually an effective path to the Queen's favour.[21] In this case there was financial aid forthcoming though there was at present no office. The money—Sidney claimed he needed £3000—was to be made available to him out of the confiscated estates of Catholics. Sidney appears to have had qualms about receiving his money from such a source; he wrote to Leicester that 'truly I like not their persons and much worse their religions, but I think my fortunes very hard that my reward must be built upon other men's punishments'.[22] Yet necessity made the difference; qualms or not (and his uncertainties may have been increased by the execution of his former friend Campion), Sidney took the money.[23]

His next attempt to procure some sort of position of service was combined with his father's effort to find some place for him in the Irish administration. In 1582, in the aftermath of the Desmond rebellion, Irish affairs seemed worse than ever. In the moment of lowest depression the former services of Sir Henry Sidney in the island were remembered, and the desire came once more to the open that he should be returned to head the administration. Someone (it is not certain who) approached Sir Henry with this possibility, and despite his earlier harsh words about Ireland, the Irish service, and indeed the ingratitude that those who laboured long and hard there seemed to get at home, Sir Henry considered it might be worth returning. A document which was sent from Sir Henry to Philip reveals clearly the main reason why he contemplated a return to the thankless charge; it was for his son.[24]

First, that the principal and chief cause that moveth him to fancy or have any liking to take the charge of the government of Ireland (if the same be offered him) is the respect he beareth to him [i.e., Philip]. So that if he will assuredly promise him to go with him hither, and withal will put on a determinate mind to remain and continue there after him, and to succeed him in the government (if it may so like her Majesty to allow him) he will then yield his consent to go; otherwise he will not leave his quiet and contented life at home, considering his years and the defects of nature, that commonly accompany age, to enter into so toilsome a place both of body and mind, but only to leave some memory and worthy mark to his posterity.

Sir Henry made other terms as well as indicating that Philip should not only join him but should succeed him in the post. Whether it was because the conditions were too extensive or whether other reasons intervened, the project was dropped. The failure of Philip Sidney to gain a foothold in the Irish administration was probably fortunate for his reputation. Few who dealt with Ireland emerged with their reputation enhanced, and even the policy of Sir Henry, which had much to commend it in comparison with that of other Elizabethans, looks poor when viewed from the perspective of the present. It would be unreasonable to expect that Philip Sidney, whatever his talents and charms in other directions, would have been able to cope with Ireland in a fashion any better than the rest of his contemporaries. And while there is little evidence that bears directly on this point, Sidney's attitudes towards Ireland and the Irish may have been even less enlightened than those of his father. This is perhaps revealed in his attempt to secure the possession of a forfeited estate in Ireland for his friend Captain Edward Denny; there was an Irish claimant for the estate, but Sidney fully concurred in the judgment that 'it is most necessary some English gentleman should have it', and he swept aside any claim that the Irish might have with the statement 'as for him that sueth for it in the court, he is indeed a good honest fellow, according to the brood of that nation, but being a bastard he hath no law to recover it, and he is much too weak to keep it'.[25] One of Sidney's biographers was surely correct in concluding that Philip 'had nothing to contribute toward the solution of the Irish problem'.[26]

If Sidney could not, then, be associated with his father in the government of Ireland, perhaps he could aid Sir Henry in his other administrative post, the government of Wales. Sidney himself took steps to try to secure such an appointment. He wrote to Edmund Molyneux in July 1582: 'Solicit my Lord Treasurer and Mr Vice-Chamberlain for my being of the council',[27] but Burghley and Hatton were unable or unwilling to do much to aid him in securing such an appointment. Philip did serve but in a completely unofficial manner as the conveyor of his father's views on the government of Wales to Lord Burghley. A fruitful employment for the state still eluded him. Under pressure both financial and psychological, Sidney began to be less squeamish about petitioning for office and pushing forward his own claims when the opportunity arose. He seems to have convinced himself gradually that he had no more to lose by pushing for office than he did by patiently standing at the side and waiting for it. At least he wrote in such a vein to one of his friends: 'Methinks you should do well to begin betimes to demand something of her Majesty as might be found fit for you. And let folks chafe as well when you ask, as when you do not'.[28]

It was through persistence of this sort that Sidney was able, after two and a half years, to gain an official position. Again, the aid of one of his relatives was used, but this time it was successful. Sidney's uncle, the Earl of Warwick, held the position of Master of the Ordnance. Warwick, appreciating the talents of his nephew, sought to have Sidney associated with him in some manner in the Ordnance. Given Sidney's inclinations towards an aggressive foreign policy, it was not an unsuitable place for him to seek employment. Acting on Warwick's request, which had been addressed to the Queen, Sidney also enlisted the aid of Lord Burghley.[29]

I have from my childhood been much bound to your Lordship which as the meanness of my fortune keeps me from ability to requite, so gives it me daily cause to make the bond greater, by seeking and using your favour toward me. The Queen, at my Lord of Warwick's request, hath been moved to join me in his Office of Ordnance, and, as I learn, her Majesty yields gracious hearing unto it. My suit is your Lordship will favour and further it which I truly affirm unto your Lordship I much more desire for the being busied in a thing of some serviceable experience, than for any other commodity, which I think is but small, that can arise of it. I conclude your Lordship's trouble with this, that I have no reason to be thus bold with your Lordship but the presuming of your honourable good will towards me, which I cannot deserve but I can and will greatly esteem.

Within a month, some action had been taken on this and Walsingham had written to the Solicitor General requesting him to make a patent for the office, but also urging him to keep the matter quiet for the time being.[30] Despite this promising beginning to the suit for office, little happened. In July 1583 Sidney wrote again to Burghley urging him to recommend to Elizabeth some action on the matter: 'I humbly crave of your Lordship your good word to her Majesty for the confirming that grant she once made unto me, of joining my patent with my Lord of Warwick, whose desire is that it should be so. The larger discoursing hereof I will omit as superfluous to your wisdom, neither will I use more plenty of words till God make me able to print them in some serviceable effect towards your Lordship'.[31]

The original desire to be associated with Warwick was not granted;

instead Philip gained some sort of subordinate appointment and was in possession of that office by 1584.[32] In July of the following year he obtained the office he had long sought, joint Mastership of the Ordnance with Warwick at a salary of 200 marks a year and allowances for clerks and other perquisites.[33] Even before he had gained this post he had been extremely active in the office preparing the defences of England as relations with Spain grew steadily more tense. The stocks of the Ordnance Office, hampered by the ever-present shortage of government revenue, were hardly sufficient, and much of Sidney's work was directed towards making good the glaring deficiencies. For example, in June 1584 he was suggested as the person most fit to superintend the work done at Dover,[34] though he was unable to undertake this commission because of the pressure of other business.[35] There is ample evidence of his active work in the Ordnance Office, both before and after he was associated with Warwick as joint Master. His own testimony as to the frequency of his contact with the Queen and of his concern in conversation with her to point out the deficiencies in her store survives in a letter to Burghley:[36]

> Your Lordship in the postscript writes of her Majesty's being informed of great wants and faults in the office where with her Majesty seemeth to charge your Lordship for lack of reformation more than your Lordship doth deserve. For my part I have ever so conceived but because your Lordship writes it particularly to me who of that office am driven to have sometimes speech with her Majesty, I desire for truth's sake especially to satisfy your Lordship if perhaps your Lordship conceive any doubt of me therein, indeed having in my speech not once gone beyond these limits, to acknowledge as in honesty I could not deny the present poverty of her Majesty's store, and therein to excuse my Lord of Warwick as in conscience I might and in duty ought to do, without further aggravating anything against any man living, for I cannot, having not been acquainted with the proceedings.

There are also surviving records of his supervision of the transportation of powder, munitions, and iron ordnance during the summer of 1585, his last summer in England.[37]

Sidney's activities of an official nature were not confined to the dull but essential work of the Ordnance Office. He also participated fully in the ceremonial life of the court, although at times such duties may have been of little pleasure to him. Among the duties which probably combined pleasure with distaste were those connected with the renewal of the French marriage negotiations. In 1581, as England's relations with Spain grew steadily worse, the old argument that an alliance with France was natural and desirable was again voiced, and with considerable effect. In January 1581, after Alençon had assumed the sovereignty of the Netherlands, Elizabeth intimated that she was ready to marry him. An embassy arrived in England from Paris with the task of revising the marriage treaty and in the course of their stay were entertained in extremely sumptuous style. Many of those who had been bitterly opposed to the match the year before were now converted to it for diplomatic reasons. Sidney's own views are not quite certain; he may have been persuaded, along with Walsingham, that the match was a necessity, but there is no indication that his low opinion of Alençon changed for the better. Because of this, he must have felt somewhat uneasy in the course of participating in the lavish entertainment for the French visitors.

Sidney's part in the entertainments was the part that might be expected of him, participation in an elaborate tournament. It was normal to stage such spectacles for distinguished visitors, and there is much evidence that Sidney delighted in their sport and pageantry on many occasions besides this one. He had taken part in a tourney in company with Sir Walter Raleigh and Sir William Russell in 1579.[38] In January 1581 he was a participant in the tournament in which the Earl of Arundel and Sir William Drury challenged all comers,[39] and he was later to take part in the Accession Day tournament of 1581[40] and in the tilt between married men and bachelors held in 1584.[41] In his sonnet sequence *Astrophel and Stella* he mentions participation in a tournament in the presence of distinguished French visitors. But of all the tournaments he took part in the most famous and the most sumptuous was the tourney before the French commissioners at Whitsun, 1581, the tournament of the Fortress of Perfect Beauty.

A detailed description of the entertainment survives in a tract published by Henry Goldwell.[42] According to Goldwell's account, the gallery at the end of the tilt-yard adjoining Whitehall was converted into the Fortress of Perfect Beauty, and this 'fortress' was then laid claim to by four challengers calling themselves the Foster Children of Desire; they were the Earl of Arundel, Lord Windsor, Philip Sidney, and Fulke Greville. On Sunday, 16 April, they delivered their challenge to the Queen; as she was coming from the chapel a messenger clad in the red and white colours of desire 'without making any precise reverence at all uttered these speeches of defiance from his masters to her Majesty'. The messenger related how there were camped not far off 'four long hapless, now hopeful fostered children of Desire' who had been assured by Desire 'that by right of inheritance even from ever, the Fortress of Perfect Beauty doth belong to her fostered children'. The four 'thus nourished, thus animated, thus entitled, and thus informed, do will you by me, even in the name of justice, that you will no longer exclude virtuous Desire from perfect Beauty'. If the Queen would not accede to their request the four foster children 'determine by request to accomplish their claim . . . upon the xxiii day of this month of April they will besiege that fatal fortress, vowing not to spare (if this obstinacy continue) the sword of faithfulness and the fire of affection'. If the Queen should chance to have champions to fight for her 'they protest to meet them in what sort they will choose, wishing only that it may be performed before your own eyes'. The contests were to be first at the tilt and then with lance and sword.

After several postponements for 'urgent causes' the elaborate tournament was begun on Whit Monday. The decorative effects of this neo-chivalry were spectacular. A 'rowling trench' on wheels had been devised, 'a frame of wood which was covered with canvas and painted outwardly in such excellent order, as if they had been very natural earth or mould'. On top of it were two wooden cannons and two men for gunners clothed in crimson sarcenet. Also on top of the device stood an ensign bearer, while within the trench musicians were concealed. When these things were all in readiness the challengers entered, first the Earl of Arundel followed by Lord Windsor, Sidney, and Greville. When one considers the ostentatious magnificence of Sidney's trappings for this ceremonial occasion it is not difficult to discern one of the main reasons for his persistent financial embarrassment. Goldwell describes his entry in these terms:

Then proceeded Mr Philip Sidney in very sumptuous manner, with armour part blue and the rest gilt and engraven, with four spare horses having caparisons and furniture very rich and costly, as some of cloth of gold embroidered with pearl and some embroidered with gold and silver feathers very richly and cunningly wrought. He had four pages that rode on his four spare horses who had cassock coats and Venetian hose all of cloth of silver, laid with gold lace and hats of the same with gold bands and white feathers, and each one a pair of white buskins. Then had he a thirty gentlemen and yeomen and four trumpeteers who were all in cassock coats and Venetian hose of yellow velvet laid with silver lace, yellow velvet caps with silver bands and white feathers, and every one a pair of white buskins. And they had upon their coats a scroll or band of silver which came scarf-wise over the shoulder and so down under the arm with this poesie or sentence written upon it, both before and behind, *Sic nos non nobis*.

When the four challengers had entered, a second defiance was addressed to the Queen. The trench was moved near to where the Queen sat and while the music 'played very pleasantly', a boy, accompanied with cornets, summoned the fortress with a song. It is probable that the words of the song (as well as much of the rest of the staging) were by Sidney; if so, they are of interest as the first of his lines to appear in print.[43]

> Yeelde yeelde, O yeelde, you that this Forte do holde,
>   which seated is, in spotlesse honor's fielde,
> Desire's great force, no forces can withhold:
>   then to Desier's desire, O yeelde O yeelde.
>
> Yeelde yeelde, O yeelde, trust not on beautie's pride,
>   fayrenesse though fayer, is but a feeble shielde,
> When strong Desire, which vertue's love doth guide,
>   claymes but to gaine his due, O yeelde O yeelde.
>
> Yeelde yeelde, O yeelde, who first this Fort did make,
>   did it for just Desire's true children builde,
> Such was his minde, if you another take:
>   defence herein doth wrong, O yeelde O yeelde,
>
> Yeelde yeelde, O yeelde, now is it time to yeelde,
> Before thassault beginne, O yeelde O yeelde.

When the song was finished another boy turned to the foster children and their retinue and sang an alarum, an intricately devised answer to the summons.[44]

> Allarme allarme, here will no yeelding be,
>   such marble eares, no cunning wordes can charme,
> Courage therefore, and let the stately see
>   that naught withstandes Desire, Allarme allarme.
>
> Allarme allarme, let not their beauties move
>   remorse in you to doe this Fortresse harme,

For since warre is the ground of vertue's love,
  no force, though force be used, Allarme allarme

Allarme allarme, companions nowe beginne,
  about these never conquered walles to swarme
More prayse to us we never looke to winne,
  much may that was not yet, Allarme allarme

Allarme allarme, when once the fight is warme,
then shall you see them yelde, Allarme allarme.

When this was ended the two cannons on the rolling trench were fired off, 'the one with sweet powder and the other with sweet water, very odiferous and pleasant', the noise of the shooting being provided by the musicians within the trench. A symbolic attack of the fortress followed, complete with 'pretty scaling ladders' and the footmen's throwing of 'flowers and such fancies against the walls, with all such devices as might seem fit shot for desire'. Then twenty-two defenders entered; each of them ran six courses against one of the challengers to complete the day's show. All performed their parts so valiantly, Goldwell records, 'that their prowess hath demerited perpetual memory and worthily won honour both to themselves and their native country'.

The elaborate show continued on the following day. This time the four foster children entered in 'a brave chariot (very finely and curiously decked) . . . made in such sort as upon the top the four knights sat with a beautiful lady representing Desire about them'. Within the chariot was carried a full consort of music playing dolefully, while the chariot itself was drawn by four horses in the white and carnation colours of Desire. Following speeches, the challengers fought at barriers and tourney against the defenders. 'Towards the evening, the sport being ended, there was a boy sent up to the Queen being clothed in ash-coloured garments in token of humble submission, who, having an olive branch in his hand and falling down prostrate on his face, concluded the 'noble exercise' by relaying from his masters, the foster children, the message that they had been overcome by the Queen's virtue and should henceforth 'be slaves to this Fortress for ever'.

No doubt Sidney much enjoyed the pageantry of the occasion and the semi-martial air of the proceedings, even if he felt less than comfortable in entertaining the French commissioners. If relations with

Alençon at a distance were disagreeable, how much more so must have been Sidney's official duties towards the Frenchman at the beginning of the following year. In November 1581 Alençon arrived in London to see to the marriage negotiations, and Elizabeth made a public show of gratifying his desires. In the presence of the French ambassador, Leicester, and Walsingham, she kissed the Frenchman and promised that he would be her husband. The Puritan activists were much alarmed by this; 'Leicester, who had begun to enter into a secret conspiracy to cross the marriage, Hatton Vice-Chamberlain, and Walsingham fretted as if the Queen, the Realm, and religion were now undone.'[45] Although Sidney's name is not mentioned here specifically, it can be assumed safely that he shared the attitudes of those men with whom he was so closely associated. The continued presence of Alençon in the country was embarrassing, and even the Queen wanted him to leave. She resorted to every device she could think of to encourage him to go according to Mendoza, the Spanish ambassador. Eventually, he did leave, at the price of an additional £10,000, a seemingly firm marriage commitment, and a splendid escort to accompany him to the Netherlands.

Among those included in the escort was Philip Sidney. Numbered in the train accompanying the Frenchman out of the country were many of Sidney's friends and associates: Leicester, Raleigh, Dyer, and Greville among them. The whole complement was over six hundred. The Queen went with them from London to Canterbury, and finally, at the beginning of February, Alençon sailed from England, never to return; fifteen ships were necessary to carry the suitor and his escort away. When the entourage arrived in the Netherlands they were given a triumphant and elaborate welcome. The Prince of Orange, representatives from various areas of the Netherlands, and the magistrates of Flushing met them when they disembarked. At Middleburg and elsewhere there was rejoicing and public spectacle, as the unlikely Alençon was hailed as the apparent deliverer of the Netherlands. At Antwerp, where the celebrations reached their gaudy climax, there were processions, gay decorations, triumphal arches, blazing bonfires, and thundering cannons to celebrate the installation of the Frenchman as Duke of Brabant.

While Sidney could have taken little pleasure indeed in the celebrations for Alençon, whom he suspected of the worst motives, this visit to the continent was not without significance for the Sidney–Leicester faction, for they were showing themselves to Orange and the Dutch at the same time that they were aiding in the celebrations for Alençon. It was the first time that Leicester, the most powerful member of the circle, ever met Orange in person, and the well-loved Sidney was present to effect the introduction. After the two had returned to England Orange was to write of the joy he had experienced in the meeting of Sidney's uncle.[46] In some ways, though the festivities celebrated Alençon, the key to the scene was the English element; it seems likely that Orange looked on the whole arrangement with favour because it seemed a possible path to English favour, and the presence of Leicester and Sidney, whose long-held sympathies for the Netherlands were well known, added to this impression. The Englishmen in attendance on Alençon were treated with considerable honour; some commented that had Leicester not been so conspicuously present, Alençon would not have been received as a friend, much less invested as the lord of the Netherlands.[47] It is indicative of the great importance which Leicester and the English were held to have that it was proposed to dedicate to Leicester the large folio which described the triumphal entry of Alençon and the rest into Antwerp.[48] It may have been an attempt to entangle England more directly in the affairs of the Netherlands, but, if so, this was something which Sidney and Leicester had long considered advisable. One person was, from Sidney's point of view, sadly absent from the scene. This was Hubert Languet, from whose teaching, kindness, and wisdom Sidney had absorbed so much. His former tutor had died at Antwerp the preceding September, and it was one more factor to cause Sidney to regard his present state duty with something less than enthusiasm. Doubtless to Sidney the only beneficial part of the trip was the opportunity to renew continental ties and to introduce Leicester directly to the men who mattered in the Netherlands. In little else could he feel the satisfaction of having done something important for either his country or his religion.

It was not Sidney's last official service in connection with France and her policy in the Netherlands. Two years later in 1584 he was again so involved. By this time, two events had changed the complexion of affairs in the Netherlands considerably. Alençon had died, and though his death was certainly no great loss to the cause of the Dutch, it removed one of the pivots around which the diplomacy of France and

England had moved. Of far more significance was the assassination of William of Orange; this did not exactly produce a vacuum in political authority, but it removed the person most able to exercise the subtle influence which kept the divergent strands of the Dutch revolt together. In conjunction, the two deaths had immense implications for English foreign policy. The death of Alençon left the Huguenot Henry of Navarre as heir to the throne, and thus opened the door to the renewal of civil strife in France. For Elizabeth this would mean shifting her tactics to balance or neutralise France, away from the policy of alliance with the French crown pursued through the on and off courtship of Alençon back to the older policy of alliance with the Huguenots. Orange's death, on the other hand, removed the man who held the Dutch rebels together, and for nearly twenty years the Dutch rebels had been England's main device for pinning down Philip II of Spain. No wonder Walsingham was to comment how greatly these matters 'importeth both the common cause and the Queen's safety'.[49] England's days of peace were drawing to a close; no longer was there a suitor to toy with diplomatically, and no longer was there an Orange to fight England's battles for her. By July 1584 the sort of policy the Protestant activists had long argued for was becoming, by the pressure of events, the policy that even Elizabeth would have to follow.

The negotiations which Sidney was to have undertaken in the summer of 1584 were part of the last effort to find some manner of preserving the old peace policy, pinning down both France and Spain through the Netherlands without involving England any too deeply either in the expenses or the dangers. As such, the negotiations could have been little to Sidney's own taste. The Queen had decided to send Philip on an embassy to the French court, with the outward purpose of conveying her grief at the death of Alençon, but in reality with the more serious purpose of inducing France to take up the cause of fighting against Spain in the Netherlands. Sidney knew, through his contacts with the French ambassador in London and the English ambassador in Paris, that such a mission had a minimal chance of success; moreover, it scarcely represented the sort of policy he was most interested in seeing Elizabeth pursue. The instructions which were drawn up for Sidney indicate clearly the nature of his mission:[50] to persuade the French King that it would be to his interests to intervene in the Netherlands and to suggest that if he did so, there would be some sort of assistance forthcoming from England. Sidney was to stress to the French King the danger that might accrue to him if he were to stand aside and let Spain have its way, for the Netherlands could not stand now without assistance, and when Philip of Spain had gathered these in, he would possess all that he needed to make him the most absolute monarch who had ever ruled on the continent of Europe. The promise of English aid was very vague; Philip was to do no more than in general words assure the French King that England would be ready to pursue a course consistent with her honour and with a due consideration of her future; under no conditions was he given power to discuss the details more directly than this, nor to suggest any particular measures by which the English aid might be implemented. If the French King were too insistent on details, Sidney was to inform him that England was suspicious of his sincerity, a charge which an envoy of England to the court of France might have found it rather difficult to deliver with a straight face in view of Elizabeth's own dealings with Alençon. However, if the French King did show some genuine interest in pursuing matters further, Sidney was to apply to Elizabeth for additional instructions and authority.

In such an atmosphere of mutual suspicion, it was, of course, extremely unlikely that any English emissary could have persuaded France to do England's work for her. It was assumed, none the less, that Sidney would depart at once on the mission to France, and he had gone as far as Gravesend when messages came from Elizabeth cancelling the mission.[51] The official reason offered for calling off the mission was that the French King was going to Lyons accompanied by only a few of his noblemen and hence was not in a position to receive a deputation; in addition, he had given up the mourning of Alençon, and as a result asked for a stay of Sidney's embassy. The real reasons for the breakdown were connected with French suspicions of the English motives and intentions; the English ambassador in Paris wrote that Sidney would not be welcome there. In consequence, the whole project was dropped. Within a matter of days, France was treating with the Netherlands in her own right, and Sidney himself was probably pleased that he had been spared the ordeal of such a fatuous mission.

One state occasion which brought Sidney reward in these years was the gaining of his knighthood in 1582. And yet even here his pleasure must have been tempered by the realisation that he gained it not exactly in his own right, that it was not the reward for service done, but a token dictated by chivalric practice. The occasion was the installation of Casimir of the Palatinate as a Knight of the Garter; the honour had been conferred on him at the time of his visit to England, but it was not until 1582 that he was installed. Unable to attend in person, Casimir nominated his young friend Sidney as his proxy, but according to the rules governing the installation, no one could act as proxy unless he was himself of the rank of knight. So that Philip could act in this respect, he was knighted and henceforth bore the title Sir Philip Sidney.[52] In this capacity he took part in the installation ceremonies, but he knew that his knighthood was no indication that either he himself or his views stood any higher in royal estimation than they had before.

It was about the same time, however, that Sidney's personal affairs did take one significant turn for the better. His closeness to Secretary Walsingham had matured into a project for a marriage between Sidney and Walsingham's daughter Frances. The first sign that such a project was under discussion appeared in a letter by Sidney to Walsingham in December 1581 in which he sent his greetings to 'your self, my good Lady, and my exceeding like to be good friend'.[53] For over a year, nothing further was to be heard of the proposal, and this is admittedly somewhat difficult to explain, but in February 1583 Burghley wrote to Walsingham to congratulate him on the news that the marriage had been arranged.[54] There has been some controversy over the marriage. It has been suggested by some that it was a genuine love match; the key argument here appears to be that since the marriage with Walsingham's daughter was not such a grand thing as the matches that had been proposed for Sidney, his choice at this time must reflect love rather than mere matchmaking. Such an argument has little validity. Sidney's stock was not so high in 1583 as it had been at an earlier date. Regardless of how great the admiration was for him as an emergent Protestant hero, his market value had declined considerably. No longer was he the heir apparent to the great Leicester, for the latter's wife had given birth to a son.[55] Nor were the Sidney family fortunes at a high level at this time. There is ample evidence, in fact, that this match, like the earlier ones proposed for Philip, was an arranged and carefully negotiated affair. Politically, of course, it made very good sense; Sidney was committed to the same sort of policy as Walsingham and had co-operated closely with him in propagating that policy. Economically it made sense too, at least to Sir Henry Sidney, who apparently hoped that a marriage alliance with Walsingham might at last be a way to securing some reward for his Irish services. Because of this, Sir Henry and Sir Francis were able to come to favourable terms for arranging the marriage of their children, the terms as much as anything else showing it was an arranged marriage, whatever else it may have been.[56]

Sir Henry for his part assured certain manors in the possession of the Sidney family to the couple; in case Philip died they were to remain solely in the possession of the widow. In similar fashion Walsingham endowed them with lands from his side. Something of the precarious financial straits of the bridegroom is revealed in the provision of the marriage settlement that Walsingham would undertake to pay or discharge the debts of Sir Philip up to the sum of £1500 and that he would allow the newly married couple and their servants their board if they would live in his house. The same worries about the financial conditions are revealed in the beginning of Sir Henry's long autobiographical letter written to Walsingham at this time.[57]

I have understood of late that coldness is thought in me in proceeding in the matter of marriage of our children. In truth, Sir, it is not so, nor so shall it ever be found; for compremitting the consideration of the articles to the Earls named by you and to the Earl of Huntingdon I most willingly agree and protest I joy in the alliance with all my heart. But since by your letters of the third of January to my great discomfort I find there is no hope of relief of her Majesty for my decayed estate in her Highness's service (for since you gave it over I will never make more means, but say, *Spes et fortuna valete*) I am the more careful to keep myself able, by sale of part of that which is left, to ransom me out of the servitude I live in for my debts; for as I know, Sir, that it is the virtue which is, or that you suppose is, in my son that you made choice of him for your daughter, refusing haply far greater and far richer matches than he, so was my confidence great that by your good means I might have obtained some small reasonable suit of her Majesty; and therefore I nothing regard any present gain, for if I had, I might have received a great sum of money for my good-will of my son's marriage, greatly to the relief of my private, biting necessity. For truly, Sir, I respect nothing by provision or prevention of that which may come hereafter, as thus:—I am not so unlusty but that I may be so employed as I may have occasion to sell land to redeem myself out of prison, nor yet am I so

old, nor my wife so healthy but that she may die and I marry again and get
children, or think I get some. If such a thing should happen God's law and
man's law will that both one and other may be provided for. Many other
accidents of regard might be alleged, but neither the forewritten nor any
that may be thought of to come do I respect, but only to stay land to sell to
acquit me of the thraldom I now live in for my debts.

There were other complications to the proposed marriage besides
the financial considerations, and not the least of these was the attitude
of the Queen. Elizabeth, who appears not to have been informed of
the negotiations, took umbrage when she discovered them and
persisted in regarding the forthcoming marriage as an offence, as she
tended to do when any of her courtiers arranged their marriage affairs
without her knowledge. Walsingham attempted to appease the Queen
through the medium of Hatton, but initially this seems to have had
little success, and Walsingham was impelled to write Hatton explaining
his reasons for withholding the information from the Queen.[58]

As I think myself infinitely bound unto you for your honourable and
friendly defence of the intended match between my daughter and Mr Sidney,
so do I find it strange that her Majesty should be offended withal. It is either
to proceed of the matter or of the manner. For the matter, I hope, when her
Majesty shall weigh the due circumstances of place, person, and quality,
there can grow no just cause of offence. If the manner be misliked for that her
Majesty is not made acquainted withal, I am no person of that state but that
it may be thought a presumption for me to trouble her Majesty with a
private marriage between a free gentleman of equal calling with my
daughter. I had well hoped that my painful and faithful service done unto
her Majesty had merited that grace and favour at her hands as that she would
have countenanced this match with her gracious and princely good-liking
thereof, that thereby the world might have been a witness of her goodness
towards me. As I thought it always unfit for me to acquaint her Majesty with
a matter of so base a subject as this poor match, so did I never seek to have
the matter concealed from her Majesty, seeing no reason why there should
grow any offence thereby. I pray you, Sir, therefore, if she enter into any
further speech of the matter, let her understand that you learn generally that
the match is held for concluded, and withal to let her know how just cause
I have to find myself aggrieved if her Majesty shall show her dislike
thereof. . . .

Postscript—I will give order that my cousin Sidney shall be forewarned
of the matter, who, as I suppose, will not be at the court before the next week.
If her Majesty's mislike should continue, then would I be glad, if I might
take knowledge thereof, to express my grief unto her by letter, for that I am

forced, in respect of the indisposition of my body, to be absent until the end of this next week.

Walsingham might well have been less surprised, and doubtless in actuality he was. A marriage between Philip Sidney, the young courtier spokesman of the Protestant activists and a relative of Leicester, with the daughter of the senior and respected spokesman of the group could not have been a matter of little concern to the Queen. Whether or not Walsingham had hoped to keep this a private, family matter, it became by the very nature of things a court concern. The son of the Earl of Rutland commented on it in letters to his father: 'I have been with Mr Secretary [Walsingham], who is somewhat troubled that her Majesty conceives no better of the marriage of his daughter with Sir Philip Sidney, but I hope shortly all will be well'.[59] Within a matter of weeks, he was able to report that matters had taken a turn for the better. 'Her Majesty', he wrote, 'passes over the offence taken with Mr Sidney concerning his marriage.'[60]

The actual wedding was postponed for some time, and this is probably to be connected with the Queen's displeasure. Nicholas Faunt, Walsingham's secretary, noted in a letter in May: 'Among other matches yet to be solemnised I had forgot to acquaint you with the full conclusion of that with Sir Philip Sidney and my master's daughter and heir, which, I think, will not be solemnised before Michaelmas'.[61] Philip was, in fact, finally married towards the end of September 1583, and the new couple availed themselves of Walsingham's offer to live at his house. It seems that the Queen's displeasure, though not extended to forbidding the marriage, did continue. A correspondent of Mary Queen of Scots mentioned later that the marriage had brought on both Walsingham and Leicester Elizabeth's jealousy.[62]

While the match was plainly one that had been negotiated, it does not follow that true love did not exist between the couple. Those who have felt that Sidney only loved his Stella, if he loved at all, have been inclined to think that the marriage was no more than a tolerable one. But there is a certain amount of evidence that the marriage was a close and happy one. Sidney made few references to his marriage, but there is no reason to believe that this indicates an unhappy union. His wife was with him in the Netherlands when he died, and that his wife's love and affection were returned by Philip is revealed in the terms of his

will. Contemporaries, too, felt that they had reason to consider
Frances Walsingham a true love of Sidney, and their view of the
situation cannot be set aside lightly. The feeling is well indicated in
the words that John Philip put into the mouth of the spirit of Sidney
in his *The Life and Death of Sir Philip Sidney*, published in 1587.[63]

> My spoused wife my Lady and my love
> Whilst life I had did know my tender heart.
> But God that rules the rolling skies above,
> Did think it meet we should again depart.
> His will is done, death is my due desert.
> She wants her mate, I from my dear am gone,
> She lives behind her lover true to mourn.

The feeling that Philip and Frances were deeply in love is also shown
by the confusion of many contemporaries over who precisely Astrophel's Stella really was. While some knew that Stella portrayed
Penelope Rich, it is striking that others, knowing full well that
Astrophel was Sidney, assumed that Stella must have been Frances
Walsingham. This is shown, for example, in the *Astrophel Elegies*
published in 1595 where Stella is very clearly Frances who comes to
tend the wounded Astrophel on his death-bed.[64] The elegy speaks of
their love in terms which confuse the identification of the Stella of the
sonnet sequence, but the important point to note is the open expression
of the love which Philip Sidney felt for his wife.[65]

> Her did he love, her he alone did honour,
> His thoughts, his rhymes, his songs, were all upon her.
> To her he vowed the service of his days
> On her he spent the richest of his wit:
> For her he made hymns of immortal praise.
> Of only her he sung, he thought, he writ
> Her, and but her, of love he worthy deemed
> For all the rest but little he esteemed.

One reason why there is little direct reference by Sidney to his
marriage is that these years were the most active ones of his life.
Denied the full opportunity to participate in the service of the state,
Sidney turned his attention in other directions, and in the last years of
his life his interest in affairs broadened and matured, his thoughts
deepened, and his concerns became far wider and more significant than
they had in the past.

Chapter 4

THE OTHER STAGE

You want another stage for your character.
Languet to Sidney (1579)
He never was magistrate nor possessed of
any fit stage for eminence to act upon.
Fulke Greville

There is a certain aptness in the suggestion that Sidney required another stage on which to act his part. His intense desires for virtuous action were persistently frustrated by the reluctance of Queen Elizabeth to let him have an important role in the affairs of England. Her suspicions of his activist leanings were no doubt the major consideration in this, and it is to Sidney's credit that he did not compromise sincerely held feelings on policy in order to ingratiate himself with his sovereign. While Sidney was as prone to the cult of the Queen as most Elizabethans, his admiration did not make him a completely pliant subject.

In view of Sidney's own ideas about proper policy, his contacts with foreign political figures tended to revolve almost exclusively around the Protestant religion and the possibility of resistance to Spain. This is revealed perfectly clearly both in his relations to the pretender to the Portuguese throne, Don Antonio, and in his relations with the Protestant lords of Scotland. There has long been a tradition that Sidney's interests in the affairs of Don Antonio had begun as early as the period when he first worked on the composition of *Arcadia*. There is certainly some plausibility to this, since the *Arcadia* was substantially the product of his year of semi-retirement after criticising the Queen over the proposed French marriage, and we have seen how the affairs of Portugal and Don Antonio were very much in the minds of those framing policy at this precise moment. By 1581 the lines of contact were much more clear. At the beginning of that year Don

Antonio was no more than a fugitive with a price on his head; his main attraction, from the English point of view, was largely one of potential nuisance value against the Spaniards, yet the Queen and her advisers were openly unwilling to do much to aid him lest they should in the bargain provoke a major clash with Spain. There was a rumour that Elizabeth had sent ships to aid him in November 1580, but there is no evidence to support this;[1] in fact, though some sort of contact with the fortunes of the Portuguese pretender was maintained by the presence of his agent da Sousa in England, for much of the time even his whereabouts were a mystery.[2] By April 1581 affairs had changed somewhat, and the interest of England in Don Antonio's fortunes sharply increased. Influenced apparently in large part by the successful return of Sir Francis Drake from his round the world voyage of plunder, Leicester and Walsingham (who both, it should be noted, had invested heavily in and profited in like measure from Drake's voyage) began to press for the employment of Don Antonio against Spanish commerce. Walsingham presented a plan with this in mind on 3 April, and there appears to have been at least one other similar scheme under discussion.[3] The plan which attracted the most favour involved sending Drake with eight ships and six pinnaces to establish a base in the Azores; there, sailing under the flag of Don Antonio, he was to lie in wait for the Spanish treasure fleet coming from the New World. The whole scheme was to be floated as a joint-stock undertaking and, though it was contemplated that the Queen would subscribe for one-quarter of the stock, the enterprise was to have the guise of a private venture and the country of England was not to be committed in any official manner.

The principal promoters of the scheme are obvious: Drake, Hawkins, and above all Walsingham. But it is apparent too that Sidney was closely involved, for about a month after the scheme was aired in England, Don Antonio wrote to Philip from Tunis giving an account of his own preparations of men and ships.[4] The pretender stressed in the letter a desire that Sidney would write to him often and would maintain a close friendship with him; he added a hope that Sidney would be able to help in person and indicated that he would value the presence of the Englishman above that of all others. Despite the evident hopes of Don Antonio, things did not proceed smoothly. Elizabeth, cautious as ever and very much occupied with the possibility of a

French alliance, decided that she could not aid the scheme unless the French agreed to co-operate with her. Despite the Queen's attitude, the joint-stock arrangements were pushed ahead; then affairs became much complicated when Don Antonio himself arrived in England. The Spanish ambassador noted his arrival on 24 June, describing him as a man 'under the middle height, with a thin face and very dark, the hair and beard being somewhat grey and the eyes green'.[5] In the circumstances Don Antonio was unlikely to receive much of a welcome from Elizabeth; Walsingham wrote to Burghley that the Queen was afraid any open reception with him would provoke a conflict with Spain and that, because of this, his speedy departure was the thing most earnestly desired by the court.[6]

Don Antonio's position in England was uncomfortable in all respects. His financial situation, like that of most pretenders, was not promising; the Spanish ambassador wrote that he even had to borrow his shirts, and his audience with the Queen was delayed while he tried to get together clothes suitable for the occasion.[7] Attempts were made to keep his presence in England a secret; they were failures, for Mendoza knew not only that the pretender was in England but also what sorts of plans were under discussion. Mendoza did his best to prevent anything fruitful coming out of the proposals and in fact persuaded Philip II to write a threatening letter to Elizabeth, telling her that he would regard any aid to Don Antonio as a warlike act.[8] The Queen needed little persuasion on this point; all along her policy and that of her more conservative advisers had been to avoid any commitment which would endanger peace. They were willing to use Don Antonio to line their own pockets, but only if they could do so with complete impunity. The Queen over and over again fell back on her demand that France must co-operate closely and irrevocably with England before any definite steps were taken. While preparations for Drake's expedition to the Azores went forward (and were still going forward when Walsingham left on a diplomatic mission to France in late July), the categorical refusal of Elizabeth to allow the ships to depart until she had the assured co-operation of France was already dimming the hopes of the activists, not to say those of Don Antonio.

Walsingham discussed the expedition with the French in the course of his mission, but even though the French were interested, they were too cautious to bind themselves to any engagement which would force them to bail England out of a Spanish war. While the negotiations thus dragged on, the preparations for the expedition were overtaken and finally overcome by the lethargy. The ships which were prepared remained idle, and the crews which had been raised consumed the supplies which had been put together for the voyage. The original sums raised were not adequate, but the Queen refused to listen to demands for more. Drake, Hawkins, and the other captains began to indicate openly their displeasure, especially since the raiding season was fast slipping away and rumours had reached England that the treasure fleet from the West Indies was already safely home and riding in Spanish harbours. At the end of August the Queen decided that she would send only four ships under the command of Hawkins; though both Drake and Hawkins appear to have backed the plan, Don Antonio refused to co-operate with it, apparently on the grounds that it did not represent sufficient aid. At this point Elizabeth gave up all intention of countenancing the affair, and on 29 August the mariners raised for the expedition were discharged and the stores of munitions sold. The completeness of her decision was underlined by the sale even of the Portuguese flags. With the failure of the expedition, the main intent of the government came to be getting Don Antonio out of England. His departure was announced by Burghley at the beginning of September, but it was not until the end of the month that he finally left. Just as Sidney had figured in the negotiations before he arrived, so too was he there at the pretender's departure. On 10 September Mendoza noted in a report that Lord Howard, Sidney, and the Earl of Oxford had received orders to accompany the Portuguese pretender who was on the verge of leaving England.[9] Several days later Don Antonio left for Gravesend in the company of the French ambassador; he was joined at that spot by Sidney, who bore a message from the Queen.

For several days Don Antonio lingered at Dover, detained by contrary winds. Sidney found himself in what he considered to be a highly ambiguous position. There is no doubt that he supported Don Antonio's schemes as part of an overall strategy of resistance to Spain, but he knew full well that Elizabeth was unlikely to commit herself or the nation deeply in the matter; the truth of this realisation had been repeatedly demonstrated during the summer's negotiations. He suspected the Queen intended that he should accompany Don Antonio, but he felt that he could serve the pretender's cause more fully if he returned to court. But he did not dare to do so without the Queen's command. Moreover, he was concerned over his own and his father's affairs and longed to have time to devote to them. In this frame of mind he wrote to Hatton on 26 September asking for his intervention.[10]

The delay of this Prince's departure is so long, as truly I grow very weary of it, having divers businesses of my own and my father's, that something import me, and to deal plainly with you being grown almost to the bottom of my purse. Therefore your honour shall do me a singular favour if you can find means to send for me away, the King himself being desirous I should be at the court to remember him unto her Majesty, where I had been ere this time, but being sent hither by her Highness, I durst not depart without her especial revocation and commandment. The Queen means, I think, that I should go over with him, which at this present might hinder me greatly and nothing avail the King for any service I should be able to do him. I find by him he will see all his ships out of Thames before he will remove. They are all wind-bound and the other that came hither, the wind being strainable at the East, hath driven them toward the Isle of Wight, being no safe harbour here to receive them, so that he is constrained to make the longer abode, if it were but to be waffed over. I beseech you, Sir, do me this favour for which I can promise nothing, seeing all is yours already.

The combination of Sidney's pleading and Walsingham's influence was enough to accomplish the desired end. The ships sailed and Sidney returned to London.

The whole experience of the Don Antonio escapade was dispiriting to Sidney, Walsingham, and those of like mind. At a time when they needed little further proof that the activist policy was officially frowned upon and was only countenanced on occasion as part of the diplomacy connected with the Queen's more cautious policy, the activists were once again frustrated. There is good reason for believing that the Queen rather than the activists was at this point pursuing the more sensible policy. Don Antonio was far too weak a foundation on which to build a destructive counter-force to Spain. His meagre resources could add little to the English stock, and weakness was hardly likely to be aided materially by further weakness. At best, Don Antonio could have been a useful diversion, but there was so little to gain from countenancing his schemes that the Queen was assuredly correct in declining to commit England to the danger of a frontal collision with Spain. The activists, as was frequently the case in their approach to foreign policy, certainly had imagination and ambition on their side;

perhaps too they had honour, but the Queen had common sense on hers, and it was sufficient to incline the balance in her favour. Of course the activists read the situation very differently. Walsingham wrote to his bother-in-law Robert Beale of the failure of Don Antonio's mission:[11]

> For the matter of Portugal I am sorry that a cause importing her Majesty so greatly as it doth should be overthrown; wherein surely the French King is greatly to be blamed and I would to God that some there [in England] also were not faulty. . . . Though there be some here that seek to lay the fault of the not proceeding in the enterprise upon her Majesty, yet have I so used the matter as her Majesty is excused and the blame lighteth upon those that have deserved it. And whereas there hath been great faults laid upon me for that the charges have grown so great, I hope I shall be with more honesty able to answer the same than they that have been the impeachers of this voyage: and if the mischief that is like to ensue thereby might only light upon the same impeachers, the harm were the less: but I fear that her Majesty and her realm shall feel of it when it shall be too late to remedy it.

Walsingham's feelings that the scheme had been foiled by the Queen's conservative advisers (including Burghley) were no doubt accurate; his suggestion that things would have been better if the plans had gone ahead seems less well founded.

Sidney's concerns with foreign relations were likewise directed to the affairs of Scotland. It was natural that this should be so, for affairs in Scotland were closely linked with the major problems that agitated his mind: the French marriage, the question of Spanish relations, the Protestant League. It was particularly in the last three years of his life that Philip took an interest in the affairs of England's northern neighbour, but, as was typical of his concerns, once interested his commitment was both deep and lasting. In fact, it might be argued (as could generally be asserted about the activist policy) that interest was so deep and commitment so sustained that a proper caution did not always guard his actions. The first real sign that Sidney was taking to a serious consideration of the affairs of Scotland came in July 1583. In that month the secretary of Henry of Navarre, de Ségur, arrived in London with hopes of bringing at last to a proper conclusion the old proposed alliance of Protestants against the Catholic threat. The ambassador was especially commended to Sidney in a letter from du Plessis Mornay, though such an introduction would hardly have been necessary to whet Sidney's appetite, for de Ségur was an active reformer, a close associate of the leading French Protestants, and a survivor of the Massacre of St Bartholomew. In any case, after de Ségur visited Wilton in Sidney's company he found himself introduced to Archibald Douglas, who had been sent to England to see to the interests of the young King James of Scotland.[12]

Although Sidney's concern with Scotland had already been aroused by this time, as witnessed by his association with Douglas, his real involvement in Scottish affairs did not come till slightly later. The politics of Scotland (and the English reaction to them) were much complicated in the early 1580s by the question of Mary Queen of Scots and her French ties and by the fact that King James VI was passed back and forth between the control of ambitious politicians and noblemen. At the time when Sidney was making his first contacts with Scotland, James had just emerged from under the control of the Ruthven Raiders; the raiders had been ultra-Protestant and generally anglophile. But in June 1583 James escaped from their grasp; he drew to his side many northerners of a more conservative complexion, and in August the Earl of Arran, who had been in prison during the Ruthven ascendancy, reappeared on the Council and rapidly emerged as the leading figure of the new regime. While the new Arran government was clearly a conservative reaction against the Ruthven group, it did not swing as far away from Protestantism and towards Catholicism as had the earlier period of ascendancy of Esmé Stuart.[13] Still, its reaction against the reformed religion was marked enough to make it extremely uncongenial to the Protestant activists in England. The Scottish Presbyterians had been closely associated with the Ruthven Raiders, and they suffered accordingly. In March 1584 Andrew Melville, one of their most outspoken preachers, fled south to England; two months later the so-called Black Acts re-established the authority of bishops and castigated 'the new pretended presbyteries'.[14]

Not surprisingly, the English activists viewed the Arran regime with distrust and usually with open hostility. Once again the activists (and Sidney among them) found themselves following a policy divergent from that of their Queen, for Elizabeth was not entirely unreceptive to the political overtures of Arran. Despite the opposition of Walsingham, the Queen appeared to incline to the advice of Lord Hunsdon who was favourable to Arran.[15]

It was at this point that Sidney began to play a conspicuous part in the manœuvring. It is to be expected that we find him, no doubt under the influence of his father-in-law Walsingham, acting as an intermediary between the Queen and the exiled Protestant lords who had fled to England. It is far more surprising, on the other hand, to find Sidney in close contact with the Master of Gray who had been sent to London from Arran to ask for the expulsion of the same Protestant lords. The incident has usually been noted as one of the less favourable in Sidney's career,[16] not because there are any suspicions that he was playing a double game but because he was so gullible in dealing with the shifty Master of Gray that he never seems to have suspected that the latter might himself be untrustworthy. To some extent the criticism offered of Sidney here is perfectly just; in much the same way that his enthusiasm for the Protestant cause blinded him to the logistical and economic obstacles to an activist policy, so too did his enthusiasm for 'the religion' lead him to grasp at the possibilities offered by the Master of Gray without investigating too closely all the issues involved. Although the Master of Gray had been in France, had been connected with Esmé Stuart's son, was high in the favour of Arran when he came on his English mission, and was, nominally at least, still in the service of Mary Queen of Scots, it was soon apparent that he was willing to play a very different game. In the first place he was far from loyal to Mary's service; he saw only too clearly the weakness of her plans and he was justifiably suspicious about the possibility of Spanish aid to place her son James more firmly in control. In the second place, though he did some of Arran's work (and was successful at least in causing Elizabeth to make the exiled lords move from Newcastle further south) and was a firm advocate of an English alliance, he was willing to listen to overtures from Walsingham and the activists to begin to undermine Arran. In fact, Arran's position was far from healthy; while he had achieved some success abroad by negotiating a league with England, at home his policy placed him hopelessly between the desires of two camps. He had inclined too much towards England to retain the full favour of the Roman Catholics, but at the same time he had been unable to gain the support or even the confidence of the strong Protestants because of his actions towards the exiled lords.

In the proposal to win over Gray to the Protestant cause Sidney played a considerable part and throughout the year 1585 Sidney's name figured prominently in the notices of Scottish affairs. He was close to Sir Edward Wotton, who was most intimately involved in negotiations for financial aid to James of Scotland, and here, once again, he found his Protestant course blocked by the Queen's tight finances. To Sidney it was not a matter for haggling: a grant would not only strengthen the Protestant cause north of the border but it would also help to thwart the machinations of the continental powers. So seriously did some of the activists take the question of the pension to the Scottish King that they even contemplated raising the money themselves if the Queen did not co-operate. Of the major activists, Leicester seems to have been the chief holdout: 'We are grown here to such an extreme kind of nearness as I see no hope to get the Master of Gray any relief from hence. I have already furnished him with £2100, delivered unto him, notwithstanding, as a thing proceeding from her Majesty, for that otherwise he would not have accepted thereof. Sir Philip Sidney hath moved the Earl of Leicester to be content to yield some present support until her Majesty may be wrought to make more accompt of the matter, than presently she doth, but he yieldeth a deaf ear'.[17] While Sidney was active in all of this he was not overwhelmingly successful, and he found that he was accumulating many expenses without much return. Walsingham reported in September that 'Sir Philip Sidney is little at the court and all men, as it seemeth weary. . . . The poor Earl of Angus and Earl of Mar receive here little comfort otherwise than from poor Sir Philip Sidney, so as our course is to alienate all the world from us'.[18] A few days later he noted that virtually the whole burden of entertaining the Scottish lords would fall on his son-in-law.[19]

Not too much should be made of the overall importance of Sidney's work with the Scots in 1585, but it is surely too strong to say, as does one of his biographers, that it is unnecessary to give a full account of Sidney's relations with the Scottish court, 'the subject being of small importance',[20] and it is almost certainly wrong to suggest, as does the same author, that Sidney was simply being deceived by the Master of Gray who was only out to serve his own purposes.[21] No one will deny that the Master of Gray was ambitious and self-seeking, but none can dispute either the evident warmth and genuine quality of the friendship between him and Sidney. Gray was considerably better than the 'contemptible time server'[22] he has been called; even the ultra-

Protestant Melville referred to him as 'a proper gentleman of a true spirit and fair speech'.[23] Nor were the matters that Sidney was dealing with here of minor importance only. The Protestant activists saw beyond the immediate situation into a future when their Queen would no longer be with them. Although much of what was said and written about Scotland in those years was couched in terms of immediately pressing issues—the Queen of Scots, the Catholic threat, the necessity of a subsidy for James—the Protestant activists were also aware of a wider problem, that of the succession. When Walsingham wrote to a colleague that 'men begin to look to the sun rising and therefore it will behoove her Majesty to make much of faithful servants'[24] it is clear that the nearness of the Scottish King to the English succession was a factor of major significance in the Secretary's calculations. And in view of the Queen's expressed unwillingness to discuss or settle the succession, it can hardly be argued that Sidney was not engaged on a task of some importance when he conducted his negotiations with the Scottish representatives.

Not all the contacts that made up Sidney's wider world were of a political nature, although usually religion and intellectual life crossed and combined closely in his mind with political attitudes. This can be seen clearly in his relations with continental intellectuals, especially with Giordano Bruno. Bruno was one of the most bizarre and misunderstood men of the sixteenth century, and misunderstanding of him has persisted. He has been called a martyr for liberalism, for science, for progress, for intellectual freedom, all this largely because some of his ideas seem to approach those of modern science and because for holding them he was condemned by the Inquisition and burnt in the Piazza dei Fiori in Rome in 1600.[25]

By the time that Bruno arrived in England in 1583 he had already achieved a considerable though suspect reputation. He had been born in 1548 in Nola in Italy. As a youth he studied in Naples, describing his course of study there as 'humanity, logic, and dialectic'.[26] In 1565, at the age of seventeen, he entered the monastery of San Domenico in Naples, was given the name of Giordano, and, after probation, took his first vows. He continued his studies at the monastery and was exposed not only to the scholastic philosophy of Aquinas and the works of Aristotle but apparently also to other classical writers such as Cicero and Ovid, to Ramón Lull, to Euclid and Ptolemy, and to the study of astronomy which he was teaching at Nola by 1576. In that year he fell into trouble for heresy, fled the Dominican order, and began a career of wandering about Europe. After a spell in Calvin's Geneva he migrated to Paris, where his public lectures attracted the attention of the King.

When Bruno crossed the Channel to England at the end of March 1583 his reputation for unorthodox and dangerous spiritual views preceded him. The English ambassador in Paris wrote to Walsingham: 'Dr Jordano Bruno Nolano, a professor in philosophy intendeth to pass into England whose religion I cannot commend'.[27] That Bruno's philosophy might have seemed dangerous is obvious. To the complacent part of the academic world, happy with its Aristotelianism, Bruno, who attacked Aristotle openly and championed the theories of Copernicus, might well seem a menace. He carried the assault on Aristotle into the University of Oxford. It seems apparent that Bruno intended to obtain some sort of lectureship at the university. In a letter to the Vice-Chancellor and Doctors of Oxford he introduced himself as 'doctor of a more abstruse theology, professor of a purer and more innocuous wisdom, noted in the best academies of Europe, an approved and honourably received philosopher, a stranger nowhere save amongst the barbarous and ignoble, the waker of sleeping souls, tamer of presumptuous and recalcitrant ignorance, proclaimer of a general philanthropy, who does not choose out the Italian more than the Briton, the male more than the female, the mitred head more than the crowned head, the man in the toga more than the armed man, the cowled man more than the man without a cowl . . . who is hated by the propagators of foolishness and hypocrites, but sought out by the honest and studious, and whose genius the more noble applaud'.[28] Bruno followed the address by a visit to Oxford itself; in June 1583 the Polish Prince Albert Laski visited the university and was entertained by plays and public disputations. In some manner or other (for he had no official connection with the university) Bruno participated in these public debates. According to his own account, his ideas were roughly, indeed rudely treated on this occasion.[29]

Go to Oxford and get them to tell you what happened to the Nolan when he disputed publicly with the doctors of theology in the presence of the Polish prince Alasco, and others of the English nobility. Learn how ably he replied to the arguments; how the wretched doctor who was put forward as the leader of the Academy on that grave occasion came to a halt fifteen times over fifteen syllogisms, like a chicken amongst stubble. Learn how roughly and rudely that pig behaved and with what patience and humanity the Nolan replied, showing himself to be indeed a Neopolitan, born and bred beneath a kindlier sky. Hear how they made him leave off his public lectures on the immortality of the soul and on the quintuple sphere.

Until recently it was supposed that the dispute was entirely a matter of the enlightened Italian and his Copernican views being rejected by an obscurantist and Aristotelian Oxford. But in fact the dispute involved more than this, and reveals there was another and more fundamental side to Bruno. Not exactly the great exponent of the new science as usually claimed, he was arguing the Copernican theory in the context of Hermetism, 'an Egyptian synthesis of Greek Platonism and Jewish tradition, a mixture of transcendental religion, Stoic science and magical gibberish, fathered on an imaginary founder, the antique Egyptian sage Hermes Trismegistus'.[30] Bruno was in many ways the last great mystical magician rather than the great modern scientist, and his use of hermetism is revealed in an account of the disputation written by George Abbott.[31]

When that Italian Didapper, who entitled himself *Philotheus Jordanus Brunus Nolanus, magis elaborata Theologia Doctor &c* with a name longer than his body had in the train of Alasco the Polish Duke seen our university in the year 1583, his heart was on fire to make himself by some worthy exploit to become famous in that celebrious place. Not long after returning again, when he had more boldly than wisely, got up into the highest place in our best and most renowned school stripping up his sleeves like some juggler and telling us much of *chentrum* and *chirculus* and *circumfererchia* (after the pronunciation of his country's language) he undertook among very many other matters to set on foot the opinion of Copernicus, that the earth did go round and the heavens did stand still, whereas in truth it was his own head which rather did run round and his brains did not stand still. When he had read his first lecture, a grave man and both then and now of good place in that university seemed to himself somewhere to have read those things which the Doctor propounded: but silencing his conceit till he heard him the second time, remembered himself then and repairing to his study found both the former and later lecture taken almost verbatim out of the works of Marsilius Ficinus.

As a modern scholar has written: 'What a marvellous scene! There is the Magus announcing the Copernican theory in the context of astral magic and sunworship of *De vita coelitus comparanda* [the work by

Ficino referred to] . . . Do they understand what it is all about? Perhaps not, but the word 'juggler' is significant, suggesting the magician.'[32] If Bruno were not suspect enough on these counts he might also have seemed a strange companion for the Protestant activist Sidney because of his connections with the French court; he came to England with letters of recommendation from the French King and he lived at the home of the French ambassador in London, Michel de Castelnau.

It is almost certain that Sidney had some contact with Bruno none the less. On the occasion of Bruno's dramatic if unfortunate debate in Oxford Sidney too was in the university city as part of the train accompanying the Polish prince in whose honour the disputations were held. It is also suggestive that Bruno wrote and printed while in London a number of his major works, two of which (*De Gl' Heroici Furori* and *Spaccio de la Bestia Triomphante*) were dedicated to Sidney. Bruno mentioned that he had first heard of Sidney while he was in Milan and that he had learned further of his reputation while in France. He goes on to say that he had made Sidney's acquaintance not long after he had arrived in England, and he lavished considerable praise both on Sidney and his close associate Greville. 'I would be untrue to myself, illustrious Sir, if I did not express my esteem for your genius and celebrate your many virtues which you made manifest to me, as time permitted, when I first came to England. . . . And although I have had occasion to rebuke others for their rudeness towards me, I must not leave without saluting you and that most generous and humane spirit Sir Fulke Greville. . . . Even as you were born and raised together in bonds of genuine friendship, so he resembles you, both in corporal and spiritual attainments. It was he who, after you, offered me his good offices, and I should have taken and he accomplished them if the jealous Erinnys of mean and malignant persons concerned had not spirited its arsenic betwixt him and me.'[33] In the later dedication of *De Gl' Heroici* Bruno again showed a familiarity with the Sidney circle and possibly even a knowledge of the Stella affair.[34] Bruno had strong anti-Petrarchan inclinations, and at this time he addressed to Sidney a violent tirade on this theme:[35]

To fix all one's thought and study upon the beauty of a woman's body is, O most generous knight, the mark of a base, brutish, and filthy mind. Good

God! what more vile, what more ignoble spectacle can present itself to a wholesome age than that of a man who is dreamy, afflicted, tormented, sad, melancholy, now hot, now cold, now fervent, now fearful, now pale, now red, with countenance now perplexed, now resolute, who spends the best part of his time, the best part of his fleeting life distilling the elixir of his brain in writing down and publicly recording the perpetual tortures, the heavy torments, the weary thoughts and speeches, the bitter meditations generated beneath the tyranny of an unworthy, imbecile, infatuated, wanton, filthy wretch of a woman.

There is one further well-known episode which is frequently taken to tie Greville, Sidney, and Bruno together. This is the Ash Wednesday dinner which Bruno described in *Cena della Ceneri*.[36] In the dedication Bruno tells of his progress along the Thames and the Strand to a supper party at Fulke Greville's house on Ash Wednesday, 1584. At the dinner an unnamed knight (usually taken to be Sir Philip) sat at the head of the table. At the opposite end was John Florio, with Greville on his right and Bruno on his left. Next to Bruno sat Torquato, an English doctor with whom he was to dispute, while opposite him sat Nundinio, another doctor. Some writers have made much of the scene just described, suggesting that it indicates the existence of a philosophical club to which Bruno was introduced; others have suggested that there was a connection between this philosophical club and Raleigh's 'School of Night'.[37] Many have, on the other hand, been sceptical about what the incident has revealed. It is true that Bruno later stated to the Inquisition that the dinner was not held in Greville's house at all but rather at the house of the French ambassador,[38] and it is equally true there is no direct evidence at all that the unnamed knight was truly Philip Sidney.

The identification of a relationship between Sidney and Bruno, then, rests on slight and on the whole circumstantial evidence. Because they have found few if any echoes of an influence of Bruno on Sidney's writings many scholars have concluded that the ties between the two were ephemeral at best and have asserted that while Sidney met Bruno on one occasion (the Oxford debate) there is no proof of further contact.[39] An argument which seems at first glance even more convincing is that Sidney was a convinced enemy of superstition and hence would have been repelled rather than attracted by the pronounced mystical element in Bruno's work.[40] Such a conclusion seems false, however, for it overlooks exactly those qualities in Bruno's thought which would have appealed strongly to Sidney. We have stressed frequently Sidney's devotion to the idea of the Protestant cause; in his later years he seems to have broadened out this interest in the direction of an ecumenical religious movement which would unite all Protestants and perhaps eventually all Christians into a common body. The hermetism, which has now been clearly identified as the central component in Bruno's thought, in its religious form tended to play down the magical element (which admittedly remains large in Bruno himself) and to emphasise elements drawn from the philosophies of Ficino and Mirandola that argued for a religious synthesis in which all Gentile philosophers pointed towards a unified Christian doctrine.[41] This much of Bruno's thought could appeal to Sidney, and he could remain an enemy to superstition and still be attracted to the mystical Nolan. That Sidney did react in such a way is clearly shown by his deep interest in the religious work of the Frenchman Mornay. Sidney began a translation of the latter's *De la Vérité de la Religion Chrétienne*, and that the work summed up the faith of Christian hermetism. 'Mercurius Trismegistus who (if the books which are fathered upon him be his indeed, as in truth they be very ancient) is the founder of them all, teacheth everywhere that there is but one God: that one is the root of all things and that without that one, nothing hath been of all things that are, that the same one is called the only good and the goodness itself, which hath universal power of creating all things, that it is impossible that there should be many makers.'[42] It is likely too that Sidney was interested in Bruno's scientific work; although Bruno may have been championing Copernicus for all the wrong reasons drawn from the mystical gibberish of his hermetism, the very fact that he was advancing new scientific ideas would have been of interest to Sidney. Sidney had an interest in science and he and Edward Dyer studied chemistry with Dr Dee;[43] here too an interest in things scientific had to override a dislike of superstition, for Dee was just as representative as Bruno of the bizarre, even dotty side of the new science and made his great contemporary reputation as a magician and astrologer.

One further element may well have been of interest to Philip Sidney in the approach to Bruno, and that was his anti-Aristotelianism. It is, of course, clear that Sidney did not reject Aristotle outright. His poetic theory, as expressed in the *Apology for Poetry*, contains many Aristotelian echoes,[44] and the very code of chivalry which he represented had as one of its chief ingredients the Aristotelian doctrine of the mean.[45] But Sidney was vitally interested as well in the work of the great contemporary anti-Aristotelian, Peter Ramus. Ramus, who lived from 1515 to 1572, created a logical system which was widely accepted in the Protestant countries of Europe in the late sixteenth century. In England it was particularly popular at Cambridge (where Sidney may have spent some time), but the works of Ramus were apparently not absent from Oxford either.[46] Certainly Sidney's name is met frequently in conjunction with those of leading Ramists. Banos dedicated to him his edition of the works of Ramus; in the course of the dedication he mentioned that Sidney had much admired Ramus when he was alive and had continued to esteem and reverence him when he was dead.[47] English Ramists too had Sidney's patronage. In 1584 William Temple dedicated his *P. Rami Dialecticae Libri duo* to Sidney, and Philip responded to the dedication in a warm and friendly manner.[48]

Good Mr Temple: I have received both your book and letter and think myself greatly beholding unto you for them. I greatly desire to know you better, I mean by sight, for else your writings make you as well known as my knowledge ever reach unto, and this assure yourself, Mr Temple, that while I live you shall have me ready to make known by my best power that I bear you good will and greatly esteem those things I conceive in you. When you come to London or court, I pray you let me see you; meanwhile use me boldly, for I am beholding.

Temple was later to become Sidney's secretary when Philip went to the Netherlands, was at his side when he died, and was remembered specifically in Sidney's will. It is worthy of note that Temple composed a Ramistical commentary on Sidney's *Apology for Poetry*, 'Analysis tractationis de poesi contextae a nobilissimo viro Philippo Sidneio Equite Aurato'.[49] From internal evidence it has been conjectured that the work was composed before Sidney died; as a composition it shows how much and how little Sidney could have gained from Ramist theories. He was probably interested in Ramus's work as a quick handbook of logic with Puritan associations, for Ramus was one of the great vulgarisers and simplifiers of his age; as an anonymous Cambridge play put it, 'For tidy Peter like a pretty primer/May well be learned ere thou go to dinner'.[50] But, as far as poetry went, Ramus had nothing to tell or teach Sidney. After a study of Temple's commentary a modern scholar concluded: 'One might go so far as to say that every time Sidney makes a useful point about poetry Temple contradicts him. Ramism would not allow for poetry at all, only for versification.'[51]

Sidney also had connections with two other prominent English Ramists, Timothy Bright and Abraham Fraunce. Bright, the inventor of shorthand, dedicated more than one book to Sidney, whom he had first seen at the time of the massacre of St Bartholomew when both had sheltered in Walsingham's house.[52] Fraunce was educated partly at Sidney's own expense[53] and he responded by dedicating his first work to 'that right noble and most renowned knight' Sir Philip Sidney; it was 'a general discourse concerning the right use of logic, and a contracted comparison between this of Ramus and that of Aristotle'.[54] Fraunce wrote other works in a similar vein, including *The Shepheardes Logike*, a summary of the logical precepts of Ramus which was dedicated to Sidney's close associate Dyer.

Sidney's connections with Fraunce are indicative of yet another facet of his wider world, and that was his recognition as a literary patron, even during the 1570s. This can be seen, as will be discussed later, in the case of Stephen Gosson who assumed his Puritan attitudes would be attractive to Sidney. Many others reacted in a similar fashion. When Greville referred to Sidney as a 'general Maecenas of learning' he was making no exaggeration. While many of the books which were dedicated to Sidney were of contemporary interest only, they are indicative of a strong feeling on the part of their authors and publishers that the Sidney name affixed to the dedication was a progenitor of good fortune. This is shown clearly, for example, in the dedication of *The Beehive of the Romishe Churche*, a Puritan satire translated from the Dutch of St Aldegonde, a statesman well known to Sidney. The dedication to the translation was signed by the publisher Stell; it praised Sidney highly and was obviously intended to draw readers to the book.[55]

This notable book . . . I have presumed to publish abroad, under your patronage and protection, not doubting that it should want credit if it were not overshadowed with the countenance of some special personage: but that for your disposition being so virtuous, as that you are a mirror among men and your course of life so praiseworthy, as that you may be well thought a blossom of nobility: your worshipful mind being beautified and enriched with such rare ornaments, as that you, among the rest, glister like a star: therefore unto your worship's hands have I been encouraged to present this worthy book . . . not in hope of any extraordinary profit . . . but that the church of Christ, being not yet grown to perfect age and strength, may reap some special benefit by the same.

By the time Stell dedicated this work to Sidney, several other books, including Henri Estienne's edition of the Greek New Testament (1576), de Banos's edition of Ramus, and Gabriel Harvey's *Gratulatiorum Valdinensium Libri IV* (Book IV) had also appeared under his patronage. From 1579 on, numerous works were published with a dedication to Sidney and they reflect clearly his wide interests, both political and intellectual.[56] An interest in continental scholarship is reflected in the 1580 dedication of Lambert Danaeus's *Geographia Poetica*; a growing awareness of the importance of English overseas expansion is reflected in the dedication of Richard Hakluyt's *Divers Voiages touching the discoverie of America* in 1582 and of Michael Lok's map designed to show the English priority in the exploration of North America. We have already noted the works connected with Ramus and Bruno which were inscribed to Sidney; a number of other scholarly books were as well: Henri Estienne's *Herodiani Historiae Libri VIII* and Justus Lipsius's *De Recta Pronunciatione Latinae Linguae Dialogus* (1586). Military activities are reflected in the dedication of Nicholas Lichfield's *A Compendious Treatise entituled De re militare* (1582), the chivalric courtier's interest in riding by Christopher Clifford's *The Schoole of Horsemanship* (1585), connections with Ireland by John Derricke's *The Image of Irelande* (1581), and diplomacy by Alberico Gentili's *De Legationibus Libri III* (1585). Sidney's patronage was, at times, more direct than simply lending his name to the book's reputation. Direct financial aid to Fraunce, verbal encouragement at least to Spenser were all part of his work, and they reflect, as one might expect, a wide diversity of interests encompassing those of both the courtier and the scholar.

There is no evidence that Sidney directly patronised artists in the same manner he did literary figures. But he was both exposed to art and interested in it. His contacts with Abraham Fraunce made him close to a man who had some skill in artistic creation, [57] and throughout the *Arcadia* there are references to paintings which suggest a familiarity with actual pictures. Even more to the point, he knew the greatest of Elizabethan miniaturists, Nicholas Hilliard, and actually discussed painting techniques with him. Hilliard has preserved a record of this in his *Treatise concerning the Arte of Limning*.[58]

I would willingly give many observations touching proportion fit to be known, but the book is great already, wherefore I omit them purposely, yet one word more in remembrance of an excellent man, namely Sir Philip Sidney, that noble and most valiant knight, that great scholar and excellent poet, great lover of all virtue and cunning: he once demanded of me the question whether it were possible in one scantling, as in the height of six inches of a little or short man and also of a mighty big and tall man in the same scantling, and that one might well and apparently see which was the tall man, and which the little, the picture being just of one length. I showed him that it was easily discerned if it were cunningly drawn with true observations, for our eye is cunning and is learned without rule by long use, as little lads speak their vulgar tongue without grammar rules. But I gave him rules and sufficient reasons to note and observe.

In these same years of widening interests, Sidney also completed his own literary work. His major literary labour was, of course, the revision of *Arcadia* on which he worked intermittently up till the time he left for the Netherlands. He also did some translating; one of the fine surviving pieces of this is the beginning of the translation of Mornay's *De la Vérité de la Religion Chrétienne*. The complete version of this was not published until after his death by Arthur Golding, who finished the work.[59] How much of the extant translation is Sidney's work, how much is Golding's, has long been a matter of dispute.[60] Golding simply noted that Sidney had 'proceeded in certain chapters therein'.[61] Golding referred to his own part of the undertaking as a great task, and this would seem to imply that Sidney had not progressed very far in the work of translation. On the basis of style, it is usually held that Sidney was responsible for the preface to the reader and for chapters one to six, while the rest should be attributed to Golding. Sidney also translated the first two books of Aristotle's *Rhetoric*; as John Hoskins records, 'the understanding of Aristotle's *Rhetoric* is the directest means of skill to describe, to move, to appease, or to prevent any mood whatsoever, whereunto, whosoever can fit his speech shall be truly eloquent. This was my opinion ever, and Sir Philip Sidney betrayed his knowledge in this book of Aristotle to me before ever I knew that he had translated any part of it, for I found the first two books englished by him in the hands of the noble, studious Henry Wotton but lately'.[62] It is probable that the translation was never published, and it has not survived. Also lost is Sidney's translation of the first *Semaine* of du Bartas, a Huguenot poet of the court of Navarre. Du Bartas's poetry, which is not of the highest quality, was much admired for its religious content and some seven different men translated parts of his works into English between 1578 and 1625.[63] Sidney's translation was entered by his literary executors in the Stationers' Register in August 1588 along with the *Arcadia* but it remained unpublished. In 1603 John Florio, in the dedication of the second book of his translation of Montaigne, called for its printing. 'That worthy did divinely even in French translating some part of that excellent du Plessis and (as I have seen) the first septmane of that Arch-Poet du Bartas'.[64] Publication was still not forthcoming, however, and one reason for this may have been a fear on the part of Sidney's executors of offending King James of Scotland who was very enthusiastic about du Bartas's poetry and had established something of a proprietary right over it.

Sidney's other major effort at translation (unfinished like his version of du Plessis Mornay) was in a well-established tradition, versification of the Psalms.[65] Sidney had already indicated in the *Apology for Poetry* that he understood the poetic nature of the Psalms.[66]

And may I not presume a little further, to show the reasonableness of this word *vates*, and say that the holy David's Psalms are a divine poem? If I do, I shall not do it without the testimony of great learned men, both ancient and modern. But even the name psalms will speak for me, which being interpreted is nothing but songs; then, that it is fully written in metre, as all learned hebricians agree, although the rules be not yet fully found; lastly and principally, his handling his prophecy, which is merely poetical. For what else is the awaking his musical instruments, and often and free changing of persons, his notable *prosopoeias*, when he maketh you, as it were, see God coming in His majesty, his telling of the beasts' joyfulness, and hills leaping, but a heavenly poesy, wherein almost he showeth himself a passionate lover of that unspeakable and everlasting beauty to be seen by the eyes of the mind, only cleared by faith?

This metrical version, which was begun by Sidney and completed by his sister, was an attempt to show that the English tongue was suitable for divine poetry.[67] Sidney's own contribution was the first forty-three of the Psalms. It is probable that this was a late work, undertaken

shortly before he left for the Netherlands, and this would explain why
he never finished the task. The Psalms, while of great interest, are not
to be reckoned among Sidney's best works, except perhaps because of
the variety and ingenuity of metre and rhyme. He was attempting to
make a new poetical rendering (to replace the English metrical version
of 1562) rather than attempting a whole new translation. Because of
this, he did not consult the Hebrew text, which he could not in any
case read, nor did he use the Vulgate or even the standard Protestant
Latin version of Tremellius. Instead, he used as his model the French
version of Beza and Marot and for his phrasing resorted to the English
prose version of the Book of Common Prayer and the Geneva Bible,
as well as consulting some recent commentaries on the Psalms, such as
that by Theodore Beza. It is important to note that in matters of
meaning and interpretation he relied most heavily on that Puritan
masterpiece, the Geneva Bible. The renditions of Sidney are something
of a virtuoso triumph, and some people, Donne and Ruskin among
them, have praised the results.[68] A modern reader, nurtured on more
familiar versions, would not be likely to agree.

The last piece of Sidney's writing which should be noted here was
in quite a different vein. This was his *Defence of the Earl of Leicester*,
an answer to a pamphlet usually called *Leicester's Commonwealth*
which had attacked his uncle viciously and accused him of a wide
variety of crimes and unsavoury schemes.[69] The libel on Leicester had
already been suppressed and the Queen had testified to his innocence,
but Sidney was not to be dissuaded from a defence. It was written
apparently for publication, though it was never printed. Sidney's
tract was a vitriolic production, full of sound and fury and reacting
with the strongest of hurt family pride. The crimes of which Leicester
was accused he passed over quickly and lightly, and he was far more
concerned with the imputation that the Dudleys were of base origin.
'Because that thou, the writer hereof, dost most falsely lay want of
gentry to my dead ancestors, I have to the world thought good to say
a little, which I will assure any that list to seek shall find confirmed
with much more'.[70] Sidney concluded the tract on a note of defiance,
bravado, and threatened revenge.[71]

But to thee I say, thou therein liest in thy throat, which I will be ready to
justify upon thee in any place of Europe where thou wilt assign me a free

place of coming as within three months after the publishing hereof I may understand thy mind. And as till thou has proved this, in all construction of virtue and honour, all the shame thou hast spoken is thine own, the right reward of an evil tongued *Schelm*, as the German especially call such people. So again in any place whereto thou wilt call me, provided that the place be such as a servant of the Queen's Majesty have free access unto; if I do not, having my life and liberty, prove this upon thee, I am content that this lie I have given thee return to my perpetual infamy. And this which I write I would send to thine own hands if I knew thee; but I trust it cannot be intended that he should be ignorant of this printed in London which knows the very whisperings of the privy chamber. I will make dainty of no baseness in thee that art indeed the writer of this book. And from the date of this writing, imprinted and published, I will three months expect thine answer.

In intensity of feeling to right a wrong, the tone is reminiscent of his short note to Molyneux threatening his life.

Sidney's continental acquaintances, especially Languet, had often expressed fears that his intellectual activity would be diverted by the courtier's life. Sidney, who saw thought and action as closely connected, increasingly felt frustration that more activity did not come his way. While in part his contacts with men like Dee can be explained in purely intellectual terms, in part too they must be explained in terms of the utilisation of knowledge, especially in these years of widening interests by active involvement in the overseas expansion of England, a movement with which Dee himself was closely connected.[72] We have already noticed Sidney taking an interest in various aspects of the expansion of his country, in the voyages of Frobisher, in the exploits of Drake, in his connection with Hakluyt. In 1582 his vague yearnings for the New World became closely involved with the plans of Sir Humphrey Gilbert, Walsingham, and (rather surprisingly) of the Catholics.[73] Gilbert can be numbered among the most distinguished English explorers of the time, and he had long been acquainted with the Sidney family, having been knighted by Sir Henry in Ireland in 1570. In 1578 Gilbert had secured letters patent from Queen Elizabeth for planting an English colony in the New World, and at the end of that year had made a short voyage. By 1582, however, he was still having great difficulty in raising enough money to finance a major expedition.

At this point the plan of Gilbert began to become involved with schemes of Sir George Peckham of Denham and Sir Thomas Gerard, the former at least sympathetic to the Catholics, the latter a convicted recusant. They too had interests in the New World, which they saw as a possible source of relief for the Catholics who were being pressed with increasing ferocity in England. Peckham himself had shown an interest in overseas voyaging in conjunction with Gilbert as early as 1574; the new anti-Catholic law of 1581 strengthened his desires, and in 1583 he and Gerard opened negotiations with Gilbert, almost certainly with the prior approval of members of the government. Secretary Walsingham took a large part in the preparations and it was to him that Peckham and Gerard sent a memorandum setting out the terms which they wanted. In the summer Peckham and Gerard were granted lands in the New World by Gilbert in return for contributions subscribed to his expedition. It seems clear what Walsingham's interest in all this was; he saw it as a scheme for ridding the realm of potentially dangerous Catholics without alienating them from England or causing them to emigrate to lands hostile to his own. In furthering the scheme (which may have been, as the Spanish ambassador alleged, his own idea) Walsingham enlisted the aid of Sidney. A draft letter of 1583, apparently of Walsingham's authorship, shows that Sidney was acting as an intermediary in trying to stir up interest in the scheme: 'I am of opinion you shall do well to hearken unto such offers as Sir Philip Sidney and Sir George Peckham will make unto you, who have sufficient authority by and under her Majesty's letters patent to perform the effect of your desire'.[74] That Sidney was acting in such a capacity is confirmed in a letter of the Spanish ambassador: 'Walsingham indirectly approached two Catholic gentlemen, whose estate had been ruined, and intimated to them that, if they would help Humphrey Gilbert in the voyage, their lives and liberties might be saved, and the Queen, in consideration of the service, might be asked to allow them to settle there (Florida) in the enjoyment of freedom of conscience and of their property in England, for which purpose they might avail themselves of the intercession of Philip Sidney'.[75] The role of Sidney here confirms what has earlier been noted about his reaction to the Catholics. He was not opposed to them in a total, bigoted way; he, like Walsingham, distrusted them politically and perhaps collectively, but was prepared to try ways to make them loyal to England, so long as such ways were consistent with the political safety of the realm.

Philip had a further and equally direct role to play in the preparations for this voyage. Since July of the previous year, Sidney had owned a New World patent of hypothetical value. An agreement had been drawn up between Sidney and Gilbert by which Sir Humphrey granted 'that said Sidney, his heirs, assigns, associates, adventurers, and people shall forever enjoy free liberty to discover anything not before discovered or inhabited by said Sir Humphrey, his heirs or assigns, and to enjoy to their own use such lands so discovered as shall amount unto thirty hundred thousand acres, with power to inhabit, people, and manure the same, together with all jurisdictions, privileges, and emoluments whatsoever for governing, peopling, etc. the same, holding same of said Sir Humphrey, his heirs and assigns, in free socage'.[76] In July 1583 this extensive grant was transferred by purchase to Peckham, Sidney thus at one stroke furthering the colonisation scheme and realising by the sale the ready cash to prepare himself financially for his marriage to Walsingham's daughter. Sidney also involved himself in the attempt to finance the voyage by agreement with the Merchant Adventurers of Southampton in December 1582, for his name appears in a list of 'High and Honourable Personages' who would make advances for the expedition in return for which they were to have 'lawful freedom and free trade or traffic of merchandise and merchandising in all and singular the countries, territories, and dominions within written now intended to be discovered in as ample manner and form as the said now Merchant Adventurers by virtue hereof hath or ought to have in the same trade or traffic'.[77]

What Sidney gained from his adventuring in this manner is open to doubt. But his interest in the scheme persisted; a year later he wrote to Sir Edward Stafford, the ambassador in Paris, 'we are half persuaded to enter into the journey of Sir Humphrey Gilbert very eagerly; whereunto your Mr Hackluyt has served for a very good Trumpet'.[78] Gilbert was already dead by the time Sidney penned these words, and they can only be interpreted to indicate a continuing interest in the various aspects of Gilbert's voyages. Sidney's interest in such schemes was a compound of a number of factors. Certainly, financial aspects loomed large; Sidney's finances, as we have had several occasions to notice, were in difficult shape, and there is no doubt that he hoped to realise some return from his investments. Certainly, too, he approved of the 'Catholic' scheme of Walsingham. The elements of sheer adventure cannot be ignored; confined in a court circle where he was unable to gain any important employment, Sidney was drawn to New World schemes as a possible way of realising his dream of a life of virtuous action. Beyond all this, Sidney increasingly saw the New World as an important factor in the overall strategy of foreign policy and his dreams for Protestant action, as his thought on such subjects matured, came increasingly to consider a focus wider than the continental struggle which had aroused his interest initially.

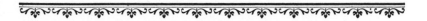

PART TWO

The Man of Letters

Chapter 5

THE EDUCATION OF AN ARISTOCRAT

A gentleman without letters, whatever his
race, will be taken for a rustic, and for myself I
would rather see young noblemen more often
with a book in their hands than a sparrow
hawk.   Alberti, *Della Famiglia* (1434)

He grew up fast in goodness and in grace
And doubly fair wax both in mind and face
Spenser, *Astrophel*

The aristocracy of sixteenth-century England was increasingly aware
of the importance of education. The courtier could be no untutored
boor; the diplomat required instruction in languages and above all in
the observation of his contemporary Europe; the budding patron
required some knowledge of the arts. Often the result of this was
still far from an intellectual, yet this was not so with Philip Sidney.
Not only does his patronage reveal taste, but his literary work reveals
an inquiring mind of the first order. Even in the business of state, he
brought more to bear on problems in the way of hard thought than
many of his contemporaries. Such qualities of mind could not grow
without proper nurture, and to understand Sidney, it is necessary to
know something of the four stages of his education—home, school,
university, and Grand Tour—and something of the men who most
influenced him in this formative period of his life.

Of Sidney's youth we know very little indeed. In fact, we might
go so far as to say that only the set on which his early childhood was
played is at all clear to us. Penshurst, where Philip Sidney spent much
of his youth, can still be visited; a vivid portrait of it is contained in
often quoted lines by Ben Jonson,[1] and Sidney's own description of
Kalander's house in *Arcadia* is often taken as an evocation of the Penshurst that he knew and loved as a child.[2] The setting for his childhood
was indeed a fine one; there is less certainty that Philip himself had a

completely happy youth. Without doubt he was a lonely child. Official duties deprived him of the company of his father for much of his youth, and the same was true to a lesser extent of his mother. Not only did Sir Henry find himself involved in diplomatic duties which drew him away from Penshurst, but from 1560 he acted as Lord President of the Council in the Marches of Wales and in 1564 he was installed as the Deputy of Ireland. Lady Sidney was called to court in the early years of the reign and remained there until stricken with smallpox.

Of the few accounts which survive of Philip's youth those which were written by Dr Thomas Moffett are the most interesting. He relates, with some evident exaggeration, that Philip was born with a 'charming and ingenuous appearance and with a stature designed for warfare—a child endowed with gifts of nature, with a strong and almost manly voice, and, in fine, with a certain consistent and absolute perfection of mind and body'.[3] Moffett also gives an interesting picture of the young Philip as a three-year-old, gazing at the moon: 'with clean hands and head covered he used to pray to it and devoutly worship it, as if in his earliest years he had compassed the heavens with his mind and wondered at the work of his creator'.[4] Already the young lad displayed the seriousness and scholarly inclinations that were to mark his life. Moffett recorded that Sidney 'would scarcely sleep or go forth' without a book.[5] Nor was his education neglected while he was a youth at Penshurst. At the age of seven he was provided with a tutor 'of suitable manners and morals' who was to instruct him in the veneration of God, then in literature, finally in public affairs and virtuous action.[6] It is noted that it was from his high seriousness and zeal for virtue that all of his interests of a studious nature sprang. There may be some backward reading in this summary of what his tutor inculcated in him; if not, it was a marvellous foreshadowing of a Protestant hero who attained a notable status in creative writing and who died nobly in the service of his country and his God.

So little information survives about the nature of his training in his pre-school years that it is impossible to generalise about its effect. More is known, however, about the second important stage in Sidney's development, the beginning of his formal education when he became a pupil at Shrewsbury School.

Philip entered Shrewsbury on the same day as his life-long friend and biographer, Fulke Greville. Already as a child, Philip had displayed intellectual interests and abilities. While many of the sons of the aristocracy were, in the sixteenth century, acutely aware of the importance of at least those aspects of education which would fit them for the service of sovereign and nation, the interests and inclinations of Sidney appear to have been somewhat unusual. Greville, in what is probably something of an overstatement, wrote of him that 'though I lived with him, and knew him from a child, yet I never knew him other than a man: with such staidness of mind, lovely, and familiar gravity, as carried grace and reverence above greater years'.[7] Greville goes on to comment that Sidney's conversation was always concerned with knowledge and that even his play tended towards those things which would enrich his mind. Because of this, even his teachers were able to find in him something to observe and something to learn beyond that which they culled from their own books. We might be inclined to dismiss all of this as exaggeration were it not for the fact that many of the details are corroborated from other sources. Sidney himself commented on this trait of his character: 'I am ready to admit that I am often more serious than my age or my pursuits require, yet I have certainly proved by experience that I am never less subject to melancholy than when I am earnestly applying the feeble powers of my mind to some high and difficult task.'[8] A letter from his father indicates too that the high seriousness of mind on which Greville commented had impressed itself on his parents as well, for Sir Henry felt obliged to warn his son to be sure 'to be merry, for you degenerate from your father if you find not yourself most able in wit and body to do anything when you be most merry'.[9] Thomas Moffett, whose life of Philip Sidney was intended as an *exemplum* to his young protégé William Herbert, noted that Philip spent the largest part of his youthful days in learning.[10] Moffett pointed out that this devotion to learning in one so young could and did draw forth the contempt of his less adult-minded friends, but, he adds, Philip 'fended out this contempt [of learning] by a greater one, directing the whole power of his mind to the matter, lest wanting knowledge he might augment the herd of brute beasts, and, acquiring nothing not shared in by vulgar minds, he might die merely inglorious and uncouth'.

The school to which Philip was sent was a natural one for him. Shrewsbury itself lay within the jurisdiction of the Lord President of the Marches, and even though it was not an ancient foundation when Sidney was enrolled, it had achieved a considerable measure of repute. There had possibly been one or more grammar schools at Shrewsbury from a very early date, but the reformation changes under Edward VI had swept away all or most of them. The Free Grammar School of Edward VI, which Philip was to attend, had been refounded during the time when his grandfather Northumberland had held sway, the charter being granted on 10 February 1552. The growth of the school into a major educational institution is largely to be associated with the tenure of Thomas Ashton, a fellow of Trinity College, Cambridge, as headmaster from 1561 to 1571. Of Ashton's ability there can be little doubt. In an age when England's educational greatness was being revealed, the age of Ascham and Mulcaster, the name of Thomas Ashton stands with justification in the ranks of the illustrious. Not only was Ashton a notable schoolmaster in the very region of the President's jurisdiction; it also seems possible that he was known to Sir Henry Sidney before Philip was sent to Shrewsbury. Ashton had been a tutor in the family of Sir Andrew Corbett, a member of the Council and a close friend of Sir Henry.

Several features of the school life were probably of special significance in the life of young Philip. Sidney was brought up during his crucial schooldays in an atmosphere of advanced Protestantism; the Puritanism of the masters at the school was well known. Moreover, there was constant provision for the spiritual life of their charges. Those with whom the students lived had a duty to see to their attendance at the parish church; a provision supplementing this adds a Puritan emphasis on preaching, for 'where there is a sermon in any other church, they shall all resort thither to the hearing thereof'.[11] In addition, in the school itself prayers were to be said and sung each morning 'devoutly upon their knees immediately after the school bell doth cease ringing'; the prayers were to be repeated before the boys left the school in the evening.

A further feature of life at Shrewsbury School which may have had a marked influence on young Sidney was the use of dramatic performances as part of the educational process. As the provision was recorded in the school orders, 'Every Thursday the scholars of the first form before they go to play shall for exercise declaim and play one act of a comedy and every Saturday versify.' Ashton appears to have been a firm believer in the educational value of the drama. The weekly Thursday play-acting for the first-formers was only a preparation for the part which the boys of the school took in the yearly performance of morality plays in a theatre on the outskirts of Shrewsbury. After Ashton became headmsater in 1560 he saw to it that his boys were themselves the actors, and although no definite connection can be made between Sidney and any of the performances, it seems likely that this experience of theatrical performances could not have helped but shape some of the lad's attitudes towards literature and drama.

Of far more interest, both to Sidney himself and to us, was the actual course of instruction which he followed. Like the curricula in other schools at the time, the prescribed course of study at Shrewsbury was almost entirely in the classics. The school orders provided for the study of Latin texts including Cicero, Caesar's *Commentaries*, Sallust, Livy, and a book of dialogues culled from Cicero and the humanist Vives by Ashton himself. For work in verse the scholars were to read Vergil, Horace, Ovid, and Terence. There was also to be some study in Greek, using Cleonardes' grammar, the Greek testament, Isocrates, and Zenophon. The school orders do not give a full sample of the materials to which Sidney was exposed. On the contrary, the accounts kept of his expenditures by Thomas Marshall indicate purchases of a number of works which reveal that the master used his prerogative to vary the set texts by suitable substitutes. Although we find Sidney in fact purchasing Ashton's dialogues from Cicero and Vives, we find in addition that he was compiling 'example books, phrases, and sentences' in French as well as Latin[12] and that a French grammar was purchased for him in the following year.[13] His Protestant inclinations were furthered by the purchase and no doubt the reading of Calvin's catechism.[14] It is interesting to note that the young Sidney seems to have been concerned with and carefully trained in penmanship. We find Marshall purchasing for him in December 1565 'three example books for the secretary hand'.[15] Perhaps this instruction serves to explain why the handwriting of Sidney stands out as a polished one compared with that of many of his contemporaries. He continued even into his adult life to take the question of his handwriting very seriously. Six years before his death he wrote to his brother Robert, 'I would, by the way, your Worship would learn a better hand; you write worse than I, and I write evil enough'.[16]

To attempt to summarise or even to conjecture as to the influence of Shrewsbury School on Philip is hazardous, but certain things do seem certain. Beyond the ordinary experience of a growing boy, beyond the Puritanism which he imbibed, beyond even the formal instruction of the classroom, it seems probable that the serious youth's already adult attitude was being further fostered and strengthened. It is good to be reminded that he was still at this point 'little Philip',[17] so serious, so high-minded, so impressed with the significance of his family had he become. He was still a boy when he left Shrewsbury to go to Oxford as a student. But he was a boy of unusual promise. Fortunate indeed in his family connections, he was also ready displaying talents and independence of mind that would make him both more and less than the government servant his father was. As Dr Moffett commented, when barely ten years old Philip yielded to none in reputation for knowledge of grammar and later of rhetorical principles, and already he was surpassing his schoolmasters in mathematical exercises and in languages.[18] The courtier was expected to have a veneer of learning, but the adolescent Sidney was beginning to display the characteristics of the true intellectual. For the rest of his life he would seek to find some path which would join an active life to his contemplative abilities, for learning was never to be with him either a show or a refuge. It was to be a tool, and a tool which he could use more skilfully than most.

When it was that Philip Sidney entered Oxford as a student is not certain. No details of his life between the last entry in Marshall's accounts in 1566 and 2 August 1568, when Sir Henry visited the university to be granted the degree of M.A., have come to light. All that is known is that sometime between the two dates Philip had matriculated at the university as a member of Christ Church. It has often been suggested that in the sixteenth century Oxford was backward and scholastic, Cambridge reforming and humanistic. While not denying for a moment that there were things wrong in the universities, we can with honesty reject the easy contrast so often made between England's two seats of advanced learning. The universities—both of them—were in fact institutions of some vigour and were going through a period of considerable growth.[19] Since the beginning of the century, when they had been beset by an intellectualism of the most sterile sort, they had rapidly freed themselves from the shackles of the old tradition, not completely to be sure and Cambridge faster than Oxford. But to suggest that Oxford was so decadent an institution that a young scholar of Sidney's ability could gain nothing from it is to misunderstand completely the importance of his university years.

As far as the formal instruction and curriculum were concerned, the picture was indeed one of traditionalism. The subjects which had been found of solid value for centuries—grammar, rhetoric, and logic—formed the staple of the studies, and the texts which were employed were not only traditional, but to some extent overlapped with those Sidney had already perused at Shrewsbury. For grammar there were readings from Vergil, Horace, and Cicero's *Orations*, for rhetoric Aristotle and Cicero, for logic Porphyry's *Institutions* or Aristotle's *Dialectics*. While resident at the universities, students were expected to engage in scholastic disputations. At first the student would simply attend and observe; gradually he would take more and more part until finally he acted as responder at least twice in the formal Lenten disputations. In such exercises Sidney proved himself to be adept. A trace of his skill is preserved in a comment of his contemporary Richard Carew. 'Being a scholar in Oxford of fourteen years age and three years standing, upon a wrong conceived opinion touching my sufficiency, I was there called to dispute *extempore* (*impar congressus Achilli*) with the matchless Sir Philip Sidney in the presence of the earls Leicester, Warwick, and divers other great personages.'[20] Carew's comment was recorded years after this scene at Christ Church in 1569, and perhaps the subsequent career of his debating opponent had coloured his recollection somewhat, but there is no reason to doubt the genuine nature of the sentiment recorded.

Traditional as the system under which Sidney studied appears in its outward forms, new life had been breathed into it in the years before he came to Oxford. On the one hand this had been effected by shifting the emphasis given to subjects within the old medieval trivium of grammar, rhetoric, and logic.[21] The medieval B.A. course had concentrated almost completely on logic, and undergraduate work then had been truly the handmaiden of the professions it was designed to prepare men for. The universities were not, however, unresponsive to the extensive humanistic criticism that was levelled at them in the course of the sixteenth century. Rhetoric had been more firmly established in the undergraduate course. Where it had once been restricted to the bachelors of arts who were engaged in work for the M.A., it was now part of the regular advanced work for the B.A. Moreover, readings from classical authors had been given more breadth. These shifts reflected the whole change in outlook that was gradually coming over the nation. No longer was the university seen as just the preparing ground for the professions; it was now the school which prepared the courtier and the statesman, the gentleman, and the local political magnate.

In outward aspect, then, Oxford may have seemed crusty and traditional as it has to generations of undergraduates since. Beneath this appearance, however, then as now there was a different reality. One crucial development in the making of this reality was the emergence in the sixteenth century of the college tutor. In looking at the formal structure of the university, we tend at times to forget the developments which were going on at the college level. The formal lectures and the formal instruction were being supplemented by the colleges themselves, and this fact, combined with the increasing accessibility of books, meant that there was in effect an 'extra-statutory curriculum'.[22] Its content and worth varied, of course, with the energy, scholarly inclinations, and pedagogical ability of the tutor. But even in traditionalist, scholastic Oxford a student could find intellectual food of the keenest delight, provided he had the right tutor.

It is important, therefore, to ask ourselves what sort of men young Philip Sidney was exposed to as tutors. The answer is that he was, on the whole, very fortunate in this regard, for at least two of his three tutors were both active and scholarly. The first was Thomas Thornton, a fine Latin scholar. Despite the fact that he was a young man (he was at this time only twenty-eight), Thornton had already well established himself as a careful and intelligent tutor. We know very little about his educational connection with Philip; it is apparent, however, that he found the brief contact with Sidney a refreshing and memorable experience, and it is to be assumed that Sidney thought equally highly of him. In later years Thornton became Vice-Chancellor of the University and Master of Ledbury Hospital. He died in the Hereford-shire town and was buried in its imposing parish church. There his monument still bears witness to the ties between him and Sidney: it notes the quality of his Latin scholarship and further comments that 'he was a sure refuge for young scholars of great hopes and parts and tutor to Sir Philip Sidney when he was of Christ Church'.[23] The truth of the statement that he aided young scholars is well attested in the relations between Thornton and the future historian Camden. Thornton saw to it that Camden, who as a student was in considerable need, was transferred from Broadgates Hall to Christ Church, and there Thornton maintained him at his own expense and in his own lodgings.

That Philip was impressed by his tutor's abilities appears in one of his earliest extant letters. On 26 February 1570 he wrote a spirited and aggressive note to Sir William Cecil.[24] From it, it becomes apparent that his enthusiasm for Thornton was such that he had somehow secured from his uncle Leicester and from Cecil a promise that when there was a vacant canonry at Christ Church it should go to Thornton. Although the vacancy had occurred, a rival candidate, Toby Matthew, had emerged. Philip wrote to secure the place for his tutor, early evidence of the zealous efforts he was frequently to make on behalf of those to whom he granted his friendship. Philip was successful in this, and Thornton received the vacant canonry; Toby Matthew was not entirely passed over either, for within a few months he too had become a canon of Christ Church.

The appointment of Thornton to the canonry occasioned a change in Philip's tutors. Within a week of the letter urging Thornton's candidacy, Philip was placed under the tutorship of the Dean of Christ Church, Dr Thomas Cooper. Cooper was an older man than Thornton; more significantly, he was one of the university's most distinguished scholars. It has been said that he was, in fact, the most distinguished man of his day at Oxford, and he was renowned both for 'his learning and sanctity of life'.[25] His scholarly reputation rested firmly on his Latin Dictionary, *Thesaurus Linguae Romanae et Britannicae*, a work of such note that it became well known outside as well as within academic circles. 'Your Cooper's Dictionary is your only book to study in a cellar. A man shall find very strange words in it.'[26]

Philip's third tutor was the least distinguished of the three, Nathaniel Baxter. He is best known as a Puritan pamphleteer and as a minor poet of very considerable volubility and very inconsiderable talent. It is, however, through his poetry that his connection with Sidney is attested. In a long, rambling poem entitled *Sir Philip Sidney's Ourania*, which set out to contain 'all Philosophie', Baxter introduced the ghost of Sidney who approached the poet and asked who he was:[27]

I was reader (quoth he) in former days
Unto great Astrophil, but now am one
Stripped, and naked, destitute alone.
Naught but my Greekish pipe and staff have I,
To keep my Lambs and me in misery.

Art thou (quoth he) my Tutor Tergaster,
He answered yea: such was my happy chance,
I grieve (quoth Astrophil) at thy disaster:
But fates deny me learning to advance.
Yet Cinthia shall afford thee maintenance.
My dearest sister keep my Tutor well,
For in his element he doth excel.

There is, of course, no evidence that Sidney actually accorded Baxter the respect which is here granted. It is hard to see what Baxter did have to offer Sidney, what element it was that he did excel in. Perhaps it was his Puritanism which would have continued to nurture seeds well planted in the youth. Certainly it was not poetry; even Sidney's worst verse shows no debt to Baxter, and likewise Baxter's best shows that he profited equally little from his ex-student.

The world in which a university student lives is, however, not composed solely of tutors and subjects. His own contemporaries form as much of an impression on the student, perhaps an even greater one, than do the majority of his teachers. Although Moffett tells us that Philip did not spend his funds on pleasures but distributed them frugally for his own use and more generously for the assistance of learned men and adds that Sidney did not pour out his love rashly on everyone,[28] there can be little doubt that it was in his undergraduate days that he formed some of his lasting friendships. The university was, in his time, far from bereft of those on whom he could dispense his friendship. Although his close friend Fulke Greville had not followed his footsteps to Oxford but had become a fellow commoner at Jesus College, Cambridge,[29] Sidney found many new and invigorating acquaintances, especially in the hall most closely connected with Christ Church, Broadgates Hall, which lay just over the road from his own college. Perhaps the most notable of these was William Camden, whom we have already seen attracting the attention and philanthropy of Sidney's tutor. Also at Broadgates were Richard and George Carew. Richard, who remembered his disputation with Philip so vividly, was a notable scholar in his own right and assisted Camden in the writing of *Britannia*, one of the most notable Elizabethan works on topography and history. George is less well known, but he too had a considerable reputation in his own time for scholarship and by 1575 was serving under Philip's father in Ireland. It is possible too that Sidney may have made the acquaintance of George Peele, the poet, who was also at Broadgates from 1571 to 1574.[30] Among his contemporaries at Christ Church was Richard Hakluyt, the publicist of England's overseas voyages. It is not certain that he and Sidney were drawn together at this time, but in later life they certainly were by their common enthusiasm for both scholarly pursuits and for the planting of English colonies overseas, and Hakluyt was to mark their association by dedicating his great book of voyages to Philip. Another figure, also to be closely connected with overseas expansion and the furthering of the Protestant cause, was Walter Raleigh, who was at Oriel College nearby. Not all Sidney's acquaintances were students. It is certain that he was on close terms with Henry Savile, who became a fellow of Merton in 1565 and was later to be warden of the college and provost of Eton. Savile has the reputation of being one of the most learned Englishmen of his time; Sidney corresponded with him after he left Oxford and termed him 'an excellent man'.[31] The friendship with Savile opens up the possibility that Sidney was also acquainted with two of Savile's closest and most distinguished friends: Thomas Bodley, who had been a fellow of Merton since 1564, and Richard Hooker, who entered Corpus Christi College in 1567. In addition Sidney must have known the brilliant young fellow of St John's, Edmund Campion. Although Campion was to become a Catholic martyr and Sidney was already a strong Protestant, Campion and the Sidney family maintained very cordial relations. Their acquaintance may have dated from Philip's first visit to Oxford in 1566 when Campion had distinguished himself in disputation before the Queen. In 1570, when Campion was forced to leave the university because of his religious views, he went to Ireland where for a year he lived under the protection of Philip's father and wrote a metrical *History of Ireland*; it was Sidney's father who saved Campion from arrest in 1571 by sending him a private warning that enabled the young scholar to scurry to the safety of the continent.

Philip's horizons were already broadening. This is apparent from his friends, his tutors, and his studies. Moffett, who tells us more about Sidney's undergraduate days than do the majority of contemporary or near contemporary biographers, states that he devoted much time to philosophy and the arts of observation. 'How many mistakes in Aristotle, how many in Plato, how many in Plotinus, and in other writers of natural philosophy did he remark!'[32] Moffett further asserts that Sidney, while showing respect for the intellectual achievements of ancient times, did not hesitate to embrace the ideas of his own time as well: 'much as he highly esteemed the first stewards of learning, yet through reverence for antiquity, he did not condemn fresh fish'.[33]

The wider world was soon to call Sidney from Oxford. Indeed, he was never separated completely from the world of the court and of politics. Those letters which survive from his undergraduate days suggest that he maintained a fairly regular correspondence with Cecil. The first marriage proposals for the young Sidney heir concerned Cecil's daughter Anne,[34] and Philip himself expressed a desire to be close to Cecil: 'the duties and the respect which I owe to you and which I wish most heartily to perform, will bind me closely to you all life long, and always I shall set before myself, ever more and more eagerly, to find my happiness in deserving well of you'.[35] As Philip stood on the verge of manhood, he desired to be regarded with favour by Cecil. In the future, when he had evolved his own ideas about England and her place in the world, he would find Cecil's views too narrow, too cautious, and very frequently opposed to his own.

Sidney left Oxford without completing his work for a degree. This does not mean his intellectual inclinations were declining; it was a common practice of the time to go down without taking a degree. There is no certainty when Philip left Oxford; it has been suggested that it was during the widespread sickness of April 1571 which caused the suspension of academic work at the university. Possibly at this time Philip migrated to Cambridge for a short while; the evidence that he had a Cambridge connection as well as an Oxford one is not overwhelming, but what there is is suggestive.[36]

What effect had the years of university had on Philip? It is difficult to judge. Much of what made up his character had been moulded before he went to Oxford. From it he drew neither his intellectual interest nor his Puritanism, although he may have strengthened, matured, and elaborated these in the give and take of university life.

Certainly too he did not derive his poetic talent or his prose style from his Oxford mentors. Oxford may have been full of distinguished men, but few save Sidney, Raleigh, and Hooker are notable in the field of composition. Yet it is clear that these were not wasted years; there is ample evidence that Philip applied himself to his work with an uncommon vigour. His own father commented, 'I fear he will be too much given to his book'.[37] Fulke Greville in his account supports this statement, and Dr Moffett, who was a learned man in his own right, also echoes the sentiments. From the future course of Sidney's achievements we may possibly divine more. His letters show that he had a formal facility in Latin, even if his English was so rough as to bear few resemblances to the work of the accomplished master. His Greek was at a rudimentary level but showed a beginning towards that accomplishment he hoped to achieve in order to have a mastery of the wisdom of the ancients. He appears to have been remarkably skilled in modern languages, though where precisely he achieved this ability is now difficult to ascertain. Italian he could handle with passable skill; French was to him a second language. Only German eluded him, and it always would; he found it a most difficult language and one for which he had very little sympathy indeed. Later he confessed that he 'despaired' of it; he felt that it had a sort of harshness and expected never to master it, though he would sometimes practise it.[38] In some ways Philip may have found the university less exciting. There is a very definite note of retrospective irritation in a letter he wrote to his brother Robert in which he complained, 'I never require great study in Ciceronianism, the chief abuse of Oxford, *Qui dum verba sectantur, res ipsas negligunt'*.[39] Dr Moffett also hints that not all which Philip hoped for in Oxford was to be found there: 'though he saw too that the University (once the home of temperance, thrift, chastity and holiness) through a gradual neglect of discipline and seizure of license had fallen almost to effeminancy and debauchery, yet by no allurements could he be led astray from the antique mode of duty'.[40] Moffett also notes the highly interesting and significant point (which clearly relates, admittedly, to a slightly later period since Sidney was not yet the close friend of Edward Dyer that he was to become) that Sidney sought out the mysteries of at least one branch of the new science, chemistry, 'led by God with Dee as teacher and Dyer as companion'.[41] His interest in the new science and his relation to men like Dee are matters which will be discussed more fully in a later chapter, but his awareness of them indicates a void he would have sensed in the teaching of the university.

The intellectual curiosity that Sidney manifested, the desire, as Moffett put it, to press 'into the innermost penetralia of causes',[42] was something which he would never abandon. Nor would he lose the good report which he had already won. Sidney was throughout his life somewhat aloof from the ordinary course of things. A natural attitude for the scion of an aristocratic family, but in him, unlike the case with many others, it was not something to be resented. Philip's enemies tended to be political and religious rather than personal, and already at the university he had displayed that winning charm which was to be his most remarked on and memorable personal characteristic. We are told that he never went to church nor to the exercise ground nor to the public assembly hall except as the distinguished one among the company of learned men. 'How genuinely both the humane, learned race of academicians and churlish, unenlightened race of townsmen loved Sidney, even as no other one.'[43]

The decision that Sidney should continue his education through foreign travel was doubtless taken for him by others such as his father and the Earl of Leicester. Sidney himself came to appreciate independently the value which such an excursion could have for the young man who aspired to the role of active servant of his country. Years later he wrote at length to his brother Robert on this very theme, and the ideas that he expressed in this letter mirror well the reasons why the young sons of England were being sent in ever increasing numbers to the continent to learn first-hand from older masters. Travelling was not simply for the sights or for the subsequent pleasure in saying that one had seen great things. 'If you should travel but to travel or to say you have travelled, certainly you shall prove a pilgrim to no saint.'[44] Travel was to be part of the general education of the courtier, and though not all who undertook it did so with the right motives in mind, yet right motives there were. The traveller was to be aware of such things as the might and riches of the countries through which he passed so he could later use this information to help his sovereign in the formulation of policy. Moreover, travel was to be an education in the knowing of things worth knowing for their own sakes: 'their religion, policies, laws, bringing up of their children, discipline both for war and peace'.[45] Above all, Sidney was to caution his brother to be careful 'what men you are to addict yourself unto',[46] for the Grand Tour provided education not just through travel and careful observation, but also in the opportunity to mingle with men of substance and stature. Companions of this sort were to be selected with great care, 'for it is certain, no vessel can leave a worse taste to the liquor it contains than a wrong teacher infects an unskillful hearer with that which afterwards will hardly out'.[47]

Sidney's early career, once he returned to England, was in state and family service, as we have seen; the Grand Tour was to influence greatly his conception of his personal duties. In May 1572, when Sidney received the royal licence to cross the Channel 'with three servants and four horses to remain the space of two years',[48] such ideas as these may already have been forming in his head. Surely one of the most remarkable features of the coming months on the continent was the rapidity with which he developed his ideas about the policies of England, the progress he made in the very sort of educational observation he later commended to his brother, and the remarkable group of men with whom he managed to come in close contact. The tour, as it was planned out for him in advance, was to begin in Paris where he was to make contact with Sir Francis Walsingham, the resident ambassador and friend of his father. Later, he was to travel on to Germany, Austria, and Italy. He was liberally supplied with funds by his father, even though the family resources were doubtless stretched hard by this expenditure; an incomplete account of money spent on his behalf compiled three years later reveals an outlay of over £1500.[49]

If one is to trust a letter from his uncle Leicester written to Walsingham the day after Sidney's licence to travel was granted Philip was still very much the young and raw student.[50] Yet the almost immediate reception of Sidney into the intellectual world of the continent, the ease with which he moved among statesmen and scholars, gives something of the lie to the assessment of his uncle. Herein lies part of the great puzzle of Sidney: how such a young man, so inexperienced even if he had such powerful connections, could have so immediately impressed his elders with his seriousness, his wisdom, and his charm. A rather different picture emerges from the reminiscences of Lodowick Bryskett, one of his personal attendants, a cultivated and intelligent

Protestant Italian who had become known to Sir Henry Sidney through his work in the civil service in Ireland. Bryskett drew attention not to the rawness of young Sidney, but to his polish and especially to his use of foreign tongues:[51]

> Sir Philip Sidney . . . was so admired by the graver set of courtiers that when they could at any time have him in their company and conversation, they would be very joyful, and no less delighted with his ready and witty answers than astonished to hear him speak the French language so well and aptly, having been so short a while in the country . . . what excellency of understanding and what staidness was in him at those years. Whereby may well be said of him the same that Cicero said of Scipio Africanus, to wit, that virtue was come faster upon him than years.

Nor was Bryskett the only one to remark on this skill of Sidney in moving at ease in the highest circles. When the scholar de Banos recollected his first meeting with Sidney, he recalled being struck by his 'excellent gifts both of body and mind' and to his memory came the old tale of Pope Gregory, 'who declared that the English whom he saw coming to Rome were angels, *non Angli sed Angeli*'.[52]

Although subsequent events were to prove very much to the contrary, it seemed at the time that the circumstances under which Sidney came to Paris were most propitious. He came in the train of the Lord High Admiral, the Earl of Lincoln, who had been dispatched to the court of Charles IX of France in order to ratify an Anglo-French treaty and to explore the possibility for negotiations for the marriage of Elizabeth with the Duc d'Alençon. The festivities connected with this embassy were magnificent, although under the surface show of enthusiasm for the English, Protestant ties lurked worries that Elizabeth would be insincere in her part of the treaties and that the Catholic party, under the leadership of the Duc de Guise, would reassert its authority in France. In conjunction with the English embassy was celebrated the approaching marriage between the King's youngest sister Margaret, and Henry, the King of Navarre, again an action pointing at the momentary dominance of the Protestant interest in the French court.

Sidney spent some three months in the French capital. No letters from him in this period have survived, and we are thus left to conjecture about his life and contacts during the period when the rosy promise gave way to bloodshed as the Catholic and Spanish interests reasserted themselves. There are occasional and revealing glimpses to be found. Sidney seems to have made an extremely favourable impression on the French king, for on 9 August, Charles IX made him a Gentleman Ordinary of the Bedchamber and awarded him the title Baron de Sidenay.[53] Even more suggestive is the favourable notice that he apparently received at the hands of the King of Navarre, the young hero of the French Protestant cause. Fulke Greville recorded that Henry, 'having measured and mastered all the spirits in his own nation, found out this master spirit among us, and used him like an equal in nature and so fit for friendship with a King'.[54]

It is known too that Sidney established some notable contacts in the worlds of letters and learning. The anti-Aristotelian philosopher Peter Ramus was in Paris during that summer of 1572, and it is relatively certain that the young Englishman became closely acquainted with him. Also perhaps to be dated from this summer was the most influential of all the friendships that Sidney was to form with continental persons, his friendship with Hubert Languet.[55] Languet was an associate of both Ramus and Walsingham and was one of the most distinguished Protestant scholars and statesmen of his generation; for a number of years afterwards he acted not only as friend but also as tutor and guide to Sidney.

Sidney's circle of acquaintances during the summer months in Paris no doubt also included some literary notables in addition to the statesmen in whose company he so often moved. It has been alleged that he met Ronsard, de Baïf, and some of the other members of the Pléiade who were making such momentous strides for French poetry.[56] It is true that they were in Paris at this time, as was the noted Italian poet Tasso, who was an acquaintance of Languet. It is possible that Sidney knew them all, but due to lack of evidence, it is not provable. The possibility is, however, increased by the fact of Sidney's association with Walsingham who was something of a patron of letters and who knew many continental writers. Certainly some Frenchmen were to remember Sidney as a poet. Du Bartas listed Sidney along with More and Bacon among the principal English authors.[57]

And (World-mourn'd) Sidney, warbling to the Thames
His Swan-like tunes, so courts her coy proud streams,

That (all with-child with Fame) his fame they bear
To Thetis lap, and Thetis, every-where

What Sidney learned from the French poets is difficult to assess, especially since it cannot be proven that he had much in the way of direct contact with them. It has been suggested that the later literary circle around Sidney, the so-called Areopagus, was an academy modelled on that of de Baïf, but such suggestions, as we shall see, are probably misleading, since the organisation, whatever it was, had no formal structure and it may have been no more than a jesting phrase. It has also been suggested that he learned some stylistic devices, notably the use of the compound epithet, 'that new elegance which sweet Philisides fetch't of late from France'.[58]

While Sidney was thus making his first real contacts with the European world of letters and learning, events in Paris moved towards a crisis. The apparently happy promise of early summer gave way to the tragedy of the Massacre of St Bartholomew's Day in which thousands of Protestant Huguenots fell victim. In the chaos that ensued Sidney was never in personal danger, though many of his French acquaintances were. The English community in Paris found shelter in the house of ambassador Walsingham and there watched, as it seemed to them, the ultimate in horror and perfidy. Deeply disturbed by the events in France, the Council wrote to Walsingham advising him to see to it that Sidney returned to England.[59] By the time the letter had arrived, Sidney had already left Paris and was on his way to Germany; Walsingham had made the arrangements for him.

Sidney's first destination was Frankfurt where he was lodged in the house of the well-known printer, Andreas Wechel. Possibly the two had known each other in Paris, for Wechel too had fled the French capital at the time of the massacre. One of the finest of the scholar-printers in whom Renaissance Europe abounded, Wechel was a close friend of both Walsingham and Languet. Throughout the autumn and winter Philip Sidney remained at Wechel's house. We can only guess that he employed the time for the furthering of his studies. Although three of his letters survive from this period, all dated in March 1573, we can glean little about his life from them.[60]

Sidney's friend Languet had, by this time, been called to the Imperial court at Vienna in connection with his duties as ambassador of the Elector of Saxony. Early in the summer Sidney followed him, on the way visiting Heidelberg, Strasbourg, and Basle. In the first two of these cities young Sidney again made important and impressive contacts. In Heidelberg he became friends with another famous scholar-printer, Henri Estienne. The impact which Sidney made on Estienne was well indicated by the latter when he dedicated his edition of the Greek Testament to Sidney in 1576.[61] The trip to Strasbourg produced a second key friendship, that with Johann Sturm, perhaps the foremost educational pioneer of the century. Sturm was a man well known to England; he had been to Roger Ascham 'the dearest friend that I have out of England',[62] and he was an acquaintance of the powerful Lord Burghley. In fact, he took advantage of a messenger from Sidney to send a letter to Burghley at this time, and in July Burghley thanked Sturm for his kindness to Sidney.[63] How direct and how deep his impact on Sidney was is difficult to judge; certainly Philip admired him greatly and later, when Robert Sidney made his tour of the continent, arrangements were made for him to lodge with Sturm. It would be rash to suppose that Sidney received his conception of the courtier's duty to take part in the government of the realm from Sturm, though this was a prime lesson that Sturm's educational programme sought to implant. It was a lesson that Sidney would have learned already in England. It is probably true to suppose, however, that such conceptions were strengthened in the course of his contacts with Sturm.

From Strasbourg, Sidney followed the Rhine to Basle, and then went on to Vienna where he joined Languet.[64] He was eagerly greeted by the diplomat and plunged almost immediately into a further phase of his education. Through Languet, Sidney was introduced to and formed contacts with many of the prominent men of the imperial court and with many of the major intellectual figures of the Empire. Sidney did not wish to confine his visit to Vienna alone. In August he set out for what was supposed to be a three-day visit to Hungary and remained away from Vienna for several weeks. Languet arranged for Sidney to stay with a friend of his, Dr Purkircher, a physician living in Pressburg. The episode of Sidney's trip to Hungary is revealing as far as the attitude of Languet towards his protégé. When Sidney did not return within three days, Languet (in the first of his extant letters to Sidney) expressed his concern and indeed the rather oppressive quality of that concern which Sidney was no doubt only too eager to escape. 'Like a buck that has broken out of its cage you make merry and wander all over the place, forgetful perhaps of your friends, and careless of the dangers which often happen in journeys of that kind. . . . I am sorry that you have no one with you who might talk to you about the difficult subjects on your journey, or instruct you about the manners and institutions of the people you visit, conduct you to learned men, and, when necessary, act as your interpreter. I could perhaps have procured you such a companion had you told me what you were going to do.'[65] Despite the closeness of this guardianship, Languet's concern for Sidney was both necessary and useful, particularly in respect to two of the points he mentioned, instruction and the acquaintance of learned men, and this utility became manifest in October when Sidney returned to Vienna.

This can be seen when one begins to compile a list of those whom Sidney is known to have frequented during his stay in Vienna. One was Théophile de Banos, 'the true image of nobility', as Languet termed him[66] and an important Ramist; de Banos subsequently maintained a correspondence with Sidney and dedicated his life of Ramus to him.[67] Another was Charles de L'Ecluse, the director of the Imperial Gardens and probably the most notable botanist in Europe. L'Ecluse was, like Languet himself, an estimable companion for Sidney in his Protestant education, for like Sidney's mentor, he too had studied under Melancthon at Wittenberg and had there been converted to Protestantism. Through L'Ecluse and Languet, Sidney was also introduced to the Emperor's physician, Crato von Krafftheim, a man of about fifty. He had also studied under Melancthon, and of even more interest had been a pupil of Luther as well. He carried on a correspondence with Sidney after the latter returned to England, and in 1575 was asking Sidney to send him books on medicinal plants from England. It is possible, too, that Sidney not only knew but lodged with the Chancellor of the University and Professor of Medicine, Dr Aicholz. This is suggested in a letter in which Languet commented 'it would be better for me if you returned to your rough old gardeners with whom you lived last year'.[68] One of those 'gardeners' was no doubt L'Ecluse; there is a strong possibility that Aicholz (with whom L'Ecluse stayed all the time he was in Vienna) was the other, since he was noted as an amateur botanist.

The early months in Vienna were fruitful and instructive, but Sidney was anxious to widen his horizons further, and he resolved to visit Italy. The plan met with little enthusiasm on Languet's part. Languet was clearly concerned lest the atmosphere of Italy should corrupt his student, and his concerns were not simply those of a fussy old man. They were shared by many of the men of the age. The strictures of sixteenth-century Englishmen on Italy are well known.[69] Yet with all this distrust and dislike for Italy there was mingled a good deal of fascination. Even Thomas Nashe, who could denounce Italy's corrupting influence in ringing words, admitted that Rome was 'the queen of the world and metropolitan mistress of all other cities'.[70] The Elizabethans were alternately attracted and repelled by Italy. Against depravity and corruption were set its learning and culture, and Sidney, in search of the best and most useful learning, was anxious to see Italy for himself. The journey to Venice, which was the first destination, was without incident and it is perhaps to this portion of the Italian journey that Bryskett later referred in charming verses:[71]

> Through many a hill and dale
> Through pleasant woods and many an unknown way
> Along the banks of many silver streams
> Thou with him yodest, and with him didst scale
> The craggy rocks of the Alps and Appenine!
> Still with the Muses sporting, while those beams
> Of virtue kindled in his noble breast
> Which after did so gloriously forth shine.

Philip had come to Venice well armed, as might be expected, with letters of introduction from Languet. Two of the most important of his acquaintances were men Languet had picked for him, the Count of Hanau and Arnaud du Ferrier, the French ambassador in Venice. Of all the Italian cities Venice long had held a keen attraction for the Englishmen, who found in it an interesting example of both commercial power and governmental structure. Its actual power had begun to decline by the time that Sidney visited it, and it is true that he was less taken by its splendours than many of his countrymen. What he called 'the magnificent magnificences of all these magnificos'[72] left him somewhat cold, and he confessed in a letter to Languet that he would relish far more a conversation with him than all that he was seeing.[73]

Languet's reply cautioned him that if he did not like Venice he would find very little indeed to admire in the whole country: 'I judge from your letter that the splendour of Venice does not equal your expectation; nevertheless, Italy has nothing fit to be compared to it, so that if this does not please you, the rest will disgust you.'[74]

The period in Italy was essentially one of a continuation of Sidney's education. It was an education composed of three ingredients: the continuing correspondence with Languet, the experience of Venice and a stay in the more liberal university town of Padua. In Venice the Count of Hanau and du Ferrier were most valuable companions. Du Ferrier was a cultivated gentleman and a friend to scholars and literary figures alike. An acquaintance of the great Venetian statesman Paolo Sarpi, he was equally intimate with some of the major poets and critics of his native France, including Guy du Faur de Pibrac. Languet recommended the latter warmly to Sidney when he came in 1574 to Venice with Henry III of France, 'a man of such intelligence, learning, and eloquence that his equal is not to be found in France',[75] but Sidney was inclined to remain aloof, since he had been a defender of the Massacre of St Bartholomew. Of course, Sidney had the friendship, too, of Englishmen: the two most notable were Robert Corbett and Richard Shelley. Corbett, whom Sidney noted was his 'very greatest friend',[76] was the brother of a schoolmate. Shelley was his cousin and had been living in Venice for some time. That Sidney was no religious bigot is well indicated in his friendship with Shelley; he wrote to Languet that his cousin was 'a man of erudition, who knows Greek, Latin, and Italian well, but he is sadly addicted to Popery'.[77] Sidney does not appear to have had many close Italian friends, despite the fact that the presence of his Italian companion Bryskett probably eased the difficulty of making contacts. On the whole, Sidney's circle of friends was largely composed of the Germans and French who moved in the society of Venice and Padua. One notable exception to the rule was Cesare Carafa: he was a Protestant member of that notable Neopolitan family and he became a close friend of Sidney. He bore some striking resemblance to Sidney and these common interests were doubtless what drew them together.[78] Carafa had literary interests and was something of a poet; though Sidney had yet to display any development along these lines, there is no doubt that he was already interested in literary matters. Moreover, Carafa was interested in a wide variety of intellectual pursuits including sciences, and here too Sidney found a mind similar to his own. Finally, Carafa appears to have been influenced by a dedicated conception of the nature of the courtier's life, and Sidney, now feeling his way towards the standards for his own life and conduct, found in the Italian a splendid example to emulate.

Sidney's Italian experience was not, of course, limited to Venice, nor to the friends he made there. It was shaped, too, by a visit to Padua. It is hard to be exact about what that influence was, but Sidney himself appears to have felt a difference and pursued his own studies there with seemingly greater diligence than he had done before. This is not to suggest that Sidney at any point totally neglected his studies, but he appears to have sharply intensified his efforts while at Padua. There is no evidence that he formally matriculated at the university. It is possible that he did; the university had a long traditional connection with English scholars and the matriculation records for the period are missing. Sidney certainly had the facility in language to become a student there, for he spoke Italian reasonably well. While in Italy, Sidney extended his language study well beyond this. He worked diligently on his Greek to learn enough, as he put it, to suffice for the perfect understanding of Aristotle.[79] It is indicative of the seriousness with which he viewed his coming career as a courtier that he thought the *Politics* the most worth reading of all Aristotle's works, but he did know other works by the Greek as well, the *Ethics* which he commended to his brother and the *Poetics* on which he almost certainly heard the Professor of Logic at Padua, Zabarella, lecture.[80]

It is possible to form some idea of the educational programme Sidney set for himself from the references he makes to books in the course of his letters to Languet. Besides Aristotle's *Politics*, there are direct references to a number of other works. It is significant, though not unusual, to find Sidney perusing volumes on the government and constitution of Venice by Contarini and Gionotti, since the model of Venice exercised a particular fascination for the English mind.[81] His interests in history and European diplomacy were further indicated by his reading of Tarchagnota's *L'Historia del mondo* (published in Venice in 1562) and by his perusal of collections of letters published in Venice in 1560 and 1562 (*Lettere de prencipi, Lettere de tredici illustri homini*). He also expressed a strong desire to possess a copy of Languet's history of the Polish election which Languet had once shown to him. Sidney further wished to obtain a copy of the French translation of Plutarch's *Lives*: this was not an unusual request, for many of the courtiers of the time sought to find inspiration in the delineation of the Greek and Roman heroes, and Languet hesitated to borrow a copy of the work from their mutual acquaintance Vulcobius 'because I see he is his favourite author'.[82] Sidney, under Languet's direction, also delved into a study of the Roman statesman Cicero; Languet suggested that such a course would be useful both to Sidney's grasp of political matters, since it would help him to understand the factors which brought the Roman Republic to an end, and to his appreciation of and facility in Latin style.[83] The cultivation of a polished Latin style was no mere academic pursuit, for Latin was still the common language of Europe and if Sidney were to emerge as a successful diplomat he would need more than an average competence in the language. It was no doubt for this reason too that Languet urged on an unwilling Sidney the study of German. Important in Languet's thinking about international politics was the idea of a union of all the Protestant powers, a *foedus evangelicum* to resist the post-Reformation resurgence of Catholicism. Again, if his protégé were to be, as he hoped, a vital cog in this, he would need to be able to converse with the German Protestant princes and their advisers, for they, in conjunction with England, seemed to be the keys to the problem.

Languet was always careful to advise Sidney on his course of study, to direct the promising youth towards those things which would be most useful to him in a career of service to his country and his religion. Facility in languages was but one aspect of the educational programme he drew up for Sidney. Knowledge of the way of salvation, to be attained through study of the scriptures, he felt was the most important of all, and next to that, Languet urged, nothing could be of greater use to Sidney than to study the branch of moral philosophy that deals with justice and injustice.[84] He also laid great stress on the study of history by which, more than anything else, he felt, the judgments of men were shaped. He confessed that he had little need to drive Philip to a study of this subject; the young Englishman's inclinations had carried him naturally to it, and in Languet's opinion he had made great progress. Philip did not entirely neglect mathematics and science. While in Italy, he dabbled in the study of astronomy, but then abandoned it with Languet's approval.[85] Geometry he took more seriously, but apparently did not spend a great deal of time on the study of it either. He mentioned to Languet that he was in two minds about that subject;[86] he longed to be acquainted with it, especially since he felt that it was necessary for the art of war, but nevertheless, he concluded, he would pay only sparing attention to it because there were so many other things he wished to learn and know.

Perhaps the real core of the educational content of Languet's letters to Sidney in this crucial formative period was the discussion of contemporary international politics. Languet had a wide and useful background for being Philip's mentor in this field, and the vast bulk of the letters was concerned with comment and speculation on the movements, doings, and machinations of princes, both Christian and Turk, both Protestant and Catholic. Behind much of the material discussed lurked the idea which Languet seems to have implanted in Sidney's mind and the idea which became crucial to Sidney's more mature thought on international relations. This was the suggestion that somehow the Protestants of Europe must come together into an alliance to forestall the day of anti-Christ, be he Catholic or pagan in his outward forms. Languet could sometimes adopt a hopeful tone in these discussions; in March 1574 he wrote to Philip: 'The Roman pontiff transforms himself into every shape to prop his falling throne, but God turns his wicked counsels to his ruin',[87] and in April he noted: 'In France the crop is ripening which was sown when you and I were there: I hope those who exulted at the sowing will reap in tears'.[88] In other letters he could be more cautious and admonitory. Many of the letters dealt with the revolt in the Netherlands against Spain, already being interpreted in the somewhat misleading light of a Protestant holy war against the Catholic enemy. Languet pointed out to Philip the implications of the revolt for England by noting the Spaniards would fall on the English as the chief authors of their misfortune (even considering the very moderate support England was offering and her carefully pursued policy of aloofness). 'See to it', Languet urged Sidney, 'that you fail not your country at so great a need.'[89] Considering the increasing involvement of Sidney with the Netherlands, this appears to have been a lesson he took to heart.

Sometime in August 1574 Sidney left Italy to return to the North, a trip to Rome unmade, his tentative plans to visit Constantinople forever abandoned. He returned in the company of one of the friends he had made in Italy, the Count of Hanau. Shortly after he arrived again in Vienna sickness overcame him and he was consequently delayed there for some time, cared for by Languet. When well enough to travel again Sidney continued his exploration of Europe and made a visit of unknown but apparently lengthy duration to Poland. The stay there seems to have revealed little to Philip; he reported to Lord Burghley that the time there 'I might perchance have employed in more profitable, at least more pleasant voyages'.[90] He had returned to Vienna by the end of November, and it is worthy of note that he used the opportunity of being back to write to both Leicester and Burghley to inform them of the political conditions he had observed on his trip and at the imperial court.[91] Sidney was following well the precept that foreign travel was an educational prelude to the life of the courtier and diplomat, and though his reports seem somewhat chatty and offhand, in an age in which diplomacy was in its infancy, this was the very stuff of which diplomatic information and government policy were made. Not that we should attribute undue importance to Sidney's early letters in the field of diplomacy; he was still an apprentice and his comments were not yet such as would shape policy, either officially or unofficially.

On returning to Vienna, once more apparently suffering in health, Sidney remained at the imperial court for the course of the winter. We know very little of his activities in these months. Certainly it was a time when Languet and Sidney were close together, when the lessons which the statesman could impart to his pupil were well taken. Sidney sought to learn others of the courtier's arts as well. In this period his friendship grew with Edward Wotton, then also living in Vienna, and together, as Sidney charmingly recounts, the two of them studied horsemanship under the direction of the formidable John Pietro Pugliano, equerry at the court. Pugliano was obviously far from restrained in his praise of the art he taught. '. . . if I had not been a piece of a logician before I came to him, I think he would have persuaded me to have wished myself a horse'.[92]

Delightful and educational as the stay in Vienna doubtless was, Philip had to begin preparations to return to England. He had exceeded the time allowance given him in his licence to travel on the continent, though that probably had been extended.[93] He did manage to find time for a visit to Prague, but by the beginning of March he was in Dresden and on his way home. Languet, as might be expected, took pains to arrange things for Sidney as he travelled back towards England. He wrote various letters of introduction for him, and even provided him with some sorely needed funds.

It is crucial to try to assess what this period on the continent, some three years of his life, had meant for Sidney. The answers that one must give to such a question are either obvious or somewhat general. No doubt Sidney did experience that 'widening of his horizons' which is the hope and excuse of every student who travels abroad. And he had formed friendships that were both useful and important. He had been in contact with some of the great and near-great intellectual figures of the continent: Sturm, Wechel, Estienne. The greatest and most influential of these was, of course, Languet himself, and yet it is his contribution to Sidney's character that is most difficult of all to judge. It would be tempting to see in the emergence of many of the most attractive features of Sidney the hand of his elderly mentor, and it is doubtless true that Languet's parental concern for the young man did much to influence him. Yet it is also true that Sidney had displayed many of these qualities before he ever met Languet. He did not need the Burgundian to develop an acute mind and a restless search after useful knowledge. Nor did he need Languet to become interested deeply in Protestantism and the Protestant cause; he had, after all, imbibed his Calvin while still a schoolboy at Shrewsbury. And Languet cannot be directly responsible for the education of Sidney as a courtier; he had been groomed for this almost from the moment of his birth by the nature of his family and family connections. And yet, in an imprecise way, Languet did contribute to all these things. They were sentiments, inclinations, aspirations that lay deep within Sidney himself, but Languet was critical in bringing them to the surface. It was he who saw to it that Sidney met the right people, that he moved in the circles most likely to enhance his future. It was he who prodded Sidney patiently along the course of useful studies, and, above all, it was he who tutored Sidney in the immense complexities of international politics and nurtured in him the idea of organising these policies in such a way as to foster the Protestant cause generally. Sidney himself was well aware of the debt which he owed to Languet. Later, while composing *Arcadia*, he interpolated a passage of praise and fond remembrance of his tutor:[94]

The songe I sange old Languet had me taught,
Languet, the shepheard best swift Ister knewe,
For clerkly reed, and hating what is naught,
For faithfull hart, cleane hands, and mouth as true:
With his sweet skill my skillesse youth he drewe,
    To have a feeling tast of him that sitts
    Beyond the heaven, far more beyond your witts.

He said, the Musique best thilke powers pleasd
Was jumpe concorde betweene our wit and will:
Where highest notes to godlines are raisd,
And lowest sinke not downe to jote of ill:
With old true tales he woont mine eares to fill,
    How sheepheards did of yore, how now they thrive,
    Spoiling their flock, or while twixt them they strive.

He liked me, but pitied lustfull youth:
His good strong staffe my slippry yeares upbore:
He still hop'd well, because I loved truth;
Till forste to parte, with harte and eyes even sore,
To worthy Coredens he gave me ore.
    But thus in oke's true shade recounted he
    Which now in night's deepe shade sheep heard of me.

Chapter 6

SIDNEY AND THE WORLD OF LETTERS

My toyfull booke I will send you with Gods
helpe by February.
     Philip Sidney to Robert Sidney (1580)

All the *Arcadia* is a continual grave of morality,
shadowing moral and political results under the
plain and easy emblems of lovers.
    The Life and Death of Sir Philip Sidney (1655)

Sidney's early career, once he returned to England, had been in state
and family service, but, as we have seen, his opposition to the French
marriage led to his departure from the court.

Sidney's immediate reaction to disfavour at court was not, however,
to withdraw to a life of quiet exile in the countryside. We have seen
how he consistently displayed a longing for active service, if not
exclusively on behalf of his nation, then on behalf of the Protestant
cause, and his actions at this time were initially motivated by this
desire. In fact, his first thought appears to have been to leave England,
go to the continent, and support the efforts of William of Orange in the
Netherlands. It was a course of action that had much to recommend it,
and Languet himself was inclined to encourage Sidney to pursue it,
particularly since he felt that it would be of great military value to the
young Englishman to learn directly in the service of Orange himself.[1]
Yet even Languet had some doubts about the proposed expedition; he
sensibly urged Sidney to resolve his mind firmly before making any
public announcements; he was thinking back to suggestions in the
past that Sidney come to the Netherlands, suggestions that had aroused
considerable hopes only to be dashed by disappointment, and he feared
a repetition of this, which might lead those in the Netherlands to feel
that Sidney lacked constancy.

Languet was thinking of even more than this, however; he had some doubts about Philip's prospects for success in the Netherlands. He pointed out that the Englishmen who had come to the country had procured only contempt for themselves and had greatly alienated the Netherlands by their quarrelling and their mutual disparaging of each other. It was true, Languet agreed, that the leaders had so much lost their reputation that the people would flock to Sidney were he to come —but what then? Sidney would be forced to deal with veteran soldiers corrupted by long-continued licence, and Languet confessed to some doubts whether Philip had the necessary severity to do so. Languet felt that Sidney by his very nature and inclination was 'formed for gentleness', but soldiers could only be retained under discipline by severity, especially in a campaign which, through previous lack of discipline, had seen warfare degenerate into a series of plundering expeditions. Languet was not alone in having some concern about the proposed expedition; du Plessis Mornay likewise suggested to Sidney that he might be unwise at this point to embark for Holland,[2] and these cautions, coupled with Sidney's concern over Alençon's probable return to the Netherlands, were sufficient to dissuade Philip from going abroad.

Instead, Philip turned his attention increasingly to literature. It would probably be wrong to think that initially he did so for much more than its diversionary value; he still thought in terms of service rather than ease, and the cautions of his friends to forbear the seductive aspects of withdrawal were, in reality, scarcely needed. Yet in this diversion Sidney accomplished that for which he is best known, and the Elizabethan age would have been less rich but for the enforced idleness which led him to write at length. This is not to suggest that Sidney had neither written nor been interested in the arts before the year of his retirement from the public scene. Sidney had already gained something of a reputation as a patron of letters and had had several works dedicated to him. While not yet fully meriting the description Greville was to give him as 'a general Maecenas of learning',[3] his interests had not passed unnoticed. Moreover, he had already begun composition. According to one source, he had started work on *Arcadia* as early as the spring of 1577 when he had just returned from his continental embassy,[4] and in May 1578 his trifling work *The Lady of May* had been presented to the Queen while 'walking in Wanstead garden'.[5] The work, which had been commissioned by Leicester as an entertainment for the Queen, involves a supplication from a countrywoman to Elizabeth in the case of her daughter, the Lady of May, who has two suitors: a forester Therion, a man of 'many deserts and many faults', and a shepherd Espilus, a man of 'verie small deserts and no faults'. The Queen was asked to make the choice, an old shepherd and a pedantic schoolmaster attempted to explain the ramifications of the contest, the merits of the two contenders were discussed. After the Queen had chosen the shepherd Espilus the entertainment was brought to a close on a note of joy.

There is little to be gained from detailed analysis of *The Lady of May*. It was an entertainment and little more, and its main interest to a reader now would probably be the comic portrayal of the schoolmaster Rombus and the opening poem, the only direct poetic tribute which Sidney paid to his Queen:[6]

> Your state is great, your greatnesse is our shield,
> Your face hurts oft, but still it doth delight,
> Your mind is wise, your wisedome makes you mild,
> Such planted gifts enrich even beggers' sight:
>   So dare I, wretch, my bashfull feare subdue,
>   And feede mine eares, mine eyes, my hart in you.

Some have professed to find more in the piece than this.[7] It is true that even a slight royal entertainment of this sort was supposed to and often did conceal a hidden or allegorical meaning. If such meaning there was to *The Lady of May* it seems to remain hidden to our eyes. Two possibilities do suggest themselves. The entertainment concerns courtship; is it not, then, an allusion to the French marriage proposals, already in the air at the time of its composition? The answer here must almost certainly be no; in this interpretation Therion would have to represent Alençon, yet Therion is allowed some good qualities, a picture sharply at variance with the manner in which Sidney treated Alençon in his letter to the Queen a year later. Perhaps closer to the hidden meaning is the suggestion that it has some connection with the programme of the Protestant activists, albeit a rather far-fetched one. Therion represents almost certainly the active life and can be taken perhaps to represent the forward policy of the activists, while Espilus would, on this interpretation, represent the contemplative life and by extension the peace policy which Leicester, Walsingham, and Sidney opposed. Given this, the injunction of the Lady of May to Queen

Elizabeth that 'in judging me you judge more than me in it'[8] would take on an important meaning, perhaps a meaning which the Queen appreciated when she picked the shepherd as the successful suitor. Perhaps, too, as has been suggested, Sidney is here already exercising something of a critical approach to writing. It has been written of *The Lady of May* that it is historically interesting as the earliest example in English of conventionalised pastoral drama,[9] but it has also been argued that the piece is a questioning of the pastoral convention itself;[10] the entertainment is seen, in this view, as returning constantly to a questioning of its own form, to a debate over the validity of the conventional antithesis of the pastoral, the contemplative vs, the active life. The view does seem to fit in well with the personal attitudes of Sidney; if *The Lady of May* really was designed to question the antithesis between action and contemplation, it was expressing a concern that Philip felt deeply, the feeling that there can be no real dichotomy between the two, the one leading of necessity to the other.

Sidney's contacts with the literary world had spread far more widely and more meaningfully by 1580 than this minor composition might indicate. Although he had little connection with the two best known poets of the court (Thomas Sackville and the Earl of Oxford) he had by 1580 formed significant friendships with Thomas Drant, Daniel Rogers, Edward Dyer, and Edmund Spenser in addition to Fulke Greville whom he had known since childhood,[11] and through their friendship (perhaps particularly that with Rogers) he had been exposed to a world of literature wider than his own realm of England. Thomas Drant, a popular preacher and advocate of the use of classical metres in poetry,[12] had perhaps had contact with Sidney as early as 1576. In the main his influence must have been slight, since he died two years later, but it has been suggested that Drant may have been the one who turned Sidney's attention towards the creation of 'a new English poetry'.[13] Closer linked to Sidney were Dyer and Greville, yet it is difficult to be precise about the relations of this 'happy blessed Trinitie'. Greville, of course, was virtually a life-long acquaintance of Sidney and had been with him on the continental embassy of 1577, but it appears that contact between the two must have been somewhat limited in the three years after that, for Greville was frequently out of the country.[14] Greville did once comment that his works were 'written in his youth and familiar exercise with Sir Philip Sidney',[15] and this may suggest a picture of close co-operation between the two writers, reading and criticising each other's works and perhaps, as a line in one of Sidney's poems puts it, 'Striving with my Mates in Song'.[16] But the evidence for an association of this sort is not great; although a few of Greville's poems paralleled themes treated in Sidney's *Astrophel and Stella*,[17] the vast majority of his works were clearly written after Sidney's death. The case of Dyer is somewhat different;[18] he was as close to Sidney as anyone at this time, and significantly he is the only person whose name was coupled with that of Sidney as a poet by contemporaries. He was close to Sidney in many of his attitudes and acquaintances as well. He had shown an interest in and some knowledge of overseas exploration; he was a confirmed Protestant and a convinced activist, and he was a confidential adviser of Leicester. The real problem is, was he a significant poet whose ideas could have had a profound influence on Sidney at this time, and to this question should probably be returned the answer, no. His verse has been adequately described as 'somewhat old-fashioned, more in the style of Tottel's *Songes and Sonettes* than in that of the new poetry of Sidney and Spenser',[19] and no more than eight surviving poems can be attributed unhesitatingly to him.[20] His influence on Sidney may have been great in some areas, but it is doubtful whether one of these was poetic creation. He and Sidney may well have discussed topics of a literary nature, but Sidney's ideas were not formed by those discussions.

The question of the relations between Sidney and Spenser is equally difficult.[21] It is true that both are prominent figures in the emergence of the new poetry, and from Spenser, Sidney did have something to learn, but was their acquaintance close enough to allow this transference of knowledge? There are really two problems here: was either of the poets a crucial influence on the other at a formative stage and was their friendship prolonged enough to be the framework for a meaningful interchange even after the formative stage? The first question must almost certainly be answered in the negative; Sidney was past the formative stage by 1579 when he first became acquainted with Spenser. He had written by this time a substantial proportion of the poems that appear in *Arcadia* and thus had already, as he put it, 'slipped into the title of a poet'.[22] Sidney did express an admiration for Spenser's work in his comment that he 'hath much poetry in his eclogues, indeed worthy the reading', but he qualified that praise markedly with the additional note, 'that same framing of his style to an old rustic language I dare not allow, since neither Theocritus in Greek, Vergil in Latin, nor Sannazzaro in Italian did affect it'.[23] In plain fact the styles and treatments of the two poets of the new school were quite different, and, as one scholar has written, 'their greatest mutual influence was to encourage each other to be themselves'.[24] Nor is the evidence for Sidney's influence on Spenser's formative stage much more substantial. Spenser did write that Philip Sidney was the person who 'first my Muse did lift out of the floor/To sing his sweet delights in lowly lays'.[25] It was also said that Sidney was the one who had induced Spenser to undertake a great work in praise of the Queen.[26] These statements may seem conclusive proof at first glance, but they will not entirely stand up. Spenser's reference to Sidney occurs in the dedicatory poem of the *Faerie Queen*; the poem was addressed to Sidney's sister, the Countess of Pembroke, and as such is open to the suspicion of being motivated by a desire to gain patronage.

Of any of the associations of Sidney at this period, perhaps the most interesting and even perhaps the most illuminating is that with the somewhat shadowy Daniel Rogers.[27] Rogers had been born in Wittenberg about 1538, but since he had been conceived in England, he always looked on himself as a native Englishman. Through his family connections he had contacts with academic circles; his mother was the cousin of Abraham Ortelius, a great and pioneering geographer. Perhaps of even greater significance in his development was the career and fate of his father who, returning to England, achieved fame as the first Protestant martyr of the Marian reaction. By 1557 young Rogers was back on the continent studying with the reformer Philip Melancthon, who had also taught Languet. In the following years Rogers studied under Languet himself and under Johann Sturm, both of whom were to be close to Philip Sidney. Rogers also managed to return to England at the beginning of Elizabeth's reign and read for a degree at Oxford. After attaining his M.A. in August, 1561, Rogers left for Paris[28] where he remained for some nine years, with the exception of a short period in Antwerp in 1565[29] when he sought to escape the horrors of the religious wars in France. Once back in Paris, he became a member of the household of the English ambassador, Sir Henry Norris, indulged in some routine diplomatic work, and in

1570, at the recommendation of Norris, returned to England, to participate full-time in diplomatic matters.

What is of particular interest in his career, beyond the contacts he made with men associated with Sidney (and he did have contacts with others besides Languet and Sturm, notably with William Camden and James Douza, the rector of the University of Leiden), is the nature of Roger's experience in Paris and the men that he knew there. It is certain that while in Paris he studied Greek language and literature under Jean Dorat, Professor of Greek at the Collège Royale de France and member of the French literary group, the Pléiade. Rogers in fact appears to have had extensive contacts with French poets; he exchanged poems with Baïf, met and conversed with Ronsard, Altarius, and Pontus de Tyard. The intellectual who seems to have made the most significant impression on him was not, however, a poet. He was the French philosopher Peter Ramus, a man of strong Protestant sympathies and pronounced anti-Aristotelian views.[30] It would be going too far to try to argue that Rogers had formed contacts with the Pléiade as a group; a number of its celebrated members do not appear in the circle of his immediate acquaintances. Moreover, we should remember that, although the Pléiade was a literary group, its concerns were not confined to poetry.[31] Some of their concerns were of a literary nature, and these have an obvious bearing on the literary interests of the circle about Sidney at Leicester House in London: they were interested in experimentation with classical metres and quantitative rules, they were concerned with an attempt to devise a poetry and a music which could successfully be integrated, they were concerned with Hellenism. The latter was rather wider than just an obvious interest in Greek language and literature and was connected with neo-Platonism and probably with magic and mysticism as well. The Pléiade was also anxious to develop a divine poetry, a poetry which could fill classical forms with a Christian content. Beyond all this, and perhaps most relevant here, they were proponents of a sort of ecumenical movement in religion. It is one of the most striking things about the group which gathered around Baïf that here, in an age we associate properly with religious tensions and controversies, both Catholics and Protestants could come together on amicable terms. The same sort of feeling is reflected in Roger's writing; his poems are addressed to both Catholics and Protestants. As far as France was concerned, these strivings for understanding and co-operation between Catholics and Protestants were to come to an end under the impact of the Counter-Reformation and the worsening religious relations in the country which culminated in the Massacre of St Bartholomew. The same movement was, however, to have a brief flourishing in England, and it was to be associated with Philip Sidney.

It was some time after his return to England in 1570 that Rogers, with his interest in poetry, his concern for classical quantitative experiments, and his connections with an ecumenical religious movement, became acquainted with Sidney. Their meeting most probably came about through the agency of their common friend Languet. Certainly Rogers was in close touch with Sidney by 1578, for in that year Sidney wrote to Languet: 'I pray you to love my friend Rogers more and more for my sake.'[32] It is apparent that their relationship was both close and significant. During the 1570s Rogers addressed some half-dozen poems to Sidney; in addition there is the testimony of the Dutch poet and historian Baudius, who thanked Rogers for introducing him 'into the *familia* of the illustrious knight Sir Philip Sidney'.[33]

What is also important to observe is that in the coming together during the late 1570s of the Sidney circle, including Rogers, Dyer, Greville, and to a lesser extent Spenser, we are dealing with something more than a literary group. There has been scholarly argument for years about how organised a group this was, whether the Areopagus referred to in the Spenser–Harvey letters was a formal English imitation of Baïf's academy or not.[34] Part of the answer to that question has been befogged by the assumption that the group was limited to literary concerns and in particular to experimenting with classical metres under the influence of Drant. Years ago one scholar made a sage observation which has been badly ignored: 'It is certainly hard to conceive the authors of the *Shepheardes Calender* and the *Faerie Queene*, of the *Defense of Poesie* and the *Arcadia* in the very years in which those works were being planned and executed finding no more fruitful basis for conversation than the "Dranting" of English verse.'[35] With the aid of newly uncovered material on Daniel Rogers, the member of the group most often overlooked in the past, we can piece together a more coherent story of this important stage in the intellectual development of Sidney.

That these men of letters did come together and discuss matters of common concern is indisputable fact, even if it is not clear that the Areopagus was formally organised like the Academy; it almost certainly was not. But in their zeal to deny the formal organisation of the Areopagus literary historians have denigrated the evidence for the actual existence of the group, some going so far as to assert that the references to the Areopagus in the Harvey–Spenser letters are no more than an Elizabethan in-joke.[36] However, in a poem written almost a year before the Harvey–Spenser correspondence, Daniel Rogers explicitly referred to the group and to his desire for inclusion in it:[37]

Nor are you without a faithful and happy circle of companions in whom, in close friendship, there abounds a pious love. In divine virtue Dyer, keeper of judgement, storer of wit, excells. Next comes Fulke whom you have known since the earliest days of manhood, Fulke, dear offspring of the House of Greville. With them you discuss great points of law, God, or moral good, when time permits these pious studies. You are all ornaments of the Court, its favourites almost—the Royal Court (Nemesis be my witness) is therefore dearer to me.

If you were to allow us to be loved as one of them, that were enough, that is the culmination of my wishes.

But where does my love for you drag me in my simple verses? Desist, Muse, such matter should properly resound in heroic verse. But it is because I, while executing the Queen's commands in this part of Belgium, have joined Languet—your Languet, and also mine. Frequently we talk of you, Sidney, and love commands me to write to you of our talks about you.

Am I wrong, or do you also—in spite of distant separation—feel the same, and does it sound from here agreeably in your ears? But I conclude and leave the rest to the Muses so that you will not say I cannot bear my happiness.

Spenser was on the fringes of this group, and it is true that the contact between him and Sidney was nowhere near so great as some have asserted. The earliest proof of Spenser's acquaintance with Sidney is his letter to Harvey from Leicester House in October 1579.[38] By the following August, Spenser had gone to Ireland, so that the total period of contact was less than a year, and there is no reason to suppose that contact was constant even during that period. But all this hardly disproves the existence of the Areopagus or of the Sidney circle.

The important thing to ask at this point is what they were doing. Certainly they did experiment with classical prosody, attempting to apply Drant's rules for this to the composition of English verse.[39] But they pursued as well the other interests which we have noticed Rogers pursuing in Paris. There was considerable interest in the subject of divine poetry, and the links of the Scottish humanist George Buchanan to the Sidney circle at this time seem a clear indication of that.[40] Moreover, it appears perfectly certain that Sidney and his friends were concerned with the creation of an integrated poetry and music, just as Rogers's friends had been in Paris; Sidney's musical directions for the eclogues in his *Arcadia*, begun by this time, seem proof of that.[41] It is not unreasonable to surmise in addition that their discussions also touched on the other concerns of the Paris group, the concerns which were of a non-literary nature. After all, Rogers referred to their discussing 'great points of law, God, or moral good'. It was thus that Sidney was exposed directly to the idea of an ecumenical religious movement, and in this respect we can perceive his thoughts on the idea of a Protestant league broadening from a mere desire to unify some Protestants against the Catholic threat to an overall desire for the reunification of Christendom. If this suggestion is correct, then some of the seeming inconsistencies in the career of Sidney may be explained. It would help us, for example, to understand why he could remain friendly to individual Catholics like Campion and at the same time appear as the staunch Protestant; it will also help to explain his relations with Giordano Bruno at a later date. Sidney's Protestantism was not so sectarian as his position of Protestant champion might seem to imply.

From the foregoing it is clear that Sidney had an ample literary base on which to build during the months he suffered under gentle displeasure from the court. He had already written; he had already engaged in the critical discussion of literature; he had begun to relate his ideas to the practice of composition. It was during the months of leisure that these elements came together in the completion of the first version of Sidney's romance *Arcadia*. As first conceived, *Arcadia* seems to have been intended for little more than entertainment; written for his sister, the Countess of Pembroke, it was, Sidney commented, an 'idle work . . . which I fear (like the spider's web) will be thought fitter to be swept away than worn to any other purpose'.[42] Admittedly much of the manner in which Sidney spoke of the work can be explained by the courtier's *sprezzatura*, the offhand and slighting manner towards his own productions and efforts which the courtier was dictated by usage to observe. But some of this lightness is perfectly justified in the case of the first version, the so-called *Old Arcadia*; it was the product of retirement, the device for passing away idle hours that Sidney would have much preferred to spend in more obvious forms of activity. Aubrey retains a picture for us of the casual composition of the work: Sidney, he says, 'was wont, as he was hunting on our pleasant plains, to take his table-book out of his pocket and write down his notions as they came into his head when he was writing his *Arcadia*'.[43] This is a picture which fits well with Philip's own description of his writing of *Arcadia*. It was, as he said to his sister, 'done only for you, only to you: if you keep it to yourself, or to such friends who will weigh errors in the balance of good will, I hope, for the father's sake, it will be pardoned, perchance made much of, though in itself it have deformities. For indeed, for severer eyes it is not, being but a trifle and that triflingly handled. Your dear self can best witness the manner, being done in loose sheets of paper, most of it in your presence, the rest by sheets sent unto you as fast as they were done.'[44]

Before turning to a consideration of the contents of Arcadia it is necessary to take a quick view of its printed history. The text, as it first reached the public, was not the *Old Arcadia* or first version that Sidney composed, but a later revision, and an incomplete one at that, cutting off, as it does, in mid-sentence. This version was put together, probably by Fulke Greville,[45] after Sidney's death. Schemes had been in the air to publish *Arcadia* within a month of Sidney's death, but it was not until 1590 that the book was issued from the press in quarto form, apparently 'overseen' by Greville. Three years later a new edition of *Arcadia* appeared, edited by Hugh Sanford under the general direction of the Countess of Pembroke;[46] it provided an end to Book III and added Books IV and V from the old and unrevised version which Sidney had first composed. The junction was hardly perfect, and little attempt was made to make it so; the edition was prefaced with the words 'how this combat ended, how the ladies by the coming of the discovered forces were delivered and restored to Basilius, and how Dorus again returned to his old master Dametas, is altogether unknown. What afterwards chanced, out of the author's own writings and conceits hath been supplied, as followeth'.[47] The edition of 1613 added a longer explanation of the relation between the parts:[48]

Thus far the worthy Author had revised or inlarged that first written Arcadia of his, which only passed from hand to hand, and was never printed:

having a purpose likewise to have new ordered, augmented, and concluded the rest, had he not been prevented by untimely death. So that all which followeth here of the work, remained as it was done and sent away in several loose sheets (being never after reviewed nor so much as seen all together by himself) without any certain disposition of perfect order. Yet for that it was his, howsoever deprived of the just grace it should have had, was held too good to be lost and therefore with much labour were the best coherencies, that could be gathered out of those scattered sheets, made, and afterwards printed, as now it is, only by her noble care to whose dear hand they were first committed and for whose delight and entertainment only undertaken.

What conclusion it should have had, or how far the work have been extended (had it had his last hand thereunto) was only known to his own spirit, where only those admirable images were (and nowhere else) to be cast.

And here we are likewise utterly deprived of the relation how this combat ended, and how the ladies by the discovery of the approaching forces were delivered and restored to Basilius: how Dorus returned to his old master Dametas: all which unfortunate maim we must be content to suffer with the rest.

The work, then, as presented to the public was a composite, two books and a fragment of a third in the form revised by Sidney after 1580, the remainder substantially in the form in which he had first composed it and sent it sheet by sheet to his sister. There was criticism that the mixture was ill-suited; John Florio commented that 'this end we see of it now is not answerable to the precedents, and though it were much easier to mend out of an original and well corrected copy then to make up so much out of a most corrupt, yet see we more marring that was well then mending what was amiss'.[49] Florio's judgment was perfectly sound, but it had no effect on the popularity of the work; edition after edition of the romance came from the press, although the text of the *Old Arcadia* was not to be known completely until the beginning of the present century when three manuscripts of it were discovered within a short time of each other.[50] So widespread was its popularity that in the seventeenth century a Puritan writer was to attack it as something diverting women from their rightful and needful tasks: 'Let them learn plain works of all kind, so they take heed of too open seeming. Instead of song and music, let them learn cookery and laundry, and instead of reading Sir Philip Sidney's *Arcadia* let them read the grounds of good housewifery. I like not a female poetess at any hand. Let greater personages glory their skill in music, the posture

of their bodies, their knowledge in languages, the greatness and freedom of their spirits, and their art in arraigning men's affections at their
flattering faces. This is not the way to breed a private gentleman's
daughter.'[51] It would be no exaggeration to assert that for a century
and a half Sidney's *Arcadia* remained the most popular work of English
fiction, its dominance only finally set aside by the rise of the novel in
the eighteenth century.[52] The great and the less great would turn to it
for enjoyment and inspiration. Shakespeare ransacked it for various
aspects of his plots;[53] Charles I quoted it on the scaffold.[54] Henry
Oxinden, describing to his friend Sir Thomas Peyton the wedding of
his cousin, composed a letter which was 'a mosaic of unacknowledged
quotations' from the *Arcadia*, a striking indication of the popularity of
the work in 1640,[55] and even John Milton, who referred to it as 'the
vain amatorious poem', could in the same sentence call *Arcadia* 'a
book . . . full of worth and wit'.[56]

What is the modern reader to make of *Arcadia?* Let us confess at
once that he is unlikely to find it enjoyable reading. Outside of the
professionally oriented, few would feel any inclination to pursue its
complexities of plot, its involved prose, and its eternal ramblings to the
end. Despite the pleas of some that there is enjoyment and enrichment
to be found in Arcadian prose, only those most committed to a study
of Elizabethan England are now to be expected to read the work with
relish. But to understand Sidney we must approach *Arcadia* and try to
extract from it material that will aid us in appreciating him and his
thought. In doing so we will not be looking at *Arcadia* in the way the
literary historian would. A favourite game of Sidney scholars has
been source-hunting in the work: from which author did Sidney draw
this element, from which that. In the course of such painstaking
investigation scholars have revealed much about Sidney as a literary
craftsman.[57] We need not follow these scholars in their researches;
suffice it to say that that Sidney drew on a wide spectrum of source
material in compiling the *Arcadia*. There is much of the Hellenism
present which was a feature of the discussions of the Sidney circle,
although how much of the classical influence is first hand and how
much absorbed through the writings of Renaissance critics is another
matter. There are elements of Italian, of Spanish, and of native English
traditions, and the most impressive thing about the craftsmanship of
the *Arcadia* is the skill with which these diverse threads are woven into

one pattern. John Hoskins, who knew Sidney personally, was one of the first to attempt to sort out the various elements involved. In his unpublished work 'Directions for Speech and Style' Hoskins pointed to an influence of Aristotle on Sidney (he suggested that his eloquence and powers of description were due to familiarity with Aristotle's *Rhetoric*) and then concluded: 'For the web (as it were) of his story he followed three—Heliodorus in Greek, Sanazarus' Arcadia in Italian, and Diana de Montemaior in Spanish'.[58] Hoskins's analysis was, in its essentials, sound, and further research has done little but to confirm it.[59]

Of far more concern to our present interest are two related questions: what did Sidney intend *Arcadia* to be and what is the connection between the *Old Arcadia* which he finished during his time at Wilton and the revised *Arcadia* which he worked on up till nearly the time of his death, but never completed? It is possible to argue that Sidney had quite different motives in mind while working on the two and that these motives were connected with a desire to make *Arcadia* more serious, to transform it from a romance into a heroic poem. This is not to argue, as has been wisely pointed out, that the two forms are mutually exclusive.[60] The element of the heroical can be present within the framework of a romance and change the one into the other, leaving the reader to extract from it what he considers its essential characteristic. And so it is with *Arcadia*; in one of the shrewdest judgments of the work Gabriel Harvey noted that it was to be commended 'for three things especially . . . for amorous courting (he was young in years), for sage counselling (he was ripe in judgment) and for valorous fighting (his sovereign profession was arms) and a delightful pastime by way of pastoral exercise may pass for a fourth'.[61]

Both elements then, the instructive and the entertaining, are present in *Arcadia*—but which was uppermost in Sidney's mind? The answer to that question has been much complicated by the conflicting attitudes of the two people who should have known the answer best, the Countess of Pembroke and Fulke Greville. Sidney's sister certainly saw *Arcadia* as a romance, though admittedly a romance with very moral overtones and not at all 'a vain, amatorious poem'. The dedicatory letter from Philip to her has helped to enshrine this approach, that *Arcadia* was an entertainment, a trifle. Greville, on the other hand, took a far more serious view of *Arcadia* as a work of instruction and of philosophy, primarily of a political nature. Years later, when he wrote of *Arcadia* in his memoir of Sidney, this was the view he took of it.[62]

> In all these creatures of his making, his intent and scope was to turn barren philosophy precepts into pregnant images of life, and in them, first on the monarch's part, lively to represent the growth, state, and declination of princes, change of government and laws, vicissitudes of sedition, faction, succession, confederacies, plantations, with all other errors or alterations in public affairs. Then again in the subject's case: the state of favour, disfavour, prosperity, adversity, emulation, quarrel, undertaking, retiring, hospitality, travail, and all other moods of private fortunes or misfortunes. In which traverses (I know) his purpose was to limn out such exact pictures of every posture in the mind that any man being forced, in the strains of this life, to pass through any straits or latitudes of good or ill fortune might (as in a glass) see how to set a good countenance upon all the discountenances of adversity and a stay upon the exorbitant smilings of chance.

It would seem prudent to suggest that Sidney, even at the beginning of composing *Arcadia*, felt that it could be used to express moral and political lessons. However, the entertaining features of it were certainly most dominant in the early form, and with the intention of transforming it into a more serious work, he began revision of it. At the same time, we might note, he much increased its complexity and greatly heightened its artistic level by making advances in characterisation and in narrative technique.[63] The revision occupied his time off and on in the years between 1580 and his death, and it was Greville who understood what was involved in this far better than his sister, for whom *Arcadia* remained a romance and little more. With this realisation in mind, we can perhaps clear up two further points about the *Arcadia*, the reason why Sidney wished it destroyed at his death[64] and the question of the sort of editing the Countess of Pembroke gave to the latter sections of it. From what has already been said, the reasons behind Philip's desire to destroy the book should be clear: begun as a work with entertainment foremost, it had taken on more serious meaning in his mind, and he had begun a revision of it with the intention of shaping it in a new way. That revision had been unfinished and too much of the light and what now seemed to him unworthy aspect of it remained for Philip to be happy with it. This seems to be the best interpretation to put on the words which Greville used to describe Sidney's attitude:[65]

Now as I know this was the first project of these works, rich (like his youth) in the freedom of affections, wit, learning, style, form, and facility to please others. So must I again (as ingenuously) confess that when his body declined and his piercing inward powers were lifted up to a purer horizon, he then discovered not only the imperfection but vanity of these shadows, how daintily soever limned, as seeing that beauty itself, in all earthly complexions, was more apt to allure men to evil than to fashion any goodness in them. And from this ground, in that memorable testament of his, he bequeathed no other legacy but the fire to this unpolished embryo, from which fate it is only reserved until the world hath purged away all her more gross corruptions.

The same considerations help to explain what may seem a problem in the textual emendations in the part supervised by Lady Pembroke. It is clear that there had been revisions from the original, and it has frequently been suggested in the past that these changes represent the work and attitudes of the Countess of Pembroke rather than the intentions and attitudes of Sidney himself, in particular that Lady Pembroke bowdlerised the final three sections of *Arcadia* because she as a woman found some of the passages on sex to be distasteful.[66] This is a completely false conception; every indication is that what changes were made were done in accordance with Sidney's own wishes. That he had not completed his ideas on revision of the last three sections is obvious enough, but he had already begun it; this is indicated by the transfer of some material from the last three books of the *Old Arcadia* to the revised *New Arcadia* which Greville edited. In fact, the changes in tone and the modifications of some of the passages is perfectly explicable in terms of what Sidney thought he was doing with the work, far more explicable indeed than the assumption that the Countess of Pembroke made the changes. For to assert she was responsible is not only to ignore the very obvious degree of reverence with which she treated her brother's work, but it is also to endow this Elizabethan lady with a very unlikely Victorian attitude towards matters of sex. It further raises the problem of how and why, if she did have such an attitude, Sidney so confidently sent the episodes to her in their original form. The emendations are, however, perfectly understandable in terms of Sidney's changing attitudes. One point that should be clear in our minds is that the moral reaction to such issues as marriage by consummation on the basis of a private betrothal (and preceding marriage by ceremony) was quite different in Elizabethan England than it would have been in the England of Queen Victoria. Such action was a convention of chivalric literature and was presented within the context as being fully compatible with the highest virtue. Hence when one of the heroes of *Arcadia* finds himself in this situation he is not placed in a position of moral degradation, as a Victorian might assert. Moreover, the sensuous details of the literary treatment given the episode would not have been offensive to Elizabethans. All this makes it very unlikely that the revision is due to a question of morality in any narrow sense on the part either of the Countess or of Philip. Rather it is due to the nature of the lesson which Sidney was attempting to draw. In the characters of the main figures of *Arcadia* Sidney was obviously attempting to delineate the supreme models of virtue. In doing so, he increasingly felt that the conduct of the two 'heroes' Pyrocles and Musidorus was in the original version inconsistent with the chivalric ideal he was trying to present; Pyrocles's conduct, for example, is changed not on conventional grounds of morality but because his conduct in the first version seemed frivolous and lacking in the vigour of purpose which a true ideal type should display.

To attempt to summarise the plot of *Arcadia* is perhaps foolish, for the many twists and turns can hardly be indicated within the scope of a few pages, and worse, compression of the romance to a plot summary reveals Sidney at what seems an absurd level and disguises the genuine skill with which he wove very diverse elements together. Suffice it to say, the plot concerns the elaborately intertwined connections of Duke Basilius and his family with two young princes, Pyrocles and Musidorus. The Duke receives a prophecy from Delphi which tells him.[67]

> Thy Elder care shall from thy carefull face
> By Princely meane bee stolne, and yet not lost;
> Thy Younger shall with Natures bliss embrace
> An uncouth Love, whiche Nature hateth moste:
> Thow with thy Wyffe adultery shalt committ,
> And in thy Throne, a forreyn State shall sitt,
> All this on thee this fatall yeare shall hitt.

Because of the prophecy, he retires to the country with his wife Gynecia and his daughters Philoclea and Pamela, leaving the kingdom in charge of his friend Philanax. The two princes, Pyrocles and Musidorus, passing through Arcadia on their way from Egypt to Macedon each fall in love with one of the daughters and adopt disguises in order to be near them, Pyrocles disguising himself as an Amazon, Musidorus as a shepherd. In the course of their pursuit of the ladies each of the prophecies in turn comes true or seemingly true. The elder daughter is stolen by Prince Musidorus, the younger by Pyrocles who, since he is disguised as a woman, seems to involve here in 'an uncouth love, which nature hateth most'. In the course of wooing Philoclea, Pyrocles is forced to trick Basilius and Gynecia so that they come together in the dark, each thinking the other is Pyrocles, and hence the Duke fulfils the prophecy 'Thou with thy wife adultery shall commit'. Basilius, moreover, inadvertently takes a potion which seems to kill him; Gynecia is accused of his murder and the princes of conspiracy and sedition. Beyond all this, Basilius's retirement from his office has brought the country to the verge of civil war, until Evarchus, the King of Macedonia, arrives suddenly to bring peace to the country and to mete out justice to the culprits. Gynecia is so remorse-stricken that she agrees to be punished; the princes admit their passion for the two daughters, but defend themselves from other charges. However, even the revelation that they are the unrecognised son and nephew of Evarchus, who is the 'foreign state' sitting in Basilius's throne, does not save them and they are condemned. At this point the supposedly dead Basilius revives, matters are set straight, and all ends happily with a double wedding. The plot itself is interspersed with a series of eclogues which both relieve the plot and supplement it; the Duke's family are entertained in the eclogues with games, verses, and tales by the shepherds, and in this way incidents falling outside the time-scope of the plot but necessary for its unfolding are introduced.

This wild, and on the surface of it ludicrous plot may seem complex enough in itself, but one should remember that this is the *Old Arcadia*, the simple version before Sidney's rewriting wove into an already complicated structure further elements. In the revised *Arcadia*, the chronological sequence of the *Old Arcadia* is abandoned and many new episodes (significantly they are frequently of a chivalric type)[68] are introduced. The main plot is still there; most of the elements of the *Old Arcadia* are incorporated in the revised version, though not always in the form and sequence in which they had first appeared. The result is, as one writer commented, 'a Chinese puzzle of enormous intricacy, by which the reader's attention and memory are kept on the strain piecing together the main and tributary stories'.[69]

To explore the many themes and ideas running through the *Arcadia*, especially in its revised form which Sidney intended to be a sort of treatise of chivalric behaviour, would require many volumes. The labours of scholars of English literature and history have been involved in this for many years, producing a copious and interesting critical literature.[70] We shall return to some of the themes when we consider the social and political attitudes of Sidney in a later chapter. Here one point alone should be made, and that involves the question of personal identification in the *Arcadia*.[71] It is tempting to try to find the auto-biographical elements in an author's writings, and it would be wrong to suggest that there are none in Sidney's *Arcadia*. We have noted how the shepherd Philisides evokes very clear memories of Philip himself and how a tribute to Languet is inserted in the text, how the description of a country house may well represent Penshurst. There no doubt are many more such identifications which can be made, but to push this sort of approach too far is extremely dangerous. There have been those who have tried. A century after Sidney's death a correspondent of John Aubrey gave him just such a list of identifications; Philoclea and Pamela become Penelope Devereux and her sister Dorothy, and so forth. The writer of this information however confessed that his key to persons 'is not worth anything' and that was the wisest of the judgments which he made.[72] The tendency in this century has been to look for a more general type of allegorical meaning in the text rather than for specific references, and this tendency would seem to be a sound one.[73] Sidney was writing with contemporary events and life in mind and there are many references which indicate this, but he was not writing an elaborate allegory in which each character consistently represented a known political personage. Sidney, the Queen, her champion Sir Henry Lee all make their appearances in disguised form. There are apparent references to the foreign policy of the activists and to the position of Mary Queen of Scots and doubtless there are other similar instances, some of which are probably beyond our recovering. Sidney's intentions were, however, general rather than specific, and for this reason if for no other, the allegory too is general and not personal.

It is far from certain that Sidney composed his *Apology for Poetry* at this same time. The date of this work, of all his prose writings the one most likely to be appealing to a modern reader, has never been determined with precision. It has been variously assigned to 1579, 1580–1, or 1583.[74] The only information which seems absolutely clear is that the work was finished sometime after the publication of Spenser's *Shepheardes Calender* in September 1579. There has been a long tradition that the *Apology* is connected with Stephen Gosson's *School of Abuse* which was published in 1579 and that Sidney wrote his work as an answer to some of Gosson's arguments. Though this connection has been recently questioned,[75] it is probably sound and because of this it is useful to look a bit into Gosson's own background.[76]

Gosson had been born in Canterbury in 1554 into a lower middle-class family of humble circumstances. After being a King's Scholar at the Cathedral School of Canterbury, he entered Corpus Christi College, Oxford, in 1572. There is evidence that Gosson contemplated a scholar's life for himself and that it was against his will that he was forced to leave Oxford and go to London in 1577 to seek his fortune. Gosson was something of a playwright, hard working but far from successful, and he soon turned his talents to a sphere more suited to them, pamphleteering. In 1579 he published *The School of Abuse*, an attack on the abuses of the stage. Two things should be noted about the work. One is that there is evidence that it was a piece of hack-work, commissioned by some of the city fathers and something for which Gosson was generously paid. The other is that it was not, in the conventional sense of the phrase, a Puritan attack on the stage, as is frequently alleged. Gosson's objections to plays were not theological; he was not so much condemning art as he was its abuse, and his objections were mainly social, economic, and political. Gosson's pamphlet was dedicated to 'the right noble gentleman, Master Philip Sidney' and told him if he would 'vouchsafe to enter the school door and walk an hour or twain within for your pleasure, you shall see what I teach, which present my school, my cunning, and myself to your worthy patronage'.[77] There is no evidence that Gosson was personally acquainted with Sidney and certainly none that in any way Sidney had authorised the dedication. It is clear, though, that Gosson hoped for approval, and from what was publicly known about Sidney at the time, he might well have expected it, especially in view of the fact that his was not the first attack on the abuses of the stage and that similar attacks had been made by John Stockwood, a schoolmaster at Tonbridge who was patronised by Sir Henry Sidney.[78] Indeed, some of what Gosson said, Sidney plainly agreed with; he, like Gosson, was critical of the contemporary stage, noting that 'our tragedies and comedies' were 'not without cause cried out against' and commenting that he spent time discussing plays 'because, as they are excelling parts of Poesy, so is there none so much used in England, and none can be more pitifully abused, which, like an unmannerly daughter showing a bad education, causeth her mother Poesy's honesty to be called in question'.[79]

Here we can begin to see the reason why Sidney, though agreeing with portions of Gosson's argument, was inspired to reject it. For reject it he did. As Spenser wrote to Harvey: 'New books I hear of none, but only of one that writing a certain book called *The School of Abuse* and dedicating it to Master Sidney was for his labour scorned, if at least it be in the goodness of that nature to scorn. Such folly is it not to regard aforehand the inclination and quality of him to whom we dedicate our books.'[80] The reasons for Sidney's rebuff to Gosson seem obvious. Even though Gosson was writing primarily about the stage and Sidney was to write in defence of poetry, there was enough in Gosson's book to provoke him. Gosson did attack poetry as such in the course of his pamphlet:[81]

> I must confess that poets are the whetstones of wit, notwithstanding that wit is dearly bought: where honey and gall are mixed, it will be hard to sever the one from the other. The deceitful physician giveth sweet syrups to make his poison go down the smoother: the juggler casteth a mist to work the closer: the Siren's song is the sailor's wreck; the fowler's whistle the bird's death: the wholesome bait the fish's bane. The Harpies have virgin faces, and vultures talents: Hyena speaks like a friend and devours like a foe: the calmest seas hide dangerous rocks. . . . Many good sentences are spoken by Davus to shadow his knavery and written by poets as ornaments to beautify their works and set their trumpery to sale without suspect. . . .
>
> Pull off the vizard that poets mask in, you shall disclose their reproach, bewray their vanity, loathe their wantonness, lament their folly, and perceive their sharp sayings to be placed as pearls in dunghills, fresh pictures on rotten walls, chaste matron's apparel on common courtesans. . . . No marvel though Plato shut them out of his school and banished them quite from his commonwealth, as effeminate writers, unprofitable members, and utter enemies to virtue.

There is probably an even more important reason, however, for Sidney's defence and that was a feeling that an attack on the abuses of one form of creative writing could be interpreted to blacken other forms as well. If plays corrupted morals, distorted truth, and were a pernicious influence, might not their enemies then argue that poetry was as well?

It would be pushing the evidence too far to suggest that Sidney's *Apology* was inspired entirely by Gosson or that it served as a pointed and detailed rebuke to him. It is more the attitude which Gosson represents than Gosson himself which is attacked, and there is merit in the argument that a man of Sidney's standing would have been under no compulsion to answer a bit of hack-work, even if it had been imprudently dedicated to him.[82] Gosson is nowhere mentioned in the *Apology*; there are a few verbal echoes of his pamphlet,[83] but in themselves they are not conclusive proof that Sidney wrote with Gosson in mind. The discussion of poetry and the defence offered for it by Sidney doubtless stems as much from the discussions he had with his friends Dyer, Greville, and Rogers as they do from Gosson. Yet to deny that Gosson's work had an influence on Sidney's composition is to err; it is not convincing to dismiss that connection because Sidney did not print his reply. To have done so would have been beneath his dignity, but he did make a clear statement of his position for his friends, and many of the charges he answered (that poetry was a waste of time, that it fostered falsehood, that it caused abuse) were precisely the charges made by Gosson. That Sidney recognised some of Gosson's points as valid is also not convincing proof that he was uninterested in replying to the arguments. It was the general attitude rather than the specific argument which most concerned him; both Gosson and Sidney realised that the good and the bad were usually mixed together in poetry. Gosson, stressing the element of the bad, would banish poetry; while Sidney, admiring the potentiality of the good, would afford it a place of honour.

The *Apology* is a carefully arranged literary form, modelled on the classical oration, and in its construction Sidney shows his mastery of classical learning and techniques.[84] The ideas that are contained in the work are not profoundly original; Sidney drew heavily on the critical writings of others such as Scaliger, Castelvetro, and Robortello, and it has rightly been said of the *Apology* that it 'is not epoch-making, but it is epoch marking'.[85]

Space does not allow a full discussion of the arguments and difficulties raised by Sidney's work. The central proposition which he seeks to maintain, he stated in these terms: 'Poesy therefore is an art of imitation, for so Aristotle termeth it in his word *mimesis*, that is to say a representation, counterfeiting, or figuring forth—to speak metaphorically, a speaking picture—with this end, to teach and delight'.[86] In advancing this thesis Sidney compared the claims of poetry to be the worthiest of all disciplines. History and philosophy might seem natural rivals, but the claims of each, as Sidney saw it, are to be set aside in favour of the claims of poetry:[87]

Since then Poetry is of all human learning the most ancient and of most fatherly antiquity, as from whence other learnings have taken their beginning since it is so universal that no learned nation doth despise it, nor no barbarous nation is without it; since both Roman and Greek gave divine names unto it, the one of 'prophesying' the other of 'making', and that indeed the name of 'making' is fit for him, considering that whereas other arts retain themselves within their subject, and receive, as it were, their being from it, the poet only bringeth his own stuff, and doth not learn a conceit out of a matter, but maketh matter for a conceit; since neither his description nor his end containeth any evil, the thing described cannot be evil; since his effects be so good as to teach goodness and to delight the learners; since therein (namely in moral doctrine, the chief of all knowledges) he doth not only far pass the historian, but, for instructing, is well nigh comparable to the philosopher, and, for moving, leaves him behind him; since the Holy Scripture (wherein there is no uncleanness) hath whole parts in it poetical, and that even our Saviour Christ vouchsafed to use the flowers of it; since all his kinds are not only in their united forms but in their severed dissections fully commendable; I think (and think I think rightly) the laurel crown appointed for triumphing captains doth worthily (of all other learnings) honour the poet's triumph.

He turns then to a refutation of specific charges against poetry, both as to its form and as to its content. Poetry, as he sees it, is not unprofitable. 'If it be, as I affirm, that no learning is so good as that which teacheth and moveth to virtue, and that none can both teach and move thereto so much as Poetry, then is the conclusion manifest that ink and paper cannot be to a more profitable purpose employed.'[88] Nor is the poet a liar:[89]

As I take it, to lie is to affirm that to be true which is false; so as the other artists, and especially the historian, affirming many things, can, in the cloudy knowledge of mankind, hardly escape from many lies. But the poet . . .

never affirmeth. The poet never maketh any circles about your imagination, to conjure you to believe for true what he writes. He citeth not authorities of other histories, but even for his entry calleth the sweet Muses to inspire into him a good invention; in truth, not labouring to tell you what is or is not, but what should or should not be. And therefore, though he recount things not true, yet because he telleth them not for true, he lieth not. . . . And therefore, as in History looking for truth, they go away full fraught with falsehood, so in Poesy looking but for fiction, they shall use the narration but as an imaginative ground plot of a profitable invention.

Poetry has been considered the nurse of abuse, but this too is a false charge. 'Nay truly, though I yield that Poesy may not only be abused, but that being abused, by the reason of his sweet charming force, it can do more hurt than any other army of words, yet shall it be so far from concluding that the abuse should give reproach to the abused, but contrariwise it is a good reason, that whatsoever, being abused, doth most harm, being rightly used (and upon the right use each thing conceiveth his title), doth most good.'[90] Finally, Sidney argues that Plato did not condemn poets in the way which controversialists have usually said; to be sure, poets were banished from the ideal state of the *Republic* as corrupting influences, but Plato was concerned with the abuse of poetry, not poetry itself. As Sidney interpreted the matter, Plato gave both 'high and rightly divine commendation to Poetry' in his dialogue *Ion*. 'So as Plato, banishing the abuse, not the thing—not banishing it, but giving due honour unto it—shall be our patron and not our adversary . . . he attributeth unto Poesy more than myself do, namely, to be very inspiring of a divine force, far above man's wit, as in the afore-mentioned dialogue is apparent'.[91]

Sidney was not unaware, as we have seen, that poetry in his own time was open to criticism because of its abuses. In a digression (which like the main text is carefully constructed in the form of a classical oration), Sidney discussed this problem, maintaining as his central proposition the view that poets must understand what they are to do and how they are to do it, if poetry is to be once again honoured. 'Marry, they that delight in Poesy itself should seek to know what they do, and how they do; and especially look themselves in an unflattering glass of reason, if they be inclinable unto it.'[92]

The digression ended, the charges against poetry refuted as 'either false or feeble', its lack of appreciation in England explained as the 'fault of poet-apes, not poets', and the English language lauded as the 'tongue . . . most fit to honour Poesy and to be honoured by Poesy', Sidney urged 'you all that have had the evil luck to read this ink-wasting toy of mine' no longer to scorn poetry nor to laugh at poets as if they were next to fools. Instead, he urged his readers 'to believe . . . that it pleased the heavenly Deity, by Hesiod and Homer, under the veil of fables, to give us all knowledge, Logic, Rhetoric, Philosophy natural and moral, and *quid non?*; to believe, with me, that there are many mysteries contained in Poetry, which of purpose were written darkly, lest by profane wits it should be abused; to believe . . . that they are so beloved of the gods that whatsoever they write proceeds of a divine fury; lastly, to believe themselves, when they tell you they will make you immortal by their verses'.[93] To those who would not believe, 'thus much curse I must send you, in the behalf of all poets, that while you live, you live in love, and never get favour for lacking skill of a sonnet, and, when you die, your memory die from the earth for want of an epitaph'.[94]

Chapter 7

ASTROPHEL AND STELLA

Our English Petrarch Sir Philip Sidney or (as
Sir Walter Raleigh in his epitaph worthily calls
him) the Scipio and the Petrarch of our time.
John Harington, *Orlando Furioso* (1591)

I that, before ever I durst aspire unto the
dignity am admitted into the company of the
paper-blurrers . . . but I, as I never desired the
title, so have I neglected the means to come
by it. Only overmastered by some thoughts,
I yielded an inky tribute unto them.
Philip Sidney

No part of Sidney's life has attracted more attention, more controversy,
and more apologetic than his alleged affair with Penelope Rich. The
circumstances surrounding the affair are, as we shall see, vague, and
their interpretation is made more difficult by the fact that they are
inextricably bound up with the greatest of all Sidney's literary efforts,
the sonnet sequence known to generations of readers as *Astrophel and
Stella*.

It would be well to be clear in our minds from the very beginning
what the history of the sonnets in their published form is. The poems
were not, in fact, published during Sidney's lifetime. Many have had
occasion to refer to the 'stigma of print' in the Elizabethan period,[1]
and it should not surprise us that Sidney, like many of the gentleman
writers of his day, did not rush his productions into print with the
alacrity that was reserved for the hack and the professional. The
important thing for the courtier was to write, not to publish, and his
poems received their normal circulation in manuscript through the
hands of his friends and relations. It was not until five years after
Sidney's death that a London publisher, Thomas Newman, circulated
the poems in printed form under the title 'Syr P.S. His Astrophel and
Stella wherein the excellence of Sweete Poesie is concluded'. Newman

indicated that he had done his best to produce an accurate edition of the poems; in fact, he cited as one of his major reasons for issuing his edition the circumstance that the poems had been circulated widely in inaccurate and corrupt manuscript copies. 'I have been very careful in the printing of it, and whereas being spread abroad in written copies, it had gathered much corruption by ill writers, I have used their help and advice in correcting and restoring it to his first dignity that I know were of skill and experience in those matters.'[2] So much for Newman's design; the final product scarcely lived up to his advertisement of care and concern. His text was as corrupt as the manuscript version of which he so piously complained, and it is not in the least surprising to find that those who had been closest to Sir Philip complained openly about the treatment his poems had received. Newman's edition was finally suppressed because of its gross inadequacies.[3]

There were subsequent editions following closely upon Newman's corrupt text. Newman himself produced a revised edition in the same year. He corrected some 350 misreadings and edited out some peripheral material from his first edition, including a preface written by Nashe and a collection of miscellaneous poems by other authors. Six years later Matthew Lownes published an edition, but since it was, in the main, a reprint of Newman's first edition, it was of small value.[4] It was not until 1598 that a satisfactory text was made available. The appearance of this had been heralded in 1593 when the overseer of the second edition of *Arcadia* indicated that the Countess of Pembroke would press beyond the editing of *Arcadia* on behalf of the memory of her deceased brother; in 1598 under her direction a collected edition of Sidney's works was printed. The Countess of Pembroke's edition was a far better one than any which had preceded it. Not only were the poems printed from what was obviously a better manuscript, but they were arranged in a slightly different and far more meaningful order and with some noteworthy additions. The 'songs' which form part of the cycle had earlier been printed in a group at the end of the sonnets; now they were scattered through the sonnets themselves, where they clearly belonged, and added greatly to the dramatic unity of the whole. One sonnet, previously omitted from the sequence (number 37), made its first appearance; while poetically it is far from the best of the poems, it is a crucial one in the biographical interpretation of the cycle, for it contains the bitter punning on the word *rich* which, as we shall see, is very significant in identifying Stella with Penelope Devereux. There were also additions made to two of the songs and one completely new song. Whether the personal nature of these additions was such that it had earlier caused them to be withheld from publication is a matter of controversy; there were enough indications in the poems already to let the knowing see the story of Philip through the fortunes of Astrophel.

In some key ways the edition of the poems as supervised by Mary Sidney must be taken to be definitive. Certainly this is true of the order of the sonnets, although in this particular there has been little argument since the order remained unchanged in the various editions of the 1590s with the exception of the songs, and all have agreed that the placing of the songs in the context of the poems rather than grouping them at the end is in agreement with the basic structure of the sequence. More important is the question of the number of sonnets in the cycle. Mary Sidney's edition contained 108 sonnets, and that number must be taken as the fixed limit for the sequence. There have been numerous attempts by scholars to graft two other sonnets on to the sequence as numbers 109 and 110.[5] Mary Sidney grouped these two with twenty-five others separately as *Certain Sonnets*, and we must respect the decision of the person who was, after all, most competent to judge the intentions of her brother's work. There can be little doubt that some of the *Certain Sonnets* are related to *Astrophel* and *Stella* and should be treated as such, but they are not part of the sequence and their connection is vital only in the information it gives us about Sidney himself, not in the assessing of the *Astrophel and Stella* sequence. Mary Sidney's edition has remained the basis for most modern editions of the sequence, although, unfortunately, the one to which many readers have been first exposed was a twentieth-century edition based directly on the worst possible source, Newman's original edition.[6] It was not until 1962 that a truly critical reconstruction of Sidney's poetry was made, and it is a noteworthy comment on the value of the Countess of Pembroke's edition that it makes only eighty-eight corrections in the 2,000 lines of *Astrophel and Stella*; this can be contrasted with the forty misreadings in the first nine sonnets alone in the Newman edition and the modern version which follows it.[7]

It is important not only to keep the printed history of the sequence in mind; it is equally vital to consider the probable date at which the poems were composed. Suggested dates have varied widely, and since the dating has an obvious connection with whatever biographical import the sequence has, it would be well for us to trace our steps carefully at this point. While it has been generally agreed that the sequence was not composed earlier than 1580, some critics have attempted to place it in the previous decade, as early in fact as 1573–4 when Sidney was on his Grand Tour in Italy.[8] There seems to be little reason for accepting this early dating; the evidence on which it is based (some allusions which are open to more than one interpretation and the obvious debts of Sidney to Italian poetry) is hardly convincing. In fact, even 1580 seems to be too early a year for the composition. All evidence suggests that *Astrophel and Stella* was composed after Sidney had completed the *Old Arcadia* and before he had begun the revision which resulted in the *New Arcadia*.

To establish the precise dating of the poems it is necessary to enter into the tangles of the scholarly debate over the biographical content of the sequence.[9] At this point let us assume that by the figure of Astrophel Sidney was portraying himself and by Stella he was portraying Penelope Devereux. Numerous scholars have doubted that the connection was this precise, and as we develop our analysis of the sequence we too shall be forced to modify it somewhat. But when a critic of Sidney writes: 'Sidney was thinking of no particular woman at all. . . . Stella merely represented the platonic ideal of love, courtliness, and beauty—a symbol of the Renaissance poetic ideal of perfection',[10] he is plainly wrong. That Sidney intended to represent himself and Penelope appears in numerous places in the sonnets. In one he refers to his father's governorship of Ireland, in another to his own coat of arms, in a third to the Devereux arms.[11] There are, moreover, the sonnets which pun viciously on the word *rich*,[12] and since Penelope Devereux had married Lord Rich, and was the only woman bearing that name who would have been intimate with the circles in which Sidney moved, there can be little doubt of the identification. Penelope also satisfies the admittedly vague physical description of Stella. Stella is described as black-eyed and gold-haired; when Henry Constable wrote sonnets praising Lady Rich he referred both to her 'black sparkling eyes' and to her hair which he described as 'waves of gold'.[13]

It is clear too that contemporaries were not unwilling to make these

identifications and that Penelope Rich herself was happy to accept
them. For example, in five of the seven books which were dedicated to
her between 1594 and 1606, the dedication plainly and openly links
her with Astrophel.[14] It would be tedious to go over all the evidence
which has been produced to show that the identification of Penelope
and Stella was one which was established among Philip's own contemporaries. A few examples will suffice. John Harington, writing of
Sidney, introduces the word *rich* into his prose in a highly indicative
manner; so does Matthew Roydon in his poem 'An Elegie, or friends
passion, for his Astrophill'.[15] Such examples could be greatly multi-
plied. While it is true that some, at the time of Sidney's death, may
have identified Stella with his wife Frances Walsingham, this is not
damaging to the theory here advanced. In the circumstances propriety
dictated that Sidney's Stella be portrayed as his wife. But for those who
still have doubts there are the words of Sidney himself, as recorded
by one who stood by his side on his death-bed. The crucial passage
has only recently come to light; in the form in which these notes of
Sidney's dying utterances have usually been circulated, the critical
words have been deleted.[16] But in one manuscript form the following
comments appear: 'He added further I had this night a trouble in my
mind. For, examining my self, me thought I had not a sure hold in
Christ. After I had continued in this perplexity a while, observe how
strangely God did deliver me (for indeed it was a strange deliverance
that I had). There came to my remembrance a vanity wherein I had
taken delight, whereof I had not rid myself. *It was my Lady Rich*. But
I rid myself of it, and presently my joy and comfort returned within
few hours.' [Italics mine] The passage should relieve any doubts that
remain about the possibility that Sidney had had more than a passing
acquaintance with Penelope Rich, and once this fact is established,
there is little reason at all to doubt the identities in the sonnet sequence.
Almost all the attempts to deny the biographical content of *Astrophel
and Stella* have stemmed ultimately from a false impression of
Sidney's own character. He has been taken to be such a paragon of
virtue that an affair with a married woman would be, for him, inconceivable. This interpretation of Sidney is false; it is compounded from
a too-ready acceptance of the stylised Sidney, the hero-knight created
by posthumous propaganda, and from a feeling that Sidney must
somehow have shared the sexual morality of an eminent Victorian.

Sidney, as becomes more and more clear, was neither a paragon of virtue in this sense, nor was he a Victorian. He was a full-blooded Elizabethan courtier, and to him the seeming sexual misconduct here touched on would have been no serious matter. He did have, as we shall see when we turn to the poems, a struggle with his conscience, but that inner tension he felt had nothing to do with the fact that he was pursuing a married woman.

If it is established, then, that Sidney was portraying in *Astrophel and Stella* at least some of the details of his romance with Penelope Devereux, we can proceed further in our attempt to date the composition of the sequence. It is crucial to establish when the pair could first have been drawn to each other. The earliest mention of a possible union between them was made in September 1576 by Penelope's father, the Earl of Essex. We have seen that Sidney and the Earl were on close terms, and four days before he died Essex expressed a desire that his daughter should marry his young colleague: 'The same day, talking of many of his friends, he spake of Mr Philip Sidney. O that good gentleman, have me commended unto him, and tell him I send him nothing, but I wish him well, and so well that if God so move their hearts I wish he might match with my daughter. I call him son, so wise, virtuous, and godly'.[17]

The important things to note about this proposal are that it neither suggests that Penelope and Philip were in love (nor indeed that they had even met) and that it is a proposal stemming from the Essex circle, not the Sidney one. Sidney's friends and relations, in fact, were inclined to look on the proposal with a certain coolness.[18] As usual, Sidney's matrimonial prospects were very much under the control of the matchmakers rather than in his own hands, and in 1576 his prospect of being heir to both of his childless uncles made his market value high. For the purpose of linking Penelope and Philip nothing can be made of this offer on the part of the dying Essex. It was simply one of several such offers for the glittering heir apparent, offers that were all turned down either for financial or political reasons. Many of Sidney's biographers have read more into the statement than they should; they have done so because they have wrongly assumed that Sidney had already met Penelope. It has been traditional to say that Sidney met Penelope for the first time in the preceding year while he was accompanying the Queen on her progress. It is true that the progress stopped at Chartley for two days and that Chartley was the principal residence of Penelope's father. But assertions that the two met at this time are the merest conjecture, and it is, in fact, extremely unlikely since it was a common practice for younger members of the family to be removed from the house on such occasions in order to make room for the Queen and her following.[19]

Many have suggested, too, that from September 1578 Sidney was frequently together with Penelope. This assumption is based on the fact that at that time Leicester married the widow of Essex, and Sidney himself was frequently with his most powerful uncle. But, again, the assumption falters when it is placed in the context of the normal pattern of Elizabethan society. It was not common for Elizabethan noble families to retain their children in the household of the mother. It certainly was not the case in the Essex family.[20] The Earl of Essex felt that his eldest son had reached a sufficient age to be withdrawn from his mother even before he was eight years old, and he further requested that after his death the child should be set under the guardianship of Burghley. This was, in fact, done, and a similar practice was observed with respect to his other children as well. Before he departed for Ireland, Essex had drafted a will which provided that Penelope and two other children were to be sent to his cousin, the Earl of Huntingdon, 'for maintenance'; as he lay dying, he wrote a letter to his legal agents confirming the arrangement: 'Provide that my Lord of Huntingdon be duly paid of the portions appointed yearly for my daughters and for Wat my boy. I have assigned them to his Lordship and to my Lady and do assure myself they will not refuse them.'[21]

From this it would seem certain that Penelope was not with her mother and Leicester and hence not of easy access to the amorous attention of Philip in the months following Lady Essex's marriage to Sidney's uncle. She was, in fact, a member of the household of the Earl and Countess of Huntingdon, and in this period they were far removed from London. Their normal seat was at Ashby de la Zouch, some 100 miles away in Leicestershire, but Penelope may have been even further removed than this, for the Earl was President of the Council of the North and hence was frequently resident at his administrative headquarters at York. This was noticeably true at this precise time, for it was a period of considerable difficulty along the Scottish border and Huntingdon was kept very firmly tied to his duties in the North.

This situation lasted from 1576 until early in 1581. Penelope was far from London, very likely in the North; Philip was in fairly constant attendance on the court in London. They could not have met, except possibly (and it is a remote possibility) during the Earl's one brief visit to London in the whole of this period, in 1579.

In 1581 the Countess of Huntingdon came to court, and with her came Penelope, now no mere child as she had been when her name was first linked with that of Philip Sidney. Records attest to her beauty and her liveliness. It is also very apparent that her guardian, the Countess of Huntingdon, wished to take the opportunity afforded by her presence at court to procure a suitable husband for her ward. She was not long in finding the one whom she decided would constitute the best match. This was the young Lord Rich, who had succeeded to the family estate and title less than a month after the Countess arrived at the court. The Earl of Huntingdon seems to have concurred enthusiastically in the choice; he noted in a letter that the late Lord Rich 'hath left to his heir a proper gentleman and one in years very fit for my Lady Penelope Devereux'[22] and asked in the same letter for the aid of Burghley and Sir Francis Walsingham in arranging the match. Young Lord Rich was equally enthusiastic; he made a special trip to Cambridge in order to win the friendship and favour of Penelope's brother, the Earl of Essex. The marriage plans went ahead quickly and smoothly. In September a gentleman usher at the court wrote that 'my lady and mistress will be married about All Hallow tide to Lord Rich'[23] and in October Lord North bought a silver cup 'to give to my Lady Penelope to her marriage'.[24] There seems no reason to doubt that the marriage was held on 1 November 1581, as the gentleman usher stated it would be.

We are now much closer to being able to date the time at which *Astrophel and Stella* was composed. It is clear from the poems that Stella–Penelope is, throughout the whole sequence, a married woman. Because of this, it seems certain that the sequence must have been conceived and the poems arranged and for the most part written after 1581. Scholars have long attempted to fix a final date for the sequence by the use of internal evidence in the poems themselves. The difficulty with this approach is that even though the sequence is a connected narrative the actual duration of time is very vague indeed. There are two references to seasons, one of which applies to June, the other to

May. But there is really nothing to indicate that Sidney was being precise in his dating here. It is possible that the first does apply to June 1582, the second to May 1583, but it is just as possible that Sidney was using figures of speech in a loose way and that in the case of May he simply employed that month because it was conventionally associated with lovers. We would do well to remember the comment of a modern scholar, 'Sidney was composing a poem, not a calendar'.[25] While attempts to date the completion of the sequence by its time span are, then, relatively futile, there is one sonnet which can be dated with some precision. Sonnet 30 deals with questions which were agitating foreign affairs at the moment of its composition:[26]

> Whether the Turkish new-moone minded be
>   To fill his hornes this yeare on Christian coast;
>   How Poles' right king meanes, without leave of hoast,
> To warme with ill-made fire cold Moscovy;
> If French can yet three parts in one agree;
>   What now the Dutch in their full diets boast;
>   How Holland hearts, now so good townes be lost,
> Trust in the shade of pleasing Orange tree;
>   How Ulster likes of that same golden bit,
> Wherewith my father once made it halfe tame;
> If in the Scottishe Court be weltring yet;
> These questions busie wits to me do frame;
>   I, cumbred with good maners, answer do,
>   But know not how, for still I thinke of you.

Taken in conjunction, the various events mentioned here (the threat of a Turkish attack, Poland's invasion of Muscovy, the feuding between religious parties in France, the Diet of the Holy Roman Empire, William of Orange's role in the Netherlands, Sir Henry Sidney's relationship to Ireland, and the turbulent politics in Scotland) could only have occurred simultaneously in the summer of one year: 1582. The fact that one of the poems can be given this date fits in well with what is known about Sidney's own movements. From 1581 till the spring of 1582, Sidney was very active in court circles. He could well, however, have seen Penelope between November and mid-December 1581, or for two or three months in the following spring. After the spring had passed Sidney retired from the court and for several months he lingered in the Welsh border region with no apparent activity. It seems more than likely that since one of the poems can be dated to this period of seeming inactivity, the rest can be also. This is not to deny the outside possibility that Sidney lingered over the composition into 1583, maybe even longer, but this does seem somewhat unlikely. The sequence shows a careful plan, and cross references from some of the earliest sonnets to some of the later ones suggest that Sidney had the general structure of the whole sequence in mind when he penned the first sonnets. It is generally agreed that the poems are the product of one sustained creation, and it is likely that they were composed as a unit within a fairly short period of time.[27]

If we are thus able to date the composition of *Astrophel and Stella* to the summer of 1582 we still have a considerable problem left, and that is to assess the precise meaning of the autobiographical content of the sequence. The opinions of contemporaries, scholars, and critics have been sharply at odds over this point. To Nashe, who wrote the preface to the first edition, the sequence was a tale of invented love, 'the argument cruel chastity, the prologue hope, the epilogue despair'.[28] To the extent to which this is an apt description, Sidney's *Astrophel and Stella* is an exercise in Petrarchan convention, and no more. It is not autobiography; it is not personal in any close sense, but it is a stylised portrayal of ideal love. Such an interpretation seems too limited; Sidney was called the English Petrarch and he was aware of the conventions of Petrarchan poetry and able to use them himself with considerable skill, but the poems themselves were more than mere exercises, more than the fulfilment of the courtier's conventional duty to write poetry. They were also the record of his love affair with a real person, Penelope Rich, and the notation of real and warmly felt emotions. Even the use of conventional forms in their writing does not effectively tell against this interpretation; the use of convention is not, after all, a necessary mark of insincerity.[29]

But in precisely what sense are they autobiographical? The answer to that question must be approached with care. It is probably true that, as more than one modern critic has suggested, the poems can tell us nothing about Sidney's life that we did not know already.[30] Few now would accept the judgment made by Charles Lamb that the auto-biographical content is their main element and that it provides a sure tale for the historian: 'they are full, material, and circumstantiated. . . . An historical thread runs through them . . . marks the when and where

they were written'.[31] Yet what we know of Sidney's affair with
Penelope and of his life in general at this time aids greatly in appreciating the poems. There are, in effect, four rather than two characters
to be considered.[32] There are, of course, Astrophel and Stella, the lover
and his desired one in the poems, but there are also Philip and Penelope.
Sometimes the characters blend together so that Astrophel really is
Philip and Stella really Penelope; sometimes they drift apart and we
are left with the figures of the Petrarchan lovers pursuing their affair in
the imaginative world of the poet's mind. The biographical element is
there, even if not always dominant; to refuse to recognise it because a
sonnet sequence 'does not exist to tell . . . a story'[33] is to overlook one
of the major ingredients of Sidney's art.

Before turning to the poems themselves, it is important to see what
ascertainable facts there are in the lives of Philip and Penelope during
the crucial years 1581 and 1582. We have seen that Penelope came to
the court in 1581; at almost the same time Sidney himself returned to
the presence of his Queen. His year of retirement at Wilton for his
part in resisting the French marriage had come to an end and on New
Year's Day when he presented his annual gift to the Queen, it was in
a form which symbolised his submission to her authority in the matter,
for his gift was a whip garnished with small diamonds, a present
valuable enough to be acceptable and symbolising the power of
command which the monarch had over her subjects.[34] In the months
that followed, Sidney pursued a busy round of official duties. He took
part in several tournaments, including the Fortress of Perfect Beauty
tournament. From January to March he was busy with his duties as a
member of parliament. He was busy too with foreign statesmen in
various capacities: with the French commissioners, with the Earl of
Angus, the head of the pro-English group at the Scottish court, and
with Don Antonio, the pretender to the throne of Portugal. It was in
these busy months that Sidney first met Penelope, who was, at the
same time, engaged in preparations for her marriage with Lord Rich.
If the poems are to be taken as autobiography these first meetings
produced no feelings of love on either part.[35]

> Not at first sight, nor with a dribbed shot
>   Love gave the wound, which while I breathe will bleed: . . .
> I saw and liked, I liked but loved not.

There can be little doubt that Sidney knew intimately of the preparations for the marriage, since many of those who were most active
in arranging the details of it were his friends and relations. His uncle
Leicester was the bride's stepfather; her guardian was his aunt.
Walsingham had been instrumental in securing the Queen's blessing
for the match. There is some evidence in the sonnets, in fact, that
Sidney himself may have taken some part in the preparations for the
marriage to Lord Rich of the woman he was to come to love:[36]

> No lovely Paris made thy Hellen his:
> No force, no fraud, robd thee of thy delight,
> Nor Fortune of thy fortune author is:
> But to my selfe my selfe did give the blow.

After the wedding Sidney was in London for only a short time; in mid-
December he left the court for Wilton where he spent Christmas with
his sister. It seems likely that he did not return to London until near
the end of January, and he was soon to leave London again in the train
which accompanied the Duke of Anjou to the Netherlands. For the
rest of the year very little can be pieced together about his movements.
We have seen how he apparently spent the summer in inactivity in
Wales. By November he was certainly back at the court, but the indications are that he had only recently arrived there.

It was in these months, in the period when he was at the court, that
his liking for Penelope grew to love. But the matchmakers among his
friends and relatives were far from idle. It is ironic to note that one of
the matches proposed for him in this very period when his attention
was fixed on Lady Rich was a match with her younger sister Dorothy.
Huntingdon noted in January 1582 that there had been 'some talk of
marriage between my well beloved nephew Philip Sidney and the Lady
Dorothy Devereux'.[37] He went on to add that as his 'hearty and earnest
wish was and is that it be so, for the great good will and liking I have
to each party . . . I do most heartily desire that such love and liking
might be between them as might bring a marriage'. He went so far as
to make provisions for an additional dowry above her father's request
and for an annual income for the prospective couple. Sidney's heart
was not moved by the younger sister of his Stella, and the negotiations
came to naught. Sidney was, however, approaching twenty-eight and
without a wife; he was aware that whatever the nature of his relation-

ship with Penelope Rich, his matrimonial cause could not be furthered in that direction, and so it was that yet another match was proposed for him, and this time it was a match in which he would accede. In December 1581 in the course of a letter to Walsingham he indicated the direction the wind was blowing by sending his 'humble salutations . . . to yourself, my good Lady, and my exceeding like to be good friend'.[38] The word *friend* was commonly used by Elizabethans to mean wife or lover, and so here Philip seems to allude to the prospect of his marrying Walsingham's daughter Frances, then only fourteen years old. For two years, as we have seen, the prospects for the match were apparently discussed no further, and it was in that two-year period that Sidney had his affair with Penelope Rich. When in 1583 the affair with Penelope was a thing of the past, references to a proposed union with Frances Walsingham began to become very common and in September 1583 the marriage took place.

Many biographers of Sidney have been so shocked by the events of these years that they have refused to believe in them. It is inconceivable enough to them that their spotless hero could have been attracted to a married woman, even more inconceivable that he could have carried on the affair even after he had indicated that he intended to marry Frances Walsingham. And added to that they have seen the character of Penelope as a sordid one and concluded from this that Philip could never have been seriously in love with such a woman. We might well ask whether this picture of Penelope is one that is entirely justified. There is little dispute that Penelope was both beautiful and clever. She had an evident interest in literature, and King James, though not always the best judge of intellectual attainment, does not seem far wide of the mark in commending 'the fineness of her wit, the invention and well writing,' of her letters.[39] Penelope was even more than this; she was ambitious and far from unskilled in the risky business of political manœuvring. Her attainments in this respect were more marked after Sidney's death than before, but it is unlikely that the talent which she showed for intrigue in the 1590s as she aided the advance of her brother Essex was something which she had acquired then and not possessed before. Essex himself gave testimony to her efforts on his part; confessing his crimes against the state, he pointed to his sister 'who did continually urge me on with telling me how all my friends and followers thought me a coward and that I had lost all my valour . . .

she must be looked to, for she has a proud spirit'.[40] What has particularly alarmed the moralists, however, has not been Penelope's evident talents for politics; it has been the nature of her married life. No one could pretend that Penelope was either well or happily married. Her husband Lord Rich, while no ogre, was certainly not a pleasant person. A modern summary of his character conveys him well:[41]

He was a little man who played things safe, and was willing to sacrifice self respect for advantage. He was given to bluster, but would retreat at any sign of opposition. He had no part in decisions of state, no influence with people in power. When he wished a favour at court, his wife approached the holders of patronage; when a lawsuit threatened his estates, he sent for his wife to bring influence upon the judges. In an age when every nobleman was expected to be a soldier he kept aloof from martial affairs. He was zealous in religion and affected the air of a Puritan, but like Malvolio he was more of a 'time-pleaser' than anything else. . . . He was morose and censorious, and certainly did not enjoy his situation; but because he did not have the courage to snarl he took refuge in sneers.

It is little wonder that Penelope sought excitement and love elsewhere, and she found it not in Philip Sidney but in one who had fought with him in the Netherlands, Sir Charles Blount (Lord Mountjoy). While married to Rich, she bore him a number of children. Eventually she secured a divorce from Rich but the settlement prohibited a re-marriage. Illegally, she married Blount anyhow, and William Laud, who as Blount's chaplain performed the ceremony, was for the rest of his life to observe the anniversary of the event by a day of penance.

There is much in the life of Penelope Rich to horrify those of a conventionally moral cast, despite her death-bed disclaimer of the marriage with Blount and her sending for her first husband to ask his forgiveness. Moralists would still wag their heads; Penelope may have died penitently, but she had much to be penitent about. There can be no doubt that she did violate the moral standards of both her day and ours, and yet it is not impossible to see in her conduct tragedy rather than sinfulness. In an age when marriages were frequently arranged as a business transaction she was sold early to a high bidder. With him she was far from happy, and when she found true love with Blount she remained faithful to him despite the scandal of their association and the illegality of their marriage until he was in his grave and she was on her death-bed. And in Blount she found that warm care and love for herself and her children that she never received from Rich; Blount, it was said, 'was very tender and careful of the said Lady and of her children, and his greatest care was for their advancement and preferment'.[42] So it may be that even in her sinning Penelope was not so disreputable as the historians assert. In any case, two further points should be remembered about Penelope Rich when she is talked of in conjunction with Philip Sidney. One is that it was he, rather than she, who was more active in furthering the relationship. As is obvious from the sonnets themselves, Sidney felt for Penelope a sexual attraction which he himself was unhappy with; for her part there is no evidence from either the poems or from other documents that she unduly encouraged him. All this may somewhat change our picture of Sidney; he felt the attraction of her beauty and he succumbed to it, not without moral misgivings on his own part. Moreover, we should remember that the Penelope to whom Philip was drawn was a somewhat different person from the Penelope of later years. There can be little doubt that there is only a small similarity between the character of Stella and the character of Penelope, yet it is not impossible that Penelope was an apparently different sort of person when Sidney knew and loved her, for she was then still young and she was fresh from the household of Sidney's uncle, the Earl of Huntingdon, where she would have been brought up in the Puritan tradition to which Sidney himself owed allegiance.[43]

The relations of Sidney and Penelope form the background of the sequence, but they are not all of it, nor is the sequence the whole tale of Sidney's life in these years. In 1581–2 Sidney was indeed active and the life of service for which he yearned seemed to be opening before him. Yet the absence of autobiographical mention of some of the key events of these years is almost as striking as the presence of the ones related to Penelope. And the tale of the sequence is also more, for it is an imaginative not a strictly factual recreation of their love, and in it Astrophel and Stella are wider than Philip and Penelope.

The progression of the lover's tale is slow at first. It opens with an affirmation of sincerity on the poet's part.[44] It will not be his guise to echo the words of others, to cull conventional conceits from equally conventional sources; rather he will find his inspiration in the contemplation of his own true love, and firm in that inspiration, he will write.[45]

Loving in truth, and faine in verse my love to show,
That the deare She might take some pleasure of my paine:
Pleasure might cause her reade, reading might make her know,
Knowledge might pitie winne, and pitie grace obtaine,
  I sought fit words to paint the blackest face of woe,
Studying inventions fine, her wits to entertaine:
Oft turning others' leaves to see if thence would flow
Some fresh and fruitfull showers upon my sunne-burn'd braine.
  But words came halting forth, wanting Invention's stay,
Invention, Nature's child, fled step-dame Studie's blowes,
And others' feete still seem'd but strangers in my way.
Thus great with child to speake, and helplesse in my throwes,
  Biting my trewand pen, beating my selfe for spite,
  'Foole,' said my Muse to me, 'looke in thy heart and write.'

As we have seen, this was no love at first sight. Astrophel 'saw and liked . . . liked but loved not'. Yet his love grew until it became a passion. It was a passion which Astrophel–Sidney felt compelled to analyse, for he found in it a conflict with what others called truth and beauty. All their arguments smacked of truth, and the paradox both intrigued and puzzled him.[46]

It is most true, that eyes are form'd to serve
The inward light: and that the heavenly part
Ought to be king, from whose rules who do swerve,
Rebels to Nature, strive for their owne smart.
  It is most true, what we call Cupid's dart,
An image is, which for our selves we carve;
And, fooles, adore in temple of our hart,
Till that good God make Church and Churchman starve.
  True, that true Beautie Vertue is indeed,
Whereof this Beautie can be but a shade,
Which elements with mortall mixture breed:
True, that on earth we are but pilgrims made,
  And should in soule up to our countrye move:
  True, and yet true that I must Stella love.

It is interesting to note, however, that despite the claims to avoid imitation with which Astrophel–Sidney began, the early poems in the sequence abound in conventional conceits, such as the paradox of black beauty in sonnet 7 ('When Nature made her chiefe worke, Stella's eyes/In colour blacke, why wrapt she beames so bright?'[47]) or the use of classical myth in sonnet 13 ('Phoebus was Judge betweene

Jove, Mars, and Love'[48]). In some ways it is possible to see Astrophel
in this first section of the sequence experimenting in literary techniques
of which he was a master only in the end to come full circle to his first
call to look into his heart. The sonnet which ends the opening section
echoes the message of sonnet 1, and once again the poet is turned in on
himself, on his own resources, and on the image of Stella which he
bears in his heart in order to express his love.[49]

> Morpheus, the lively sonne of deadly sleepe,
>   Witnesse of life to them that living die:
>   A Prophet oft, and oft an historie,
> A Poet eke, as humours fly or creepe,
> Since thou in me so sure a power doest keepe,
>   That never I with clos'd-up sense to lie,
>   But by thy worke my Stella I descrie,
> Teaching blind eyes both how to smile and weepe,
>   Vouchsafe of all acquaintance this to tell,
> Whence hast thou Ivorie, Rubies, pearle and gold,
> To shew her skin, lips, teeth and head so well?
> 'Foole,' answers he, 'no Indes such treasures hold,
>   But from thy heart, while my sire charmeth thee,
>   Sweet Stella's image I do steale to mee.'

By the time the opening section is completed the reader's picture of
Astrophel–Sidney is reasonably complete. He is a man skilled in the
conventional attributes of poetry, yet he finds these unsatisfactory.
More importantly, he is a lover who is troubled by his love. There can
be little doubt that throughout the sequence Astrophel is drawn as a
person affected by the physical attractions of Stella. And yet, and yet
he wishes that his love could be more. His friends are critical of the
effects of sensuous love; it will lead him from the path of virtue, from
his duty as a courtier, from his life as an active man.[50]

> Your words my friend (right healthfull caustiks) blame
>   My young mind marde, whom Love doth windlas so,
>   That mine owne writings like bad servants show
> My wits, quicke in vaine thoughts, in vertue lame:
> That Plato I read for nought, but if he tame
>   Such coltish gyres, that to my birth I owe
>   Nobler desires, least else that friendly foe,
> Great expectation, weare a traine of shame.
>   For since mad March great promise made of me,

> If now the May of my yeares much decline,
> What can be hoped my harvest time will be?

But Astrophel, though cognisant of what they say, is resolute.[51]

> Sure you say well, your wisdome's golden mine
>   Dig deepe with learning's spade, now tell me this,
>   Hath this world ought so faire as Stella is?

And he twists his friends' arguments to his own purpose, elevating by doing so his concept of love till it is seen as shaping his manners, his faith, his honour.[52]

> Alas have I not paine enough my friend,
>   Upon whose breast a fiercer Gripe doth tire
>   Then did on him who first stale downe the fire,
> While Love on me doth all his quiver spend,
> But with your Rubarb words yow must contend
>   To grieve me worse, in saying that Desire
>   Doth plunge my wel-form'd soule even in the mire
> Of sinfull thoughts, which do in ruine end?
>   If that be sinne which doth the maners frame,
> Well staid with truth in word and faith of deed,
> Readie of wit and fearing nought but shame:
>   If that be sinne which in fixt hearts doth breed
>   A loathing of all loose unchastitie,
>   Then Love is sinne, and let me sinfull be.

When his friends press him for advice and opinion on the great international affairs of the day he returns them answer, but his mind is elsewhere: 'I, cumbred with good maners answer do/But know not how, for still I thinke of you.'[53]

The second section of the sequence concerns the progress of the love which Astrophel feels for Stella. It opens with rebuke, first for Astrophel's inability to act sooner and more forcefully in his demonstration of love for Stella, then of himself again for involving himself passionately in an affair that turns him from his normal life. He 'could not by rising Morne foresee/How faire a day was neare, o punisht eyes,/That I had bene more foolish or more wise'.[54] Even more indicative of the mood of Astrophel–Sidney is the following sonnet, number 34.[55]

Come let me write, 'And to what end?' To ease
A burthned hart. 'How can words ease, which are
The glasses of thy dayly vexing care?'
Oft cruell fights well pictured forth do please.
'Art not asham'd to publish thy disease?'
Nay, that may breed my fame, it is so rare:
'But will not wise men thinke thy words fond ware?'
Then be they close, and so none shall displease.
'What idler thing, then speake and not be hard?'
What harder thing then smart, and not to speake?
Peace, foolish wit, with wit my wit is mard.
Thus write I while I doubt to write, and wreake
My harmes on Ink's poore losse, perhaps some find
Stella's great powrs, that so confuse my mind.

The confusion and tumult of Astrophel's mind gives way to appeal to his Stella to recognise his love and merit and not to destroy that which exists only to serve and honour her.[56]

As good to write as for to lie and grone.
O Stella deare, how much thy power hath wrought,
That hast my mind, none of the basest, brought
My still kept course, while others sleepe, to mone.
Alas, if from the height of Vertue's throne,
Thou canst vouchsafe the influence of a thought
Upon a wretch, that long thy grace hath sought;
Weigh then how I by thee am overthrowne:
And then, thinke thus, although thy beautie be
Made manifest by such a victorie,
Yet noblest Conquerors do wreckes avoid,
Since then thou hast so farre subdued me,
That in my heart I offer still to thee,
O do not let thy Temple be destroyd.

The appeal is followed by a scene of the chivalric Astrophel–Sidney at his most resplendent, engaged in a ceremonial tourney such as we know Sidney himself excelled in. It is probably not possible to identify the exact tournament in question, despite the reference in the sonnet to the presence of French ambassadors, but this is no serious matter. It is the nature of the occasion rather than the occasion itself which is of importance here. Astrophel the gallant is pictured overcoming all through the power which his love for Stella gives.[57]

Having this day my horse, my hand, my launce
 Guided so well, that I obtain'd the prize,
 Both by the judgement of the English eyes,
And of some sent from that sweet enemie Fraunce;
Horsemen my skill in horsmanship advaunce;
 Towne-folkes my strength; a daintier judge applies
 His praise to sleight, which from good use doth rise;
Some luckie wits impute it but to chaunce;
 Others, because of both sides I do take
My bloud from them, who did excell in this,
Thinke Nature me a man of armes did make.
How farre they shoote awrie! the true cause is,
 Stella lookt on, and from her heavenly face
 Sent forth the beames, which made so faire my race.

While Astrophel-Sidney's attitude towards Stella here seems both clear and reconcilable with his fears for his honour, the inner tension which he has already expressed is by no means resolved. In sonnet 47 he turns again to relentless questioning, fearing now that he has sacrificed all for his love and become a mere slave to her and to his passion as a result.[58]

What, have I thus betrayed my libertie?
 Can those blacke beames such burning markes engrave
 In my free side? or am I borne a slave,
Whose necke becomes such yoke of tyranny?
Or want I sense to feele my miserie?
 Or sprite, disdaine of such disdaine to have?
 Who for long faith, tho dayly helpe I crave,
May get no almes but scorne of beggerie.

Yet the mood of doubt is again fleeting. Resolved to put Stella from his mind, he cannot, and the mere sight of her changes him back again to the impassioned lover.[59]

 Vertue awake, Beautie but beautie is,
I may, I must, I can, I will, I do
Leave following that, which it is gaine to misse.
Let her go. Soft, but here she comes. Go to,
 Unkind, I love you not: O me, that eye
Doth make my heart give to my tongue the lie.

Astrophel is in fact now resolved to win Stella's love despite the fears that he and his friends had earlier expressed. It is his passion which will prove his case; conventional behaviour, conventional language no longer are sufficient to express that which is within him. When criticised by others precisely because he ignores the conventional approach to love with its symbolism and constant swearing of affection, Astrophel answers in a deeply felt tribute to the power of love, a power over and beyond the shallow protestations of love made by the conventionally affected.[60]

> Because I breathe not love to everie one,
>   Nor do not use set colours for to weare,
>   Nor nourish speciall lockes of vowed haire,
> Nor give each speech a full point of a grone,
> The courtly Nymphs, acquainted with the mone
>   Of them, who in their lips Love's standerd beare;
>   'What he?' say they of me, 'now I dare sweare,
> He cannot love: no, no, let him alone.'
>   And thinke so still, so Stella know my mind,
> Professe in deed I do not Cupid's art;
> But you faire maides, at length this true shall find,
> That his right badge is but worne in the hart:
>   Dumbe Swannes, not chatring Pies, do Lovers prove,
>   They love indeed, who quake to say they love.

The assurance of his love is further expressed in the first of the interspersed songs. Stella, and Stella alone, is his concern. There is little in his attitude of the accomplished courtier writing verses simply to amuse; he is writing to convey his love as deep and true. Poetry itself is not his concern; Stella as flesh-and-blood person is.[61]

> Doubt you to whom my Muse these notes entendeth,
> Which now my breast orecharg'd to Musicke lendeth?
> To you, to you, all song of praise is due,
> Only in you my song begins and endeth.

It is with this mood of serious love that the final section of the sequence opens. If hope for the success of his endeavours keys the beginning of the section, joy at seeming fulfilment marks its middle, and depression at ultimate rejection marks its end. Here in the final sequence is the whole of Nashe's summary epitomised: a prologue of hope, an argument of cruel chastity, an epilogue of despair. Astrophel is hopeful that Stella will be his; no longer does she seem to be entirely the cruel mistress, but signs of kindness and affection are breaking through. 'Hope, art thou true, or doest thou flatter me?/Doth Stella now begin with piteous eye,/The ruines of her conquest to espie'.[62] In sonnet 69 this mood reaches a peak; the tentative signs of reciprocity from Stella are now interpreted by Astrophel–Sidney to mean that she is truly his.[63]

> Gone is the winter of my miserie,
> My spring appeares, o see what here doth grow.
> For Stella hath with words where faith doth shine,
> Of her high heart giv'n me the monarchie:
> I, I, o I may say, that she is mine.

Admittedly, Astrophel qualifies his joy in the end. Stella has given her word only conditionally, and Astrophel is led to the ironic comment, 'No kings be crown'd but they some covenants make'.[64] Stella may love as well as be loved, but she, like Astrophel's friends, insists that the course of his passion follow a virtuous track.

The mood of joy gives way rapidly to one of impatience; Stella is his and yet not his. Sensual thoughts drive him on; virtue alone is not enough for him. ' "But ah", Desire still cries, "give me some food." '[65] Astrophel comes upon Stella sleeping and steals a kiss.[66] He is rebuked for his audacity, but his lyrical passion reaches a height in seven sonnets celebrating the kiss he has stolen.[67]

> How falles it then, that with so smooth an ease
> My thoughts I speake, and what I speake doth flow
> In verse, and that my verse best wits doth please?
> Guesse we the cause: 'What, is it thus?' Fie no:
> 'Or so?' Much lesse: 'How then?' Sure thus it is:
> My lips are sweet, inspired with Stella's kisse.

Astrophel is now determined to win from Stella more than these tokens of love; referring to her husband, he comments, 'Is it not evill that such a Devill wants hornes?'[68] and he embarks on a trip to Stella's country house with the expressed intent of seducing her. In this he is doomed to failure. Stella rebuffs his advance.[69]

> That you heard was but a Mouse,
> Dumbe sleepe holdeth all the house:

> Yet a sleepe, me thinkes they say,
> Yong folkes, take time while you may:
> Take me to thee, and thee to me.
> 'No, no, no, no, my Deare, let be.'

The reiterated *no* of Stella is to be her final answer to the entreaties of Astrophel. The climax of the whole sequence is reached in the eighth interspersed song. Astrophel still pleads for his Stella, is still moved deeply by his love for her—'Stella soveraigne of my joy'[70]—and he seeks still the consummation of that love: 'Graunt, o graunt but speech alas'.[71] Stella is not unmoved by the lamentations of Astrophel. Her answer indicates that on her part too there is genuine affection, but her resolve is still the same:[72]

> 'Astrophil' sayd she, 'my love
> Cease in these effects to prove:
> Now be still, yet still beleeve me,
> Thy griefe more then death would grieve me.
>
> 'Therefore, Deere, this no more move,
> Least, though I leave not thy love,
> Which too deep in me is framed,
> I should blush when thou art named.'

And with her refusal once again expressed, the pair is separated.

> Therewithall away she went,
> Leaving him so passion rent,
> With what she had done and spoken,
> That therewith my song is broken.

John Buxton has noticed the highly significant change in pronouns here.[73] Astrophel and Stella are parted; because of this the poet's song is broken off. Here clearly the interplay of real and imaginary is underlined. Astrophel is not exactly the same as Sidney, yet he is at the same time so close that the virtual end of his love affair strikes home to the poet as well.

The sequence continues beyond this point, and the keynote now is grief. Gone is the blissful spell of remembering the kiss; all too present is the thought of separation and of absent love. Astrophel moves now on the fringes of Stella's world, anxious for sight and touch of her.

The world seems to move about him rather than he through it. He hears rumours linking his name with that of Stella and is ready to admit that the rumours have a basis in fact.[74]

> Your morall notes straight my hid meaning teare
> From out my ribs, and puffing prove that I
> Do Stella love. Fooles, who doth it deny?

He sees her pass on the Thames, he hears that she is sick, but she is far removed from him. He makes one last attempt to see her, a meeting at night echoing the meeting when she had returned to him her decided no. This time Astrophel is not confident; he expects no other answer than the one he has already received, and this is precisely what he hears. His despair is now complete, and the sequence ends with a series of sonnets lamenting his lot.[75]

> So strangely (alas) thy works in me prevaile,
> That in my woes for thee thou art my joy,
> And in my joyes for thee my only annoy.

It is perhaps true that the sequence merely ends rather than concludes. There is no total resolution of Astrophel's situation. He is left only with his acceptance of the lasting frustration to which love has brought him. There have been many attempts to add a more conclusive ending to the sequence through the addition of two of Sidney's *Certain Sonnets*.[76]

> Thou blind man's marke, thou foole's selfe chosen snare,
> Fond fancie's scum, and dregs of scattred thought,
> Band of all evils, cradle of causelesse care,
> Thou web of will, whose end is never wrought;
>
> Desire, desire I have too dearely bought,
> With price of mangled mind thy worthlesse ware,
> Too long, too long asleepe thou hast me brought,
> Who should my mind to higher things prepare.
>
> But yet in vaine thou has my ruine sought,
> In vaine thou madest me to vaine things aspire,
> In vaine thou kindlest all thy smokie fire;
>
> For vertue hath this better lesson taught,
> Within my selfe to seeke my onelie hire:
> Desiring nought but how to kill desire.

Leave me o Love, which reachest but to dust,
And thou my mind aspire to higher things:
Grow rich in that which never taketh rust:
What ever fades, but fading pleasure brings.

Draw in thy beames, and humble all thy might,
To that sweet yoke, where lasting freedomes be:
Which breakes the clowdes and opens forth the light,
That doth both shine and give us sight to see.

O take fast hold, let that light be thy guide,
In this small course which birth drawes out to death,
And thinke how evill becommeth him to slide,
Who seeketh heav'n, and comes of heav'nly breath.
  Then farewell world, thy uttermost I see,
  Eternall Love maintaine thy life in me.

If these are included the picture of Astrophel–Sidney becomes different from what the sequence has given us. Here he is shown as rejecting all the passion and heat of his affair with Stella and turning to a 'nobler' or 'more elevated' view of love consistent with his honour and position. Such a picture would be a false one in more than one way. There is, as we have seen, no direct evidence that the sonnets were intended by Sidney to complete the sequence. Moreover, they do not correlate in time with the *Astrophel and Stella* poems. It has now been established that all or all but two of the *Certain Sonnets* were completed before Sidney began the writing of *Astrophel and Stella*,[77] and with this in mind it becomes very hard to argue that the two poems quoted above are intended to fill out our picture of Astrophel. Sidney may have, in fact, reached a position somewhat akin to the thinking in these sonnets when he looked back over his affair with Stella–Penelope; his death-bed reference to Lady Rich can be interpreted in this way, but it was not a design he wove into the fabric of the sequence. No matter what one may want to make of this, Sidney had not in 1582 purged himself of the sensual aspects of the affair as these sonnets would suggest. It would be a gross misreading of his character to make him do so, for whatever Philip Sidney was, he was not a Victorian Christian gentleman.

It is not the place of a biographer to attempt a literary analysis of Sidney's poetry. Scholarly studies of the techniques and merits of the sequence abound, and it is to these that the reader should turn if he wishes to pursue this aspect.[78] But it is impossible to avoid making some general comments on the sequence as poetry. It was a crucial turning point, or at least indicative of a crucial turning point in the literary history of Elizabethan England. The great popularity of the sonnet sequence as a form was something that followed the trail blazed by Sidney. Sidney's work itself stands in a sense with one foot in the past, in the older tradition, with another in a later and more introspective age. It is not without significance that many critics have found foreshadowings of Donne and the metaphysical poets in Sidney's work.[79] But what perhaps strikes the modern reader most on encountering the sonnets for the first time is the simplicity of the diction.[80] Beneath the metrical complexity and behind the skilful use of poetical device there is a straightforward employment of the English tongue for poetical purposes. It has been truly said that 'Sidney did more than any other writer to make the continental experience and practice of poetry and criticism accessible to his own countrymen while at the same time speaking in his own voice as an English poet'.[81] The effect of this is enhanced by a quality of individuality, hard to define but finding expression in flexibility of form and direct language. The nervous intensity of broken lines and varied phrases is a frequently employed device to achieve this. So too are the ironic and direct statements that can turn a whole sonnet in meaning in the course of a single line, such as that at the end of sonnet 71. For thirteen lines Sidney paints an abstract picture of love and attendant virtue; in line fourteen the sensual soul of desire breaks through to make a criticism of the harmonies that have been appreciated before.[82]

> Who will in fairest booke of Nature know,
>> How Vertue may best lodg'd in beautie be,
>> Let him but learne of Love to reade in thee,
> Stella, those faire lines, which true goodness show.
> There shall he find all vices' overthrow,
>> Not by rude force, but sweetest soveraigntie
>> Of reason, from whose light those night-birds flie;
> That inward sunne in thine eyes shineth so.
>> And not content to be Perfection's heire
> Thy selfe, doest strive all minds that way to move,
> Who marke in thee what is in thee most faire.
> So while thy beautie drawes the heart to love,

As fast thy Vertue bends that love to good:
'But ah,' Desire still cries, 'give me some food.'

Astrophel and Stella is the only piece of Sidney's writing that is likely to be much read by people now. And in its survival is the surest test of its success. Individual sonnets such as number 31 are as fine as any of the lyrics produced in the Elizabethan age.[83]

With how sad steps, o Moone, thou climb'st the skies,
    How silently, and with how wanne a face,
    What, may it be that even in heav'nly place
That busie archer his sharpe arrowes tries?
Sure, if that long with Love acquainted eyes
    Can judge of Love, thou feel'st a Lover's case;
    I reade it in thy lookes, thy languisht grace,
To me that feele the like, thy state descries.
    Then ev'n of fellowship, o Moone, tell me
Is constant Love deem'd there but want of wit?
Are Beauties there as proud as here they be?
Do they above love to be lov'd, and yet
    Those Lovers scorne whom that Love doth possesse?
    Do they call Vertue there ungratefulnesse?

Only the awkward inversion of the last line mars what is otherwise a splendid piece. Sidney may have thought less of these poems than he did of his *Arcadia*; some of his contemporaries, like Fulke Greville, certainly did. To him they may have been no more than an 'inky tribute', but their impact and success was such that few would wish Astrophel's wish to come true that there should not be 'graved in mine Epitaph a Poet's name'.[84]

Chapter 8

A LEARNED KNIGHT

In court he liv'd not like a carpet knight
Whose glory is in garments and his tongue
And not alone in poesie he did pass,
But ev'ry way a learned knigh t he was.
G. Whetstone, *Sir Philip Sidney*
His Honorable Life

To write of Sidney's ideas is perhaps somewhat misleading, for he left behind no systematic treatises expressing his thoughts; though a man of ideas, he was not a systematic thinker. But it is possible by utilising such sources as Greville's *Life* and the *Arcadia* to form some impression of Sidney's approach to foreign policy, social and political relations, science and superstition. It would be wrong to think that Sidney was either a profound or an original thinker.[1] Many of the views which he held, probably the great majority, were commonplaces for the circles he moved in, and there is little in his view of social and political relations, for example, which would set him apart from the vast majority of radical Protestants. In his attitude towards science, magic, and superstition he was perhaps more enlightened (or should we say more sceptical) than many of his contemporaries, while in foreign policy his views were generally those held by the Protestant activists. To the extent to which his ideas about English policy and action differed from those about him it was usually in the direction of greater ambition and less common sense. None of the Protestant activists seem to have taken into full account the real weakness of England, the financial difficulty which made any sort of ambitious policy the wrong one. Sidney, in his enthusiasm for an active policy, crossed this line of reason more often than most and was willing, as we shall see, to make sweeping claims and assertions about the loyalties and interests of other nations, claims which in the long run were not very likely to be realised.

This is not to say that all of Sidney's thoughts on foreign affairs, as they were recorded by Fulke Greville, were empty-headed. Sidney, after all, was in constant contact with men like Walsingham and from them he could not help but obtain some sound grasp of the relative strength and weakness of England's neighbours. Moreover, it is apparent that he gave long and serious thought to foreign relations, especially in the years of disappointment when his widening interests and maturing mind found so few outlets in the service of the state. As Fulke Greville commented,[2]

Whereupon, when Sir Philip found this and many other of his large and sincere resolutions imprisoned within the plights of their fortunes that mixed good and evil together unequally, and withal discerned how the idle-censuring faction at home had won ground of the active adventures abroad, then did this double depression both of things and men lift up his active spirit into a universal prospect of time, states, and things, and in them made him consider what possibility there was for him that had no delight to rest idle at home of repropounding some other foreign enterprise, probable and fit to invite that excellent Princess's mind and moderate government to take hold of. The placing of his thoughts upon which high pinnacle laid the present map of the Christian world underneath him.

As Sidney saw 'the present map of the Christian world' his own country had greatness of worth and place, but this was counterpoised by the arts of power and favour. He had considerable admiration for the spirit and powers of his countrymen, but argued that they needed constant testing through strife to remain at their best; they were, he said, 'apt indifferently to corrupt with peace or refine with action', and from this he concluded that the best way to keep them from what he termed 'rust or mutiny' was to undertake foreign adventures.[3] Starting from such a premise, it was logical to go on to criticise the policy pursued by his Queen. She was blessed, to be sure, and he was, as always, deeply loyal to her, but her policy was, to his way of thinking, misguided: 'because she resolved to keep within the decorum of her sex, she showed herself more ambitious of balancing neighbour princes from invading one another than under any pretence of title or revenge apt to question or conquer upon foreign princes' possessions'.[4] He criticised such an approach on the grounds that it only involved the nation in a species of defensive war from which no real gain to England could ever come. There is a total lack of awareness here of the real success of Elizabeth's balancing policy and of the major contribution it had in giving England some sort of leverage in foreign affairs which she could never have had on straight military grounds alone.

When he turned to consider nations other than England, Sidney was struck, as any observer would have been, by the Spanish power and the apparent threat it constituted. Among most other nations Sidney discerned 'a fatal passiveness'.[5] France he saw as apt to fall under the control of the strongest 'undertaker' (as indeed it was to do under Henry of Navarre) or else prone to endless splitting up in the manner of the Swiss cantons. The Empire rested 'as in a dream upon an immovable centre of self-greatness'.[6] The power of the papacy, he admitted, was a threat, but the real danger of both Austria and Rome was, Sidney thought, the fact that Spain called the tune behind the scenes. And so on through the countries of the continent he pursued his analysis, leading to the conclusion that 'all these Princes lived thus fettered within the narrowness of their own estates or humours'. Spain was the great exception to this general pattern. 'Spain, managing the Popedome by voices and pensions among the Cardinals and having the sword both by land and sea in his hand, seemed likewise to have all those western parts of the world laid as a *tabula rasa* before him, to write where he pleased *Yo el Ré*'.[7] That which made this gloomy prospect even more probable was the Spanish control of the rich New World treasure mines. These not only supplied the material base for the Spanish military threat but allowed Spain to terrify and corrupt the other nations of the continent.

Sidney considered Spain a threat to all princes, but especially to England itself and concluded that the danger was unlikely to be prevented except by a general league among European princes 'to undertake this undertaker at home'.[8] The present policy of England, with its half-hearted support of the revolt in the Netherlands, was, Sidney had come to think, the least likely way to achieve a limit to Spain's ambitions. Here we can see Sidney's ideas changing rather markedly from his original concept of foreign policy. Initially, he had seemed to think that the struggle in the Netherlands was the basic one in the world, the arena where the Spanish beast could be most successfully baited; this was a view in which he was encouraged by Languet. Towards the end of his life, however, he came to think that no matter how grand the involvement of the Protestants in the Netherlands, this was simply the wrong place to attempt to engage Spain. 'He providently determined that while Spain had peace, a Pope, money or credit, and the world men, necessity, or humours, the war could hardly be determined upon this Low Country stage'.[9] Sidney calculated that Spain was, in plain fact, better prepared to resist armed attack in the Netherlands than she was anywhere else in her extensive empire. It was a place 'where all exchanges, passages, and supplies were already settled to his best advantage, and so a force bent against him even where himself could wish it'.[10] Flanders was a province well supplied with both offensive and defensive arms and fortified by a considerable number of large cities, with the result that invading armies must either waste much time reducing them one by one, or else proceed while leaving enemy bastions untouched behind them. Nor could England expect much aid in such a campaign, as Sidney saw things. The French, who were nearest, might well be suspicious of English intentions: 'our neighbourhood upon the same continent [would not be] over-welcome to them'.[11] Other nations would have to come too far to be of much aid; the passage of their troops to Flanders would be difficult, would involve a major loss of time, and might well result in a lack of discipline among their troops.

What, then, was to be done to counter the Spanish threat if an attack in Flanders in conjunction with the Dutch rebels offered so little promise? Sidney decided there were two possible courses open for the other powers to follow: 'the one that which diverted Hannibal and by setting fire to his own house made him draw in his spirits to comfort his heart; the other that of Jason by fetching away his Golden Fleece and not suffering any one man quietly to enjoy that which every man so much affected'.[12]

The first approach he summed up as a design 'to carry war into the bowels of Spain and by the assistance of the Netherlands burn his shipping in all havens as they passed along'.[13] An important part of the plan was to surprise, take, and if possible keep 'some well-chosen place for wealth and strength'.[14] Sidney had Seville in mind as such an objective, 'a fair city, secure in a rich soil and plentiful traffic, but an effeminate kind of people guarded with a conquering name and consequently a fair bait to the piercing eyes of ambitious generals, needy soldiers, and greedy mariners'.[15] Another possibility he mentioned was the former English possession of Calais. Sidney felt that there was much to commend such a plan. The fleet thus engaged would be useful for defensive and offensive purposes. Should such a scheme prove to be too costly, the least England could do in Sidney's estimation was to keep a strong and active fleet on her birthright, the Narrow Seas, and attempt to forge an alliance with the Protestant party in France, hoping thus 'to reap a reasonable harvest out of that well-chosen seed time by receiving Rochelle, Brest, Bordeaux, or any other place upon that continent distressed for religion into her absolute protection'.[16] Sidney added (though the argument would hardly have convinced the French) that this absorption of territory was not to be done with any intention of reconstituting parts of England's former continental empire, 'but only to keep those humble religious souls from oppression in that super-Jesuited sovereignty'.[17] Sidney may well have believed this, but the argument sounds only too like those for the 'wars of liberation' with which the twentieth century has become so familiar.

Sidney appears to have been extremely naive when he considered what the reactions of other countries to such a policy might have been. The hope for any sort of a firm alliance with France on such a basis was simply illusory, but this was not the least of Sidney's illusions. He hoped that an 'exposure' of Spanish motives would lead to the inaction of even her strongest allies and that in this way Europe would achieve a 'true balancing design'.[18] Italy itself would rise to aid in the cause:[19]

> Again, shall we [said Sir Philip] in these collections of particulars forget the state of Italy itself? Which excellent temper of spirits, earth, and air, having long been smothered and mowed down by the differing tyrannies of Spain and Rome, shall we not be confident they would, upon the approaching of these armies, both stir up those benumbed sovereignties which only bear the name of free princes to effect their own manumission and help to chase away those succeeding and oppressing garrisons whose forefathers for many years had sold life, liberty, and laws for eight pence the day, and so resolutely oppose those Spanish-born or Spanish-sworn tyrannies which have for divers ages lorded over that most equally tempered nation?

Sidney even suggested that the Pope would not be hostile to such a scheme; in doing so he recognised that Spain was not so much the arm of Rome as Rome was one of the swords of Philip II, but again he exaggerated the possibilities: 'he made a query whether the Pope himself would not (like a secular prophet) to keep his becoming chaplain a little the farther off either wink, or at least delay his thundering curses or supplies of Peter-pence against these qualifying armies, only to moderate the over-greatness of this Spanish monarchy?'[20]

Sidney admitted that the plan might seem of 'too high a nature or too many chargeable parts',[21] and because of this he had a second (and he thought preferable) line of approach to curbing Spain. This second plan, which involved invading, possessing, and inhabiting 'some well chosen haven in Peru, Mexico, or both',[22] is indicative of the extent to which his view of foreign affairs had extended beyond the confines of Europe. It was basically the same policy that the elder Pitt was to follow two centuries later, assailing the European enemy in his most vulnerable spot, his overseas possessions. It is interesting to observe that Sidney had another reason besides expense for advocating this scheme; rightly surmising that many in England would oppose such active policies, he was drawn to the scheme of a colonial attack because he felt that there was less chance that 'the freedom of choice . . . be taken away or at the least obstructed by fatal mists of ignorance or factious counsels reigning among the ministers of Kings'.[23] Some of the reasons which Sidney used to support his argument for overseas adventure were not very convincing, for example the argument that men would gain honour more easily abroad than at home just as prophets were better respected in countries other than their own; he was also convinced that honour could be obtained more easily at sea than on land. Some of the arguments were more sound; he was correct in arguing that the vast distance between Spain and the New World would hinder any Spanish attempts to suppress the English adventurers, though he appears to have rather neglected the fact that the distance could serve as a hindrance to the English efforts as well. He hoped, too, that the English would be aided by a native reaction against the viciousness of the original Spanish conquest. This may well have been wishful thinking, for the native strength was so reduced as a result of the conquest and the disease which followed in its track that it was in no real position to be a consistent aid, no matter how deep the resentment, no matter whether the natives would have trusted a new European invader after being badly deceived by the first one. Part of Sidney's calculations rested on a psychological interpretation of the Spaniard which was far from uniformly true; he cited 'the pride, delicacy, and security of the Spaniard, which made him live without discipline'. They trusted more, he felt, the greatness of the Spanish name abroad than 'any strength, order, courage, or munition at home'.[24] One of Sidney's arguments was an interesting anticipation of a common defence of colonies in the next century: that they were useful for the disposing of elements of the population. The reasoning that carried him to such a conclusion is interesting, too, for it postulated the union of Scotland and Ireland with England. In this he thought he foresaw 'that if this multitude of people were not studiously husbanded and disposed, they would rather diminish than add any strength to this monarchy, which danger (he conjectured) could only by this design of foreign employment or the peaceable harvest of manufactures at home be safely prevented'.[25]

One final reason weighed heavily on the mind of Sidney and it shows that beneath the political level there was still an intense religious justification for what he proposed. Sidney, like many in his own time and since, was appalled by the cruelty of the Spanish conquest and the nature of the colonial rule which was subsequently established. 'What little difference tyrants strive to leave between the creation, use, and honour of men and beasts, valuing them indifferently but as counters. ... Tyrants be not nursing fathers, but stepfathers and so no anointed deputies of God, but rather lively images of the Dark Prince, that sole author of dis-creation and disorder who ever ruins his ends with over-building.'[26] But not only were the Spanish iniquitous; they were also, he felt, hypocritical and because of this subject to the vengeance of God which must 'necessarily hang over those hypocritical cruelties, which under colour of converting souls to him sent millions of better than their own they cared not whither, and instead of spreading Christian religion by good life, committed such terrible inhumanities as gave those that lived under nature manifest occasion to abhor the devily character of so tyrannical a deity'.[27] In short, the Spanish had trans-gressed divine and natural law by attempting to fit them to their own uses, and the vengeance of God would surely fall on them, aided in this world by the arms of England.[28]

The method of effecting this vengeance was to capture Nombre de Dios or some other New World haven; if the conquest should not proceed smoothly the accompanying fleet would at least wreak havoc among the Spaniards in the region. Greville asserts that Sidney's scheme actually proceeded well into the planning stage, that he had persuaded the United Provinces to assist in the plan to the extent of sending a fleet of their own, and that he had persuaded thirty of the magnates of England to provide funds for the expedition (though Greville's total subscription figure of £3000 was, of course, ridiculously out of proportion to the actual cost of such an operation.

So far Sidney's scheme was no more firmly rooted in reality than his European plan; it was simply the policy of the activists stated clearly but took little account of actual costs and overestimated the ease of the operation, just as England was to do under Cromwell in the 1650s. His idea of what was to be done with the land thus taken in the New World was also somewhat out of touch with reality; he tended to ignore the pressures that would have arisen for religious conformity and monopolistic trade restrictions. Because of this his vision of England's New World empire had a very noble and admirable element in it. 'He contrived this new intended plantation not like an asylum for fugitives, a *bellum piraticum* for banditi or any such base *Ramas* of people, but as an emporium for the confluence of all nations that love or profess any kind of virtue or commerce.'[29] On one aspect of this plan Sidney was firmly rooted in reality; he understood the motives that might lead men to indulge in such adventures. He knew they were various, and he was prepared to court them all. To those anxious for gain he would offer an argument of quick returns; in general, he admitted, 'the word gold was an attractive adamant to make men venture that which they have in hope to grow rich by that which they have not'.[30] To those of martial inclinations he offered the hopes of glory and conquest. To the religiously oriented Sidney presented the scheme as 'a new apostolical calling of the last heathen to the Christian faith, a large field of reducing poor Christians, misled by the idolatry of Rome, to their mother primitive church'.[31] To the industrious he displayed the New World as well stocked in a variety of natural resources and manufactures to work on, to the curious as 'a fruitful womb of innovation'[32] and to the oppressed as a haven of liberty.

Sidney's thoughts on foreign relations were shared by many of his Protestant activist contemporaries. So too were his ideas on political thought.[33] Just as his colonisation scheme appealed to a certain group and alarmed the more conservative elements in the government, so did his political ideas which closely resembled those of the French Huguenots he admired and of his friend Mornay in particular. Sidney never attempted to write a treatise on political thought, but the versions of *Arcadia* contain some important comment on political relations, the earlier version being somewhat more radical than the revision. Clearly Sidney believed in the commonplace *salus populi suprema lex*, and he was willing to draw from it what seems its inevitable conclusion, that if the government becomes debased or unworthy and neglects the well-being of its people, then they are entitled to use force against it. We have seen how Sidney was convinced that the Queen was following wrong courses in policy, and there are echoes of criticism of her (though not a direct portrait) in his characterisation of Basilius. Basilius's greatest 'crime' was neglecting public affairs, and Sidney felt that Elizabeth was doing something of the same when she refused to follow the lead of the activists.

The most important political idea which Sidney raises and discusses in *Arcadia* is the question of the right of resistance by insurrection. In dealing with a revolt of the commons, a rebellion against established authority in the name of freedom and justice, with the intention of reforming the state, Sidney seemingly followed closely the ideas of Mornay as expressed in his *Vindiciae contra tyrannos*.[34] Because of this outlook Sidney did not condemn the rebellion outright. He saw the essential safeguard of the state not so much in the person of the King himself as in laws which would restrain the King's unilateral power, in the existence of a strong magistracy which could guard the laws of the land and protect its constitution, in the recognition of the rights of the people, even to the extent of rebellion under proper and authorised leadership of the magistrates. Sidney is here advocating a variety of the mixed state, the dream and ideal of much political thought from classical times on, a form of state which would balance monarchy, aristocracy, and the popular element to produce a government which would rule in the best interests of all. The interests of governor and governed, of prince and people, are identical, and the good prince will make this identification clear, as Sidney indicates in his comments on the model King Evarchus:[35]

And therefore, where most princes (seduced by flattery to build upon false grounds of government) make themselves (as it were) another thing from the people and so count it gain what they can get from them; and (as if it were two counterbalances, that their estate goes highest when the people goes lowest) by a fallacy of argument thinking themselves most kings when the subject is most basely subjected: he contrarywise, viruously and wisely acknowledging that he with his people made all but one politic body, whereof himself was the head, even so cared for them as he would for his own limbs, never restraining their liberty, without it stretched to licentiousness, nor pulling them from their goods, which they found were not employed to the purchase of a greater good, but in all his actions showing a delight to their welfare, brought that to pass, that while by force he took nothing, by their love he had all.

It was logical to conclude from such a premise that the welfare of the community stood over and above all other political goals, and Sidney was not afraid to draw such a conclusion. The position of the King in this scheme was bound to be a bit ambiguous. People, Sidney seems to assert in one place, created monarchs in the very beginning for their own convenience[36] and this explains in part the continuing hold which the people have over their ruler through the right of rebellion. Yet Sidney also felt that the institution of civil government was of divine origin, so that as long as a prince rules well, his person is to be considered sacred, for he embodies a civil authority which is heavenly in its origin. When he rules poorly, however, he ceases to share in the divine nature of the office and becomes subject to the coercion of the better elements of his country.

Sidney qualified the right of rebellion and the power of coercion carefully, and he did so in a manner very similar to that employed in the *Vindiciae*. Under conditions of sufficient provocation, especially if the people are oppressed because of religion or tyranny, the magistrates, even those who have been commissioned by the King, may oppose their sovereign by force of arms and refuse to obey his commands. We should note that Sidney did not allow the mass of the people any significant role in the process of casting off political authority. The duty of the people is to obey if not the King then the superior sort who will lead them in revolt. Sidney was no democrat; to him the common people were the mob or the rabble, the ever-dangerous multitude which must be kept firmly in its place low down the social hierarchy.

This sort of interpretation of Sidney's political thought has not passed unquestioned. His following of the advanced Protestant line has been queried as most unlikely, and it has been asserted by some that Sidney's social and political views were far closer to what one might expect of an Elizabethan gentleman. It has been suggested, for example, that Sidney reached conclusions not unlike those of Machiavelli, though he was appalled by what he considered the lack of moral content in Machiavelli's thought.[37] Such an interpretation is not, however, fundamentally at variance with the view that Sidney's political thinking closely resembled that of the *Vindiciae*. Those areas on which Sidney and Machiavelli agreed were not incompatible with the Huguenot theory: the belief in a mixed state, the feeling that the state should not be a private possession but should benefit the whole community, the idea that the preservation of order is desirable and is a major function of the state (though Sidney advocated the right of rebellion, he never denied the importance of civil order; rebellion is allowed, in fact, only as a means to the restoration of proper harmony). It is true that Sidney's views on this matter seem to have modified slightly after 1580. In the *Old Arcadia* the right of rebellion is not criticised, but changes made in the revised version play down the rightful element in the commons' revolt, although they do not ever completely repudiate the doctrine that the right of resistance is implicit as a check in the well-ordered state, and certainly Sidney did not waver from the suggestion that the government must rule in the interests of all rather than in the interest of itself. This retreat towards conservatism on Sidney's part is explicable in terms of the political conditions of 1580. The justification of the commons' rebellion in the *Old Arcadia* had too close a reference to the activists' opposition to the French marriage alliance. As the activists withdrew from open opposition, and especially as Sidney himself sought to regain court favour, such a redefinition of his views was to be expected.[38]

Some have gone so far as to query whether Sidney ever believed in the rightness of insurrection. Such a view would stress the growth of a concept of kingship in Tudor England which considered the King to be God's representative on earth and hence someone to be unconditionally obeyed no matter what his course of action. Sidney, of course, did grow up in the court circle where this doctrine of absolutism and passive obedience was most strongly supported, and it has been argued that, whatever his sympathy for the Protestant cause, he was repelled by any element in Protestant policital thought which allowed for armed insurrection against a King who did not fulfil his obligations to the people.[39] Certainly in the revised version of *Arcadia*, where Sidney is more conservative politically, views approaching those in the Tudor absolutist tracts are expressed by characters who are supposed to be exemplary. This is implicit in Pyrocles's address to the rebels, where he argues that the prerequisite of good government is obedience and that the allowing of the right to question the action of princes would lead to endless rebellions for petty and self-seeking reasons.[40]

> Imagine, what could your enemies more wish unto you, than to see your own estate with your own hands undermined? O, what would your fore-fathers say if they lived at this time and saw their offspring defacing such an excellent principality which they with so much labour and blood so wisely have established? Do you think them fools that saw you should not enjoy your vines, your cattle, no, not your wives and children without govern-ment: and that there could be no government without a magistrate, and no magistrate without obedience, and no obedience where every one upon his own private passion may interpret the doings of the rulers?

The attempt to portray Sidney's thought as being consistently on the more conservative and absolutist side is, however, quite uncon-vincing. Particularly is it unconvincing when one considers the political theorists with whom the Sidney circle had its closest con-nections. Of their closeness to the advanced continental thinkers like Languet and Mornay no more need be said. But it is crucial to note that the Sidney circle had contacts in addition with two of the most outspoken advocates of the right of rebellion in the British Isles, Christopher Goodman and George Buchanan.

Christopher Goodman had been notorious as an advanced Puritan since his exile from England during the Marian reaction. He had com-posed a radical political tract, *How Superior Powers Oght to be Obeyd*, which was even more blatant about the right of resistance than the French tracts. It has been called 'one of the most elaborate arguments for tyrannicide written'.[41] Goodman argued that if rulers really were God's representatives, they should reign only so long as they fully obeyed the divine will. Included in the divine will was an obligation to follow the dictates of established law and natural procedure, and should they deviate from this, they forfeited their right to receive obedience from their subjects. The King, as Goodman analysed it, was subject to the same natural laws as any man and hence was liable to punishment for transgressing them, just as the lowliest of his subjects. Goodman was at his most radical when he suggested that tyrannicide was justified if the monarch's crimes were great ones. Even when Goodman finally did return to England in 1565, he was still in trouble because of his extreme nonconformity and was twice called to recant before the Ecclesiastical Commission in 1571. But Goodman was throughout this defended and aided by both the Dudley and Sidney families for more than twenty years.[42] Sir Henry Sidney especially worked on Goodman's behalf; Goodman served him in Ireland and Sir Henry urged his appointment as Dean of St Patrick's: 'he hath been in my house almost a year; if ever man on earth since the apostles' days deserved to be held a saint, he is one. Sir, the whole church of this realm shall be bound to pray for you if you prefer [him] to that place, and I shall think it a great grace done to myself so to place him.'[43] In 1570 Philip Sidney solicited on his behalf a living at Alford, near Chester;[44] Goodman held this for a short while, was finally forbidden to preach further, and died there at an advanced age.

The association of Sidney with a man holding views like those of Goodman is indicative of Sidney's own political outlook. Equally indicative are the relations of the Sidney circle with the Scottish thinker George Buchanan. We have already noted one sort of link between Buchanan and the group around Sidney, their interest in divine poetry. But it would be wrong to think that this was all that attracted Philip and his friends to the Scot. It is perfectly clear from laudatory passages on Buchanan's work in the *Apology for Poetry* that Sidney knew and appreciated his literary work, but the fact that his interest was wider is indicated in the one surviving letter from Sidney to Buchanan:[45]

> Sir, although unknown to you, yet knowing your virtue and loving it, I have sent this bearer, my servant, unto you, and to desire such favour and friendship of you as ye think may be bestowed upon a young man that desires to do well. If my estate did well suffer it, I have not been without desire to see you and kiss the hand of the young King in whom many have laid their hopes. God prosper him and make him learn by you that goodness is the greatest greatness. . . . My man can show unto you as much as I of the matters concerning Monsieur and purpose of his marriage, *hactenus hesitamus.*

Two references in the letter are worthy of particular note. One is the very offhand reference to the French marriage proposals; since

Buchanan had at this time nowhere expressed himself publicly on this subject, it seems certain that Sidney was aware that an extensive correspondence had existed between Buchanan and their mutual friend Daniel Rogers on this precise subject.[46] The further comment on the proposed marriage, *hactenus hesitamus*, indicates the uncertainty and tension felt by the activists at this juncture.

The interest of the Sidney group in Buchanan was even wider than an appreciation of his views on the French marriage. In particular they were also drawn to him as the tutor of the young James VI whom they were already anticipating as the future King of England, and they hoped that with a tutor like Buchanan James would be educated in the tradition of statecraft associated with the Protestant humanists like Mornay whom they so much admired. Mornay himself hailed Buchanan as the educator of a new Constantine who would deliver the world from its twin afflictions of tyranny and superstition.[47] In supporting Buchanan's views on statecraft Sidney was again clearly associating himself with the doctrines of left-wing Protestantism. Buchanan's major political work, *De Jure Regnis apud Scotos*, aroused an almost universal hostility in England, with the notable exception of the Sidney circle, who hailed it as a great work. The main argument of the book was in favour of limited monarchy and the right of resistance to tyranny, and many of the ideas current in the Sidney circle which were apparently borrowed from Mornay could have been borrowed with equal facility from Buchanan.[48] This is true, for example, of Walsingham's lecture to James VI in 1583, especially in its 'recommendation to the King to take council with his people as represented in parliament, upon matters of government, in its insistence upon his subservience to the law and his obligation to rule justly, in its broad hints at the right of his subjects to depose him if he did otherwise'.[49] It is equally true of the political thought contained in Sidney's *Arcadia*. As a modern scholar has concluded, 'to Sidney, then, the ideas in *De jure regni* would not necessarily have seemed strange and alarming, but on the contrary would have been ideas which he had incorporated and developed in his own work'.[50]

Sidney and his circle had one further interest in Buchanan, and it is a concern which indicates another significant, although occasionally overlooked, aspect of Sidney's thought—his very real concern with the writing and understanding of history. Although Buchanan's

Rerum Scoticarum historia was not published until 1582, it had been long known to be in preparation. Buchanan's work was more critical of ancient sources incorporating legendary traditions, like the compilation of Geoffrey of Monmouth, than the work of many of his contemporaries, and in the 1580s, when the sort of critical scepticism represented by Buchanan was generally unpopular in England, his work was frequently and violently attacked. Again, however, the Sidney circle stood aside and found in the Scot's work a subject of admiration. Though the evidence on this point is admittedly scanty, it can be conjectured that a 'modern' critical attitude towards legendary history was characteristic of the Sidney circle.[51]

Sidney occupied a more important place in the development of the Elizabethan attitude towards history than simply being an apparent admirer of the critical work of Buchanan.[52] During the course of the sixteenth century men changed the reasons they gave for writing history, and in this change of direction Sidney, although he wrote no history himself, played a significant part. In the beginning of the century it was common to view history as a branch of moral philosophy, but by the end of the century history to some extent had become a branch of politics. When Sidney came to make comments on the writing of history in his *Apology for Poetry* he was faced with a long-established tradition that history was a teacher of morality; in his defence of poetry his chief attack on history is precisely that it does not have this power or nature to instruct in moral lessons. He argued, as we have seen, that in this sphere poetry's invention was of far more utility than history's fact, for poetry could always cause virtue to triumph, while history, with its respect for the actual, was doomed to record the ever too frequent triumph of sin. But to say this was not, as some have thought, to condemn history outright. It was merely to point out properly a function which history cannot fulfil. Elsewhere, notably in a letter to his brother Robert, Sidney commended the study of history with enthusiasm.[53] In doing so he was not contradicting his attitude towards history as expressed in the *Apology* but merely further defining the area in which history could be useful. What Sidney reflects here is the change of attitude towards the utility of history; while doubt was growing about its moral utility, faith was increasing as far as its political usefulness. For the future statesman the study of history was of more utility than poetry, particularly the sort of history which went critically beyond the mere events themselves to an analysis of the causes of events.

Sidney's contribution to the development of historical writing is, then, two-fold. Most importantly, in the brief passages on history and morality in the *Apology for Poetry*, he constructed one of the best critical arguments on the nature of history which was written in Tudor England and demonstrated with both wit and insight the futility of seeing history as the inculcator of morality. In his letter to his brother, on the other hand, Sidney was able to show what sort of utility a critical history and the careful study of it could have in so far as it could give specific instruction to men of action. In doing so it might possibly teach morality, but this was only an accidental by-product and could not be relied on. In teaching men how to behave politically, however, it was teaching by example a lesson that poetry, for all its moral power, could not. Sidney himself on occasion revealed that he had grasped in a practical way the points he made here about history. Sections of his defence of his father's policy in Ireland show an awareness of the sort of practical lessons which history can teach. Perhaps Sidney's greatest contribution to historical writing is that which is hardest to assess. How much impact his ideas about morality and history had is not open to an easy answer, but if one assumes they were read, discussed, and understood, then Sidney's role cannot have been a minor one. Sidney's fellow scholar and friend William Camden was probably the best historian of the time. When he came to explain his motives for composing history Camden relegated instruction in morality to a secondary place and suggested the real motive was the exploration of reasons and causes, the exact aspect of history which Sidney himself commended.[54] It would not be too sweeping to suggest that it is this very relegation of the moral lesson and the search to explain causation which elevates Camden's work above that of his predecessors. In this vital shift of emphasis it is probable Sidney played no small role.

One final aspect of Sidney's thought might well be treated briefly here, and that is his attitude towards superstition and science.[55] One of the apparent paradoxes of Sidney's whole career is that he is, on the one hand, an apparently critical and non-superstitious mind, an attitude reflected even in his approach to history where he applauded a sceptical study which investigated as fully as possible the legendary background of the British Isles. He stressed the importance of rationality in his approach to religion as well.[56] He felt that nature was impregnated by reason and by the goodness of God. His feeling that religion and rationality were compatible is shown clearly in the much discussed episode in the revised *Arcadia* in which Pamela attempts to refute the atheism of her aunt. Pamela confined herself to purely rational arguments, and emerged from the discussion as a good pagan who had reached the truth by natural reason. The aunt's atheism was treated in effect as a sort of blinding caused by faith in the supernatural. On the other hand, Sidney is seen to be the friend and intimate of men like Dr John Dee and Giordano Bruno, who are, at best, bizarre and, at worst, representative of the ascendancy of the superstitious mind over critical reason. The apparent incongruity of such friendships with his own attitudes has led some so far as to deny that Sidney had any meaningful contacts with Dee and Bruno, but, as we have seen, the evidence is reasonably clear that he did. How are we to explain this? Perhaps the answer is to look more closely at Sidney's attitudes towards superstition and science and also to look carefully again at his reasons for association with such men.

A convincing case can be constructed that Sidney was basically an opponent of all forms of superstition. It is reasonably clear, for example, that Sidney conceived the true hero to some extent at least to be the master of his own destiny. Such a view is implicit in the purpose of the revised *Arcadia*, which was, as Greville so pointedly reminds us, to be a handbook of statesmanship and self-discipline. It is not stretching a point too far to argue that a negative corollary to such a view would be that those who resorted to soothsayers and other occult arts to handle the problems of life which they themselves could not face were making a serious blunder. The mere fact that the oracle's prophecy to Basilius in *Arcadia* comes true does not commend the use of oracles by rulers; the point that is being made is surely the opposite, that by being over-influenced by the oracle Basilius allowed the dire prophecies to come true, endangered the internal security of his country, and by withdrawing from an active participation in affairs, ceased to be an admirable ruler. One could extend the argument further and suggest that Sidney may be implying here a criticism of Queen Elizabeth's reliance on the soothsaying of Dr John Dee; after all, it has been said that his house at Mortlake was her Delphi.[57]

Other evidence could also be marshalled to suggest that Sidney was a consistent enemy of superstition. A most important piece of information is contained in Moffett's *Nobilis*. While Moffet was quite unilluminating about Sidney's literary work and was well caught up in the legend of the Protestant hero, he was in a very good position to know something about Sidney's attitude towards magic and soothsaying, and what he has to say about this is very specific. Moffett noted that Sidney devoted much time to philosophy and to the arts of observation, but that he could never be so far misled as to taste astrology 'even with the tip of his tongue'. 'In fact,' Moffett continues, 'as a young man precisely excellent and inspired with true religion, he feared lest, too receptive to the fables of soothsayers, he might in rashness diminish the Divine Majesty (always held in reverence) and tie down Divine Providence (everywhere and always the disposer of all things) to particular modes and means'.[58] Then, too, there is the evidence of the *Astrophel and Stella* sonnets. Sonnet 26, with its astrological terminology, is sometimes taken as proof that Sidney was not only conversant with the language of astrologers but that he was also interested in their occult arts.[59]

> Though dustie wits dare scorne Astrologie,
> And fooles can thinke those Lampes of purest light,
> Whose numbers, wayes, greatnesse, eternitie,
> Promising wonders, wonders to invite,
>   To have for no cause birthright in the skie
> But for to spangle the blacke weeds of night:
> Or for some brawle, which in that chamber hie,
> They should still daunce to please a gazer's sight.
>   For me, I do Nature unidle know,
> And know great causes, great effects procure:
> And know those Bodies high raigne on the low.
> And if these rules did faile, proofe makes me sure,
>   Who oft fore-judge my after-following race
>   By only those two starres in Stella's face.

This may seem evidence for a view different from the one being argued here, especially in view of the fact that many Elizabethans did take such astral influences seriously and Sidney was himself enough influenced to have his horoscope cast.[60] But it seems possible to argue that the sonnet should be taken as evidence of quite a different sort. In the first place the astrological treatment here may well have been suggested by some lines of Du Bartas whose poetry Sidney knew and admired.[61] In the second place it can be suggested that the resort to astrology here is the result of poetical expediency and that no more should be read into it than that. It is rather hard to imagine a sequence of 108 sonnets to Stella without some recourse to astrology for the imagery, and the fact that Sidney only does so on one occasion and makes the slightest use of the technical jargon of the subject would suggest that he was not totally sympathetic to the occult arts. *Arcadia* offers similar negative evidence. Sidney borrowed heavily in composing *Arcadia* and he borrowed extensively from works which abound in references to the supernatural and the occult. Yet *Arcadia* itself is remarkably free from enchantments, sorcery, or other superstitious content, and when they are introduced they tend to be treated in a sceptical manner, as is the case, for example, with the prophecies at the birth of Musidorus.[62]

For scarcely was Musidorus made partaker of this oft-blinding light when there were found numbers of soothsayers who affirmed strange and incredible things should be performed by that child; whether the heavens at that time listed to play with ignorant mankind, or that flattery be so presumptuous as even at times to borrow the face of divinity. But certainly so did the boldness of their affirmation accompany the greatness of what they did affirm (even descending to particularities, what kingdoms he should overcome) that the King of Phrygia (who over-superstitiously thought himself touched in the matter) sought by force to destroy the infant, to prevent his after-expectations, because a skilful man (having compared this nativity with the child) so told him. Foolish man, either vainly fearing what was not to be feared, or not considering that, if it were the work of superior powers, the heavens at length are never children.

Finally, Sidney's rejection of the superstitious use of verse in the *Apology for Poetry* might be noted among the evidences that he was an opponent of superstition. Referring to one such case, Sidney commented, 'it were a very vain and godless superstition, as also it was to think that spirits were commanded by such verses'.[63]

The case, then, that Sidney opposed superstition seems reasonably well proven. We are still left, however, with the problem of how to explain his relations with Dee and Bruno. With the latter we have already suggested an answer: interest in science, interest in anti-Aristotelian conceptions, and perhaps, above all, an interest in a pan-

Christian movement. Some of the same reasons apply to his relations to Dee. The interest in science is most obviously a case in point; Dee delved seriously into the occult, but much of the significant scientific work of the period was done by those who in a more sceptical age appear to have been somewhat mad. The existence of a mad streak in men like Dee should not blind the modern to the fact that they were, albeit often for the wrong reasons, treading the path of investigation towards modern science. If John Napier, for example, was really most interested in the number of the Beast he none the less performed a valuable task in the development of logarithms and the slide rule to help his calculations. And if Dee sought to commune with spirits he also performed notable work in chemical investigation and in the development of cartography and navigation, far more notable work than was being performed by anyone within the traditional educational centres of Oxford and Cambridge. It was for enlightenment in such matters that Sidney sought out Dee; he could set aside the mumbo-jumbo to attempt to get what seemed to him vitally important—an understanding of the nature of things. In the same passage where he mentions Sidney's rejection of astrology Moffett goes on to say that Philip 'pressed into the innermost penetralia of causes' and that with Dee as a teacher and Dyer as a companion he learned something of the secrets of chemistry.[64] Moffett also asserts (though no evidence seems to survive of this) that Sidney made corrections in the works of various scientific authors and that by his careful methods he led many to write on science in a more correct fashion or at the very least to make their observations in a more scientific fashion.[65] In short, as Moffett had it, though Sidney as a scholar reverenced antiquity, 'he did not condemn fresh fish'.[66]

One particular aspect of Dee's fertile teaching must have especially appealed to Sidney in the last years he was in England. This was Dee's interest in New World exploration. We have seen how Sidney's mature thoughts on foreign policy inclined more and more to action in the New World. In Dee he would have found one who would readily agree with such schemes.[67] No man in England was in fact better suited to act as technical adviser for overseas voyaging than Dee was, and by 1573 Dee had begun to dream of England as the mistress of a northern empire based on a firm command of the seas. By 1581 Dee's thought was largely centred on America, and he apparently wrote a vast tome in Latin on the propagation of the Christian faith among the infidels of the New World. Such thinking was not far removed from that of Sidney. Perhaps here too we can discern a further reason why Sidney drew close to men like Dee, for to Dee the overseas search was a part of something even deeper, a part of a probing for the heart of all knowledge, for the understanding of the infinite and the unknowable. To Sidney, who also wanted to press into the 'innermost penetralia of causes', Dee was a suitable guide. In the days just before he was called to the Netherlands Sidney was to make one last effort to realise the great American scheme he had come to hold most dear, and as he did so there can be little doubt that he had his lessons from Dee planted firmly in his mind.

PART THREE

The Man of Action

Chapter 9

SIDNEY AND THE NETHERLANDS

I must advise you now and then to reflect that
young men who rush into danger incautiously
almost always meet an inglorious end and
deprive themselves of the power of serving
their country.　　　Languet to Sidney (1578)

The smallest fear was held that day a shame.
G. Whetstone on the Battle of Zutphen

By 1585 the prospects at last seemed favourable for Sidney to enter the life of active service he had so desired. His work in the Ordnance Office placed him closer to the centre of activity than any post he had held before. His developing ideas on foreign policy afforded him a bolder scheme of action, and the changing international situation, with its menace to England, seemed at last to give more logic to the desires and aims of the activists. Moreover, in March the United Provinces, which had long been courting the direct aid of France in their revolt against Spain, received a final and definite no to their offer of the sovereignty of the Netherlands to the French King, Henry III. It did not take a particularly acute statesman to realise that this decision had momentous implications for England as well as for France and the United Provinces. For the better part of her reign Elizabeth had depended on France as the crucial weight in the continental balance and had skilfully played that nation off against Spain and the Catholic threat. Now it was apparent that the Catholic party in France, represented in the Guise family and the League, had gained too secure an ascendancy for such a policy to be feasible any longer. One whole pivot of English foreign relations had disappeared, and in its place was precisely the threat the policy of cautious balance had been designed to avoid: a continental Catholic league. Once again the logic of necessity at last seemed to favour the activist policy; if a Catholic league was about to be created, England's most obvious policy was to place herself at the head of a Protestant league.

In such conditions it was logical, too, that negotiations should be resumed for more direct English aid to the Netherlands. A few days after the final collapse of the French negotiations Ortel, the Dutch agent in London, was summoned by Walsingham to his house to reopen negotiations for a treaty between Queen Elizabeth and the United Provinces. It was an occasion which marked a significant turning point in English policy.[1] For years, small groups in England and the United Provinces had worked for an alliance, only to be thwarted again and again by those who actually determined policy. In 1585 the diplomatic dallyings became a matter of deadly earnest, and, even though the Queen might still have doubts about the policy of intervention and wish to erect strict limits and safeguards around the English aid, the fact of alliance was a necessity. As Leicester expressed it, he was prepared to support the Dutch cause with 'his own body, goods, and credit' if the Dutch would send ambassadors with full power to treat and 'make a proper representation' of the cause to the Queen.[2] The cautious Queen herself, impressed by the seriousness of the military situation in the Netherlands where the Spanish general Parma was besieging Antwerp, promised not to delay a treaty with the provinces. Within remarkably short time an embassy of many of the most distinguished Dutch politicians was ready to cross to England to make the final arrangements. The embassy was, however, then held back by delays, and when it finally did sail it was rapidly forced back to seek shelter until an English fleet could come to escort them to Gravesend. They were not finally welcomed officially to England until 6 July.

Despite the obvious urgency of the situation and the promise of the Queen that there would be no delays, the negotiations proceeded at a very slow pace. Lord Talbot wrote to his father from court in mid-July that 'as for the news here, they are more uncertain than the weather, and it is not possible your Lordship should know anything but doubtfulness of the proceedings in the Low Country matters as yet, but within a very few days they will be resolved, and in the meantime everyone may guess as he list, and I for my poor part believe that some five or six thousand footmen shall be sent, and no horsemen, although Sir Philip Sidney be so far prepared to take the charge of five hundred'.[3] The activists like Sidney tended to take a very dim view of the delays, and their reaction was to blame them on the Queen, whose cautious policy had so often defeated them in the past. To be honest, the Queen was responsible for some of the delay; even if she admitted the necessity of English intervention she was unwilling to accept what seemed to most the best scheme for carrying it out, the plan whereby she would accept the sovereignty of the Netherlands and appoint a governor-general with full military and civil power. Only in such a way was there likely to be a sufficiently authoritative hand in control of the somewhat disorganised United Provinces. But to do so involved in her mind more than a change from the policy of balance. It involved the usurpation of the title of a legally anointed sovereign, and whether Philip II was an enemy or not, as a monarch Elizabeth was emotionally and psychologically incapable of siding fully with rebels against their rightful ruler. Moreover, such a scheme would have involved the creation in effect of another English court, another fount of honour, another source of patronage outside her island and headed by one of her greatest nobles, the ambitious Leicester, the only person seriously considered as commander-in-chief. Finally (and here she was reverting to the thinking behind the policy of balance) such a scheme would create enormous expense and could well shatter the fragile financial system of England. One cannot deny that the Queen was probably correct in the last two of these points and that, given the prevailing social and political attitudes of her times, there was much logic in the first point as well.

In fact, however, much of the blame for the delay must come from the Dutch themselves.[4] The States General of the United Provinces were lax in sending necessary final instructions to both their own deputies and the English Queen. As a modern scholar has commented: 'The time wasted before the terms of the treaty were put into practice was largely due to the fault of the Dutch who, for various reasons, were excessively slack in confirming the arrangements, procuring securities, and providing the funds they had agreed to raise.'[5] The Queen was, to be sure, bargaining for strict terms. In the formal negotiations the issue of sovereignty was out of the question, although informal negotiations of which the Queen was not fully aware did raise the possibility of investing the English general with the same *de facto* authority the Queen was refusing. The English demand for control of the so-called cautionary towns (Flushing, Brill, Fort Rammekens) to be held by England as security for whatever sums they were advancing also proved a stumbling block, although the Dutch eventually conceded the demands. Finally there was the problem of who was to go on the expedition. It was uniformly assumed that Leicester would be in command, but in the course of the negotiations the Queen wavered. Leicester wrote to Walsingham in September that the Queen did not desire him to leave the realm, and the name of Lord Grey was proposed as an alternative.[6] There was also doubt who would be the governor of the cautionary town of Flushing; the Dutch were extremely desirous to have their long-time friend Sidney placed in this position, but the Queen was at first evasive about this and seems to have favoured Thomas Cecil for the post.[7]

All this led Sidney to make a dramatic decision. Already convinced in his mind that intervention in the Netherlands was a second-best course and that overseas adventuring would be far more effective and now apparently being thwarted even in gaining major command in the second best scheme, Sidney resolved to voyage to the New World. Walsingham reported to the English ambassador in the Netherlands in mid-September: 'Sir Philip hath taken a very hard resolution to accompany Sir Francis Drake in this voyage, moved thereto for that he saw her Majesty disposed to commit the charge of Flushing unto some other; which he reputed would fall out greatly to his disgrace, to see another preferred before him, both for birth and judgment inferior unto him. The despair thereof and the disgrace that he doubted he should receive have carried him into a different course.'[8]

The fullest account of this escapade is contained in Greville's memoir, but there some of the details are garbled, especially as to what role Sidney himself played in the planning of the voyage. According to Greville's account, the whole expedition was of Sidney's 'own projecting, wherein he fashioned the whole body with purpose to become head of it himself'.[9] It was to be a combined land and sea operation, and to this purpose, Greville continued, Sidney chose as officers 'the ablest governors of those martial times'.[10] His arrangement with Drake was that they should be equal commanders of the expedition once they had left England's shores, but until then 'Sir Francis was to bear the name, and by the credit of Sir Philip have all particulars abundantly supplied'.[11] There can be no doubt that Sidney favoured Drake's schemes, especially since his own concept of New World conquest had been so precisely echoed in a letter which he had received from Ralph Lane, an old friend of the family who had been left in the New World as the governor of the Roanoke colony.[12]

If her Majesty at any time find herself burthened with the King of Spain we have by our dwelling upon the island of St John and Hispaniola for the space of five weeks so discovered the forces thereof, with the infinite riches of the same, as that I find it an attempt most honourable, feasible, and profitable, and only fit for yourself to be the chief commander in. . . . To conclude, finding by mine own view his forces at land to be so mean, and his terror made too great amongst us in England, considering that the reputation thereof doth altogether grow from the mines of his treasures, and the same in places which we see here are so easy both to be taken and kept by any small force sent by her Majesty, I could not but write these ill-fashioned lines unto you, and to exhort you, my noble general, by occasion not to refuse the good opportunity of such a service to the Church of Christ, of great relief from many calamities that this treasure in Spaniards' hands doth inflict into the members thereof, very honourable and profitable for her Majesty and our country, and most commendable and fit for yourself to be the enterpriser thereof.

No doubt from his side Drake welcomed at least the Sidney name to his plans as an inducement to investment. But that he actually agreed to share command with Sidney seems inconceivable; perhaps he was counting on the Queen forbidding Sidney to go, perhaps on Sidney having an assured place in the Netherlands.

In any case, the sequence of events which transpired, though reasonably clear in their details, are difficult to explain fully. Drake had gone with his fleet to Plymouth. There he was to wait until the fleet was ready for sea and attending only a favourable wind; when this happened he was to send a private messenger to Sidney to join him. The message reached Sidney towards the end of August; at the same time news also reached him that his old friend Don Antonio was on his way to England. Sidney was able to use this latter information as a convenient excuse for leaving the court, and he departed with haste in the company of Fulke Greville, ostensibly to meet Don Antonio, in actuality to sail with Drake to the New World. Sidney appears to have kept his plans secret even from some of his closest associates.[13] Walsingham himself was writing at almost this very moment of his son-in-law as the

Governor of Flushing, and when he did learn of Sidney's relations with Drake it was after Sidney had already been recalled, though he was not let in on that news either, probably because the court wrongly suspected that he was aware of the whole scheme from the beginning. When Sidney and Greville arrived at Plymouth they were feasted on the first night by Sir Francis 'with a great deal of outward pomp and compliment'.[14] Greville, however, was convinced that there was something wrong. 'I . . . observing the countenance of this gallant mariner more exactly than Sir Philip's leisure served him to do, after we were laid in bed acquainted him with my observation of the discountenance and depression which appeareth in Sir Francis, as if our coming were both beyond his expectation and desire.'[15] Sidney was not inclined initially to share his friend's doubts; his spirit, 'not apt to discredit others, made him suspend his own and labour to change or qualify my judgment',[16] Greville recalled. But within a few days even Sidney had to agree that something was amiss. The fleet was not, in fact, ready to sail, 'nor possibly to be made ready in many days'.[17] and Sidney began to note that there was an underlying friction between Drake and himself. On 7 September Don Antonio arrived in Plymouth, and to the consternation of Drake, who already had obvious doubts about the wisdom of taking the idealistic Sidney along, announced that he too intended to join the expedition. Drake, as Greville commented, 'watched an opportunity to discover us without being discovered'.[18] An opportunity was found, and Drake sent secretly to the Queen to inform her of the real purpose of Sidney's absence from the court. The Queen's action was quick; she sent three letters back by messenger, one to Sidney, a second to Drake, the third to the Mayor of Plymouth, all ordering that Sidney return at once to the court.

Sidney's determination at this point is well illustrated by the next step in the story. A letter written to the Earl of Rutland contains part of the tale. 'Sir Philip Sidney's departing with Sir Francis Drake was so fully advertised her Majesty as it pleased her to command Mr Vice-Chamberlain to write three letters. . . . If they were already gone, some bark should be sent after with the letters. The messenger was one Hyts, whom I think your Lordship know, one serving my Lady Drury, who was despatched accordingly, and when he was within four miles of Plymouth, he was surprised by four mariners and his letters taken from him, the which being opened and read were sent him again.'[19] Greville tells us more about the incident, in which Sidney himself had more than a casual hand.[20]

For within a few days after [Drake had decided to notify the Queen] a post steals up to the court, upon whose arrival an alarm is presently taken: messengers sent away to stay us, or if we refused to stay the whole fleet. Notwithstanding this first Mercury, his errand being partly advertised to Sir Philip beforehand, was intercepted upon the way, his letters taken from him by two resolute soldiers in mariner's apparell, brought instantly to Sir Philip, opened, and read. The contents as welcome as Bulls of excommunication to the superstitious Romanist, when they enjoin him either to forsake his right or his holy Mother Church, yet did he sit this first process, without noise or answer.

The second summons from the court could not be handled in such high-handed fashion, however. This 'more imperial mandate' was borne to Sidney by a peer of the realm, 'carrying with it in the one hand grace, the other thunder'.[21] The proffered grace was 'instant employment' under Leicester in the Netherlands as Governor of Flushing, while the thunder was a threat to prevent the sailing of Drake's fleet so long as Sidney remained with them. Sidney, faced with the ultimatum, gave in with grace and tact, even if he would have far preferred the voyage to America. A messenger from among Don Antonio's men was sent to the Queen to inform her that 'Sir Philip never meant to go, but stayeth there to see the ships set forth'.[22] Some apparently knew the longings of Sidney's mind well, for rumours persisted in London and among many courtiers that Sidney had gone with Drake notwithstanding.[23] But Sidney knew his duty as a servant of the Queen better than this: 'how unwillingly soever he yielded up his knowledge, affections, public and private ends in that journey, yet he did act this force in a gallant fashion'.[24] Before leaving Plymouth he instructed Drake in the details of his grand scheme for the New World, encouraged the whole force assembled there with a promise of unstinting support, cleared Drake himself from any disfavour that might hamper his operations, and even justified the Queen's policy in the Netherlands on the grounds that it was a visible token of her great concern to engage herself 'more ways than one against the Spaniards' ambition'.[25] Drake's fleet sailed from Plymouth on 14 September, still not fully ready for sea,[26] and a week later Sidney was back at court.

The proposed voyage with Drake is one of the most celebrated episodes in Sidney's career, but it is not easy to make a balanced judgment of it. The role of Drake himself remains something of a mystery. What sort of agreement did he really make with Sidney? Why did he encourage Sidney to come to Plymouth and then secretly inform the court in an attempt to get rid of him? The results of Sidney's not going with the expedition seem more open to analysis. Greville, in looking back on the affair, could only lament that his friend had not had a chance to put his ambitious schemes into practice. 'That heroical design of invading and possessing America, how exactly soever projected and digested in every minute by Sir Philip, did yet prove impossible to be well acted by any other man's spirit than his own, how sufficient soever his associates were in all parts of navigation, whereby the success of this journey fell out to be rather fortunate in wealth than honour'.[27] But a modern judgment vindicating Drake's resolve not to have Sidney nor Don Antonio sail with him is far more acute: 'Drake was right: naval experience was essential to the success of the enterprise, and a fleet commanded by a sailor, an idealist, and an exiled prince would have steered straight to disaster'.[28] One can almost tell exactly where the trouble would have come. The central point of Sidney's plan was the seizure of a foreign base; he could never have agreed with Drake that it was militarily necessary to abandon Cartagena after it had been taken, but for all the subsequent activist criticism of Drake for doing so, he was surely in the right.

Sidney was quickly restored to favour on his return to the court; the Queen had no reason not to be magnanimous to one she had so decisively defeated, and the official story that Sidney had never really intended to go on the expedition was accepted as the truth. A signal of the Queen's favourable attitude to Philip at this point was her willingness to serve as godmother to his daughter, named Elizabeth in honour of England's Eliza.[29] For the next two months Sidney was busy himself in making preparations for his departure to the Netherlands. Even before he had made his attempted flight with Drake the final arrangements between England and the United Provinces had been worked out and embodied in the Treaty of Nonsuch. The Queen had also caused to be published in five languages *A Declaration of the causes mooving the queene to give aide to the . . . lowe countries*. It was the final step in the enunciation of the new English role. Elizabeth had succumbed to the activists and committed her nation to support the rebellious provinces against Spain. The letters patent confirming Sidney's appointment were issued on 9 November, and the following day, from Gravesend, Sidney sent the Queen a cipher for messages of a confidential nature and assured her of his desire to serve her well.[30]

> Most gracious sovereign. This rude piece of paper shall presume because of your Majesty's commandment, most humbly to present such a cipher as little leisure could afford me. If there come any matter to my knowledge the importance whereof shall deserve to be so masked I will not fail (since your pleasure is my only boldness) to your own hands to recommend it. In the meantime I beseech your Majesty will vouchsafe legibly to read my heart in the course of my life, and though itself be but of a mean worth, yet to esteem it like a poor house well set. I most lowly kiss your hands and pray to God your enemies may then only have peace when they are weary of knowing your force.

He departed six days later for the Netherlands, though his company of two hundred Welsh soldiers were left behind and his friend Greville, who had been given a command of horse by Leicester, lingered in disfavour at the court. On the 18th he reached the Netherlands; the rough weather made his arrival less than triumphant. Forced to land four miles from Flushing, he had to approach his new post on foot, 'with as dirty a walk as ever poor governor entered his charge withal'.[31] He was none the less warmly received by the inhabitants, though one correspondent observed he 'was not so entertained and received as I think he should have been if the weather had not fallen out so foul'.[32] On the following Sunday he was honourably entertained at the State House and took his oath; the next day he was again at the State House and the representatives of Flushing took their oaths to the Queen and to Sidney as her governor.

Sidney was well aware that he had been given an important and formidable task. It was clear that Flushing was a site of major strategic importance, especially in view of the fact that it commanded the mouth of the Scheldt River and was an effective check on Antwerp which had recently fallen to Parma's Spanish troops. Consequently, a major portion of Sidney's work would be to see that the defences of his charge were built up and secured. Sidney was aided in his handling of Flushing by the co-operative attitude of Maurice, the son of William of Orange, in whose territory Flushing lay. Maurice willingly turned over the town to the English governor and asked Sidney to consider him as his brother and companion in arms. On other fronts, however, the situation was far less favourable. The potential leader of the Dutch was St Aldegonde, with whom Sidney had earlier had contact, but the Antwerp burgomaster was now very much under a cloud, suspected of treachery by many in the nation for his action in surrendering Antwerp. There was considerable disunity and jealousy among the other leaders in the Netherlands, and the arrival of an English governor was not welcomed by all. Of some of his problems, Sidney was unaware. He did not appreciate the extent to which the activist policy would still be curbed by a cautious scheme even after it had been put into operation. He was not fully aware that the English had been instructed to fight essentially a defensive war, and this was bound to cause friction between his adventurous spirit and the way the Queen wanted war to advance.

What Sidney was only too well aware of was the very serious condition of Flushing. The fortifications were insufficient, the men badly paid and badly disciplined. Edward Norris, who had been in command at Flushing, was exonerated by Sidney; he had performed his task 'very well and soldierly' but the companies themselves were 'indeed very sickly and miserable'.[33] Of the six hundred men in the garrison, nearly two hundred were in the hospital. Their pay was far in arrears, and some of the men were quite literally starving. It is little wonder that the garrison was termed 'the worst accomodated of all our soldiers, amongst a people of a froward and perverse disposition'.[34] The muster master described them as 'weak, bad-furnished, ill-armed, and worse trained'.[35] Sidney, from the very beginning, was conscious of the weakness of the garrison. 'The garrison is far too weak to command by authority', he wrote to Leicester, 'which is a pity for how great a jewel this is to the crown of England and the Queen's safety I need not write it to your Lordship who knows it so well'.[36] The weakness of the fortifications matched the bad conditions of the garrison. The muster master reported that the ramparts and bulwarks were in a bad state, that the barriers in many places had fallen to the ground, and that the sentinel and guard houses were in extreme need of repair. He concluded pessimistically that it was 'utterly impossible with this garrison to hold it against any royal force', no matter how qualified the new governor might be.[37] The actual situation of the town was not, on the other hand, badly suited to defence, since it commanded a large area of low ground around it. The muster master recommended extensive repairs to bring the town into a semblance of order, though he cautioned that an overall scheme for rebuilding the fortifications was extremely desirable.

Sir Philip had not arrived in Flushing any too soon. 'I think truly if my coming had been longer delayed some alteration would have followed, for the truth is the people is weary of war, and if they do not see such a course taken as may be likely to defend them they will in a sudden give over the cause'.[38] He also brought some £7000 with him which helped to ease the dire financial situation, although he subsequently complained that the treasurer was paying the men at a depressed exchange. 'The Treasurer here pays our Zealand soldiers in Zealand money which is five in the hundred loss to the poor soldiers who, God knows, want no such hindrances, being scarce able to keep life with their entire pay'.[39] The victualling situation was as unsatisfactory as the pay. Sidney reported to Walsingham 'as concerning victuallers, for ought I can yet perceive I may better furnish myself either here or in England than by taking myself to anyone, and for Brown and Bruin, I assure you, Sir, they do as yet but badly satisfy the soldiers, and in my opinion are merely hurtful after a Gomorrah fashion by means of friendship of the officers forcing the poor men to take it dearer than here they might provide themselves'.[40]

The feeling which perhaps worried Sidney the most at this juncture was that the Dutch would abandon him and his men unless they were convinced that English aid was really forthcoming in a significant fashion. This was why he was so anxious for the arrival of his uncle. To Leicester he wrote that his coming was 'here longed for as Messiah is of the Jews'. 'Good my Lord', he continued, 'haste away, if you do come, for all things considered, I had rather you came not at all than came not quickly, for only by your own presence those courses may be stopped, which, if they run on, will be past remedy.'[41] To Burghley, Sidney wrote in a very similar fashion. 'For my part, I am in the midst of the worst tempered people, but while they hope of her Majesty's taking their part, so long I comfort myself with opinion that they will continue constant but when that begins to fail, it is time that both the garrisons [*i.e.*, Flushing and Brill] were better replenished.'[42] Sidney was not entirely despondent and hoped that a reformation of abuses, both English and Dutch, would remedy things. 'I am more and more fully persuaded that with that proportion which her Majesty alloweth the country is fully able to maintain the wars if what they do be well ordered and not abused as it is by the States.'[43] If Sidney needed any further demonstration that the situation was precarious, he received it in the course of the first military action his soldiers were involved in. As if the problems of Flushing were not enough, he received news that the veteran commander La Motte had advanced to Blankenburg and was on his way to lay siege to Ostend, one of the most important towns outside Spanish control. He also received letters from the governor of Ostend, Captain Errington, an old friend of his, stating that munitions and food were scarce and that he feared an internal rising against his troops. Sidney acted quickly; he sent messengers to the States General and the general of the Dutch forces asking for supplies, sent another agent off to buy armour, and dispatched a force under his brother and others to encounter La Motte. La Motte did, in fact, besiege Ostend, but shortly afterwards withdrew. The danger and predicament were pointed up by communiques from Errington and Robert Sidney. Errington had been so afraid that the population of Ostend might rise against his garrison that he had not permitted his soldiers to leave the town to fight La Motte.[44] Robert Sidney, for his part, gave a dismal picture of the face of war on the area: 'This garrison hath so spoiled the country hereabouts that almost for twenty miles riding every way there is never a house standing nor ever a man out of a walled town to be seen. . . . Here is want of all things—no victuals in store for above twenty days; if a soldier should break his pike or his halbert not any here to furnish him; of powder not 12,000 weight whereof five is not serviceable.'[45]

It was confidently expected that the arrival of the great Leicester would cure all things. This was hardly to be the case. Leicester himself was never to display the drive, skill, or tact necessary for such a post; even more important, his arrival placed directly in the open the very vexed question of what precisely his office entailed. The anti-English party in the Netherlands were already worried about it, and their hurried election of Maurice as Stadtholder of Holland and Zealand represented their response to Leicester's coming. Maurice himself was less inclined to be anti-English and Sidney was able to write of the election that it 'only grew by the delays of your Lordship's coming, but I cannot perceive any meaning of either diminishing or crossing your

Lordship's authority, but rather that the Count means wholly to depend upon your Lordship's authority'.[46] The real difficulty was to come from a quite different direction, from England and Elizabeth. All through the negotiations with the United Provinces, Elizabeth had insisted that the governor-general was to have a very limited authority. In the informal and secret discussions, however, the activists had pressed for and secured the point that the governor-general was to have a full authority in the same manner as his Spanish predecessors had had. What emerged from this decision was, in effect, a conspiracy against Queen Elizabeth by her councillors; they would keep from her news of what precisely Leicester was doing and what power he was assuming until he had secured all. Only then, when the Queen's hand was fully forced, was she to be presented with the true facts as a *fait accompli*. The conspiracy went through several carefully planned and executed phases.[47] Stage I involved elaborate welcomes for Leicester and a triumphant progress from Flushing, where he was received by Sidney, to The Hague, where he was to establish his 'capital'. The progress was a succession of magnificent pageants, carefully planned and staged, each town vying to outdo the rest, and even The Hague, then not much more than a village, managed a sumptuous state entry on a scale unparalleled since the entry of Philip of Spain there over thirty-five years before. Leicester, as one writer noted, was being welcomed like a second Charles V, and he himself reported that the people 'will have it that her Majesty shall have in her hands the whole bestowing as well of their money and contribution as of their men of war . . . they will no other authority but under her Majesty, nor that their treasure nor lives shall be at the disposing of any but her Majesty'.[48] Phase II of the plan was an elaborate charade in which Leicester considered the offer of full power from the Dutch. He pretended to be surprised; for a fortnight he withdrew and conducted careful negotiations and consultations through the intermediary offices of Sidney and Davison. Sidney played a large part in the proceedings and conducted a very difficult task with considerable skill; it is certain he approved of the idea that the governor-general should have a full power, but it is less clear that he understood how contrary to the Queen's wishes all the negotiations were. In January 1586 Leicester accepted the rule and government general of the Netherlands.

Phase III involved telling the Queen the news. This was not done directly, but was gradually leaked to her. All expected an angry response from the Queen, but few expected one quite so violent. The Queen was irate not just because her policy had been crossed. She was particularly irate because her 'creature' Leicester had done it, and had done it with the connivance of her closest councillors, who had kept the news from her until it was too late to do much except bluster. Her anger with Leicester is well indicated in the stormy letter she addressed to him.[49]

How contemptuously we conceive ourself to have been used by you, you shall by this bearer understand, whom we have expressly sent unto you to charge you withal. We could never have imagined, had we not seen it fall out in experience, that a man raised up by ourself, and extraordinarily favoured by us above any other subject of this land, would have in so contemptible a sort broken our commandment, in a cause that so greatly toucheth us in honour; whereof, although you have showed yourself to make but little account, in most undutiful a sort, you may not therefore think that we have so little care of the reparation thereof as we mind to pass so great a wrong in silence unredressed: and, therefore, our express pleasure and commandment is, that, all delays and excuses laid apart, you do presently, upon the duty of your allegiance, obey and fulfil whatsoever the bearer hereof shall direct you to do in our name: whereof fail you not, as you will answer the contrary at your uttermost peril.

The Queen's anger was further heightened because Leicester's action came just at the point when she was, behind the back of the Dutch alliance, opening peace negotiations with Spain. Finally her ire was increased because of her continued fears of a second and rival English court, and the news that the Countess of Leicester, with her full train that rivalled that of the Queen herself, was about to join her lord in the Low Countries did nothing to calm her temper. Angrily she demanded Leicester's resignation and would have dispatched Sir Thomas Heneage with a letter to that effect had not the Council opposed her. Davison was sent back from the Netherlands to the Queen to attempt to explain things, and Leicester fell back on the excuse that he had been pressured into the decision to accept full power by the arguments of Sidney and Davison. Once in England, Davison found himself placed in an extremely awkward position by Leicester's conduct. Leicester, in an unfair letter to Davison, complained 'how hardly' he was drawn to accept the position without consulting the Queen.[50] Davison sarcastically noted in the margin: 'Let Sir Philip Sidney and others witness.'[51] To Leicester's angry, 'You did chiefly persuade me', Davison retorted with accuracy, 'His end in coming over, with some other circumstances, may decide this question.'[52]

Sidney, too, was placed in a very uncomfortable position by the bitterness of phase III of the plan. He found himself along with Davison labelled a principal actor and persuader in the affair,[53] and thus under heavy censure from the court; there were even hints that he might be removed from the governorship of Flushing. Sidney found himself acting as a middleman between some of the aggrieved parties. Angry as he was to fall from favour because of it, he approved the step taken by Leicester as the one most likely to bring military success in the Netherlands, and he felt obliged to stand by his uncle. 'I beseech your Excellency not to be discouraged with the Queen's discontentments, for the event being anything good, your glory will shine through those mists, only if it please you to have daily council taken of your means, how to increase them and how to husband them. And when all is said, if they can serve, you shall make a noble war.'[54] Moreover, he felt obliged to try to make peace between Leicester and the affronted Davison. He wrote a very careful letter to Davison, indicating his trust in him, but at the same time stressing his loyalty to Leicester.[55]

My Lord thinks great unkindness in you, being advertised from thence, that you greatly disclaim from his defence, which now your absence from court seems much to confirm, but of your faith I will make no doubt while I live, only I think you answered not the point of her Majesty's mislike, for you answered only upon the necessity, but should have argued withal upon the nature, which is not absolute as her Majesty took it. Well, a great blow is stricken; things went beyond our expectation, I doubt me hardly to be redressed.

Above all, Sidney was worried, and with good cause, about the effect which the uproar would have on the effectiveness of the English aid to the Netherlands. The dispute was at best unedifying; at the worst it could undermine all the essential authority that was needed if the English were to have any impact. When Heneage did arrive with a much modified message from the Queen (a message which represented what compromise could be scraped out of the differing views of the

Queen and Leicester) all his care and honesty could not repair the damage. As Sidney reported to Burghley,[56]

I have written to my Lords of the Council in answer to theirs where, because I was fain to be long, I will not trouble your Lordship with any repetition, but only humbly beseech your Lordship to give your hand to the helping of the money's sending over, for truly, my Lord, else there will some terrible accident follow, particularly to the caution towns, if her Majesty mean to have them cautions. The news here I leave to Sir Th. Heneage who hath with as much honesty in my opinion done as much hurt as any man this twelvemonth hath done with naughtiness, but I hope in God when her Majesty finds the truth of things, her graciousness will not utterly overthrow a cause so behooveful and costly unto her, but that is beyond my office.

He wrote later to Walsingham stressing the same point that the Queen's reaction to Leicester had had a disastrous effect on the hopes for military success. 'We shall have a sore war upon us this summer wherein, if appointment had been kept and these disgraces foreborn which have greatly weakened us, we had been victorious.'[57] In April he wrote again to Davison, still apologetic about the effect of the quarrel, but still firmly in Leicester's camp.[58]

I am heartily sorry with the unkindness you conceive of my Lord, and more at the cause thereof. I know by letters thence and some speeches here that he was much incensed because he had heard that you had utterly and with tears disclaimed him with dislike of the acceptacion but I did never think he had written touching you into England. For my part, I will for no cause deny (and therefore you shall have my handwriting to prove I am no accuser of you) that I was ever of opinion he should accept it without delay, because of the necessity, without sending to her Majesty because of not forcing her in a manner to be further engaged than she would, which had been a piece of undutiful dutifulness. The odds was that some others were of opinion the authority was not enough; you liked of this as it is, and I only leaned to your opinion therein. Well, cousin, these mistakings sometimes breed hard effects, but I know he in his judgment loves you very well, howsoever in his passion he have written, and so I end assuring you that I am still one toward you as one that know you and therefore love you.

Sidney was learning fast under such pressure. In one of the most interesting of all his letters he confided his feelings to Walsingham. He showed in it a total devotion to the cause of the reformed religion and of the Netherlands; in doing so he comes as close as he ever did to expressing a sort of crusading spirit. In the midst of the shady dealings, corruption, and ambitious back-stabbing that characterised the political life of his day the spirit of Sidney that shines through his words has a considerable nobility. For all his shortcomings, he, more than any other, did have the makings of the Protestant hero knight.[59]

I receive divers letters from you, full of the discomfort which I see and am sorry to see that you daily meet with at home, and I think such is the goodwill it pleaseth you to bear me that my part of the trouble is something that troubles you, but I beseech you let it not. I had before cast my count of danger, want, and disgrace, and before God, Sir, it is true that in my heart the love of the cause doth so far overbalance them all that with God's grace they shall never make me weary of my resolution. If her Majesty were the fountain I would fear, considering what I daily find, that we should wax dry, but she is but a means whom God useth and I know not whether I am deceived but I am faithfully persuaded that if she should withdraw herself, other springs would rise to help this action. For methinks I see the great work indeed in hand against the abusers of the world, wherein it is no greater fault to have confidence in man's power than it is too hastily to despair of God's work. I think a wise and constant man ought never to grieve while he doth play, as a man may say his own part truly though others be out, but if himself leave his hold because other mariners will be idle he will hardly forgive himself his own fault. For me I cannot promise of my own course, no nor of the my [?] because I know there is a higher power that must uphold me or else I shall fall, but certainly I trust I shall not by other men's wants be drawn from myself.

Therefore, good Sir, to whom for my particular I am more bound than to all men besides, be not troubled with my trouble for I have seen the worst in my judgment beforehand, and worse than that cannot be. If the Queen pay not her soldiers she must lose her garrisons; there is no doubt thereof.

But no man living shall be able to say the fault is in me. What relief I can do them, I will. I will spare no danger if occasion serve, I am sure no creature shall be able to lay injustice to my charge, and for further doubts, truly I stand not upon them. . . . I understand I am called very ambitious and proud at home, but certainly if they knew my heart, they would not altogether so judge me.

His first and last winter in the Netherlands could hardly have been a happy one for Sir Philip. The tangle over the governorship was bad enough; added to it were the continuing bad condition of his troops, the well-founded rumours that Elizabeth was negotiating for a peace with Spain, and the general lack of activity by the English. It was reported that Sidney was in good health, but melancholy.[60] He had good reason to be so, for the supposed allies were more active in squabbling among themselves than they were in combating the enemy. A clear case in point involved Sir Philip directly. Many of the leaders of the Dutch were angered by offices being given to Englishmen, and when Sidney was given command of the Zealand regiment, Count Philip von Hohenlo, a German adventurer who had long been fighting on the Dutch side, took violent exception. Sidney reported to Davison 'upon my having the Zealand regiment, which you know was more your persuasion than any desire in me, the Count Hohenlo caused a many handed supplication to be made that no stranger might have any regiment, but presently after with all the same hands protested they meant it not by me to whom they wished all honour, etc. The Count Maurice showed himself constantly kind towards me therein, but Mr Paul Bus hath too many Busses in his head, such as you shall find he will be to God and man about one pitch. Happy is the conjunction with them that join in the fear of God.'[61] Sidney, as he indicated in the letter, was able to smooth over the difficulties, and Greville noted the affair as a particular instance of the tact with which Sidney was able to keep affairs going. Sir Philip 'through himself wrought, if not a kind of unity between the Earl of Leicester and the Count Hollock, at least a final surcease of all violent jealousies or factious expostulations'.[62] In short, Sidney was gradually proving himself indispensable in the sorry business of keeping the allies together. Gradually, all came to realise his usefulness, just as they came to appeciate the selflessness with which he dedicated himself to the task. The changing attitude of Leicester towards his nephew is instructive on this point. After Sidney's death, and shortly before his own, Leicester told Greville that 'when he undertook the government of the Low Countries, he carried his nephew over with him as one amongst the rest, not only despising his youth for a counsellor, but withal bearing a hand over him as a forward young man'. In the course of the campaign Leicester 'saw this sun so risen above his horizon, that both he and all his stars were glad to fetch light from him, and in the end acknowledged that he held up the honour of his casual authority by him whilst he lived and found reason to withdraw himself from that burthen after his death'.[63]

To the disappointments stemming from ineffectiveness and lack of action, Sidney added deep personal loss at the end of this sorry winter.

In early May his father Sir Henry died as a result of a chill caught while travelling by barge from Bewdley to Worcester. Philip received the news of his death at Arnhem and applied for leave to return to England to settle family affairs and to see his mother, also in ill-health. The leave was refused by the Queen, a last token of disservice to the family of Sir Henry Sidney whose great labours for his sovereign had been so persistently unrewarded.[64] Before the summer was out Sidney had lost his mother as well, her last days lacking even the comfort of the presence of her three sons, all of whom were serving in the Netherlands.

The bitter blow of his father's sudden death was only partially compensated for by the arrival of Sidney's wife in the Netherlands, and with the arrival of spring and the renewal of military activities Sidney had fresh cause for despair. Even with the campaigning season upon them, the pathetic, ill-paid, and disorganised English force continued to rot in idleness rather than shape itself into an effective arm of the Protestant cause. Sidney had long argued for a more aggressive strategy. In February he had openly criticised the inactivity of Leicester's troops in letter to his uncle. 'Here are no news in Rotterdam but that you band is of very handsome men, but merely [?] and unarmed, spending money and time to no purpose.'[65] And again, 'The enemy stirs of every side, and your side must not be idle, for if it be, it quickly looseth reputation.'[66] Sidney's one effort to take the offensive had been an attack on Steenberg by which he had hoped either to win the town or at least to cause Parma to raise the siege of Grave. Sidney had a thousand men under his command to accomplish the task, but a sudden thaw set in and ruined the scheme.[67] He also consulted at the same time with Gianbelli, a famous Italian siege engineer who had achieved repute in the Netherlands by destroying Parma's siege works at Antwerp with fire-ships.[68] Gianbelli had a scheme which was close to Sidney's heart, the creation of a vast Anglo-Dutch fleet which would be financed by levies in both England and Holland and would harass the Spanish colonies and interrupt Spanish trade. That Sidney's mind was still drawn to vast schemes is indicated by the last stage of Gianbelli's plan which involved an invasion of Spain itself, aided by the fomenting of risings by the Portuguese and the Moors.

Little came from modest attacks like that on Steenberg, nothing at all from the grandiose schemes like that of Gianbelli, and as the new campaigning season was to begin, Sidney was obviously in a somewhat despondent mood. His friend the Master of Gray had indicated a desire to bring over Scottish troops to aid, but Sidney discouraged him, at first indirectly and then by personal letter. He asked a message be passed on to Gray that 'I would rather wish him if he have any other enterprise in hand to go on with that first until our matters be better settled here, for I cannot as considering how things stand here wish any friend of mine whom I love as I have reason to love him to embark himself in these matters until we be assured of better harbour'.[69] The next month he wrote to Gray himself: 'My Lord is exceedingly desirous to have your presence here. But by reason there is not yet so full an established authority as there should, the moneys come in so slowly as in good faith I know not whether I should wish the coming of so dear a friend or no.'[70]

At least one of the commanders in the Netherlands, Sir John Norris, agreed with Sidney that a more aggressive policy was in order. Unfortunately for the smooth operation of the campaign, Leicester and Norris were on the worst of terms, Leicester constantly humiliating Norris and Norris in turn doing nothing to conceal the bitter contempt he felt for Leicester's policy of remaining in quarters. The already tense and unsatisfactory command situation was made worse by the arrival of Sir William Pelham in July; his ambiguous title of Lord Marshal kindled again the petty jealousies of subordinates and added to the growing feeling of the Dutch that the only commands Leicester gave were orders to advance his favourites to positions of prominence. Thomas Cecil, writing to his father, summed up the very sad state which affairs had reached: 'Our affairs here be such as that which we conclude overnight is broken in the morning. We agree not one with another but we are divided in many factions, so as if the enemy were as strong as we are factious and unresolute I think we should make shipwreck of the cause this summer.'[71]

That the summer was not entirely a shipwreck was due to the efforts of men like Norris and Sidney who managed some successes for the English army. Norris opened the campaigning season with a notable success. Ordered by Leicester to relieve Grave, he had encountered crack Spanish troops and won a handsome victory; at the beginning of April, five hundred additional troops were placed in the garrison along with supplies sufficient for a year. General elation became the mood of the moment; a correspondent of Leicester hopefully stated 'if the Spaniard have such a May as he had an April, it will put water in his wine'.[72] Elation was soon turned to stupified despair, however, for Parma renewed his activities against Grave. Much to everyone's amazement, the garrison under Governor Hemart surrendered several hours after successfully repelling a Spanish attack. Leicester was dumbfounded; he wrote to Walsingham: 'To be short, being the best fortified place thoroughly of all these provinces, none like it, being full-manned, victualed, and stored with all manner of artillery and munition, having but iii hours battery laid to it and a show of assault upon Thursday last in the morning, gave it up at afternoon. What hath corrupted them there I know not. . . . I will not complain any further, and yet will I never depart hence till, by the goodness of God, I be satisfied someway for this villain's treachery done.'[73] What had caused Hemart to surrender so easily is unknown, but his cowardice and negligence were fatal. He was tried at Utrecht on 17 June by a court martial. Sidney sat as a member of the court, and it is reasonable to suppose that he concurred wholeheartedly in the sentence of death which was passed on Hemart and several of his captains.

Parma continued with his string of successes. Despite a bold attempt by the English to rout his camp, he captured Venloo on 28 June and with it controlled the Maas River. A few days later his troops laid siege to Neuss. It was in an attempt to relieve the pressure on Neuss that Sidney achieved his most notable military coup of the war. Count Maurice had suggested in early June that a surprise attack on the town of Axel might well be the most effective form of relief. His plans were confided to Sidney and with the blessing of Leicester the two worked out the details. On the evening of 6 July, Sidney and his Zealand regiment moved to join with five hundred men of Lord Willoughby at Flushing. Then they rowed up the Scheldt River to a point about three miles from Axel where they effected a rendezvous with Maurice and his fifteen hundred men. A mile from the town, Sidney exhorted his men to do their utmost; so successful was this oration of his, the chronicler recorded, that it did 'link the minds of the people that they desired rather to die in that service than to live in the contrary'.[74] Shortly before two in the morning the combined forces reached Axel, which they took totally unawares. Forty soldiers swam the moat, overpowered the guards and opened the gates. Sidney and his men guarded the market place while the others routed the garrison; the invaders suffered no loss of life at all, and only a single man was wounded. It was a notable, if not a decisive victory; while it did not save Neuss, it was the first really successful piece of aggression against Parma on his own ground, and it gave a great morale boost to the English. Thomas Cecil reported that 'the victory . . . happened in good time, for since the fall of Grave and Venloo your Lordship [Burghley] will not think with what faces they looked upon us. This hath made us somewhat to lift up our heads'.[75] And Leicester was overjoyed: 'This town of Axel is of very great importance; we shall have way to get at Antwerp and Bruges by it.'[76] It is by the success of Axel that Sidney should really be remembered as a soldier. It was here, rather than in the careless heroism of Zutphen, that he demonstrated his ability to plan and execute a military operation. It is significant that his great admirer Greville selected this instance to illustrate at their best the martial capabilities of his hero.[77]

For instance, how like a soldier did he behave himself, first in surprising, then in executing the surprise of Axel? where he revived that ancient and secure discipline of order and silence in their march, and after their entrance into the town placed a band of choice soldiers to make a stand in the market place for security to the rest that were forced to wander up and down by direction of commanders, and when the service was done rewarded that obedience of discipline in every one, liberally, out of his own purse.

Sidney's second major military effort of the campaign was not a spectacular success; it was in most ways a failure, though the care and caution of Sidney, who was rapidly developing into a capable field commander, prevented it from being a worse disaster. In terms of overall strategy, the English were much concerned with keeping the Spanish from having a free access to the sea. Reports reached the English of Spanish preparations for an assault on the coast; Italian carpenters were said to be at work in Antwerp churches building flat-bottomed boats, and Elizabeth herself felt impelled to write the States of Zealand warning them that an attack on Ostend and Sluys was in the offing. The securing of the town of Gravelines might have been a way of thwarting the Spanish plan, and it was with all this in mind that Sidney entered warily into a scheme, the soundness of which he appears to have doubted from the very beginning. Agents who came from

Gravelines reported that they were prepared to surrender the town to the English; Sidney had developed a distrust for such isolated adventures, and particularly since the overtures came from the enemy and the redoubtable veteran La Motte was in command of the town, he was inclined to view the proffered surrender as a trap. Under instructions, however, Sidney proceeded to the town and cast anchor before it on 16 July. The signals which had been prearranged were exchanged, but then, instead of the hostages which had been promised, Sidney was confronted with a servant of the Walloon captain who had proposed the surrender. The servant brought a letter offering explanations for the change in plan and still assured Sidney that Gravelines was his for the taking. A Captain Smith was sent to make a preliminary investigation and returned to report that all was well. Sidney remained suspicious and finally decided to send a small advance party ahead; the choice of leader for the party was made by a throw of dice on the drumhead. The leader was instructed by Sidney that if he discovered treachery on the Spanish part, he was straightway to throw down his arms and surrender; Sidney guaranteed to ransom him at once or to avenge his death severely should the Spanish break quarter. When the party reached the town, they discovered everything apparently in order, 'every street safe and quiet according to promise, till they were past any easy recovery of the gate'.[78] Then they were charged by both horse and foot. The leader, following Sidney's commands, threw down his arms and was taken prisoner. The rest of the company attempted to withdraw in the direction of the English ships but were cut off by the pursuit of the enemy. Although aided where possible by fire from Sidney's ships and displaying considerable heroism on their own part, some forty-four men were lost in the encounter, the rest 'bringing home even in the wounds, nay ruins of himself and company, reputation of courage and martial discipline'.[79] The best that can be said of the attempt on Gravelines is that Sidney had shown discretion in only risking a small number of men; his caution certainly saved the lives of many. As he confessed to Davison, all the rest was a sorry tale: 'the long practice of Gravelines which was brought unto us is proved a flat treason I think even in them that dealt with us'.[80]

Sidney returned from the Gravelines fiasco to his duties at Flushing. Though he longed to be active in the field, he was also very anxious about the security of his town. He was aware of discontent among the inhabitants, and once again money and supplies were short. He appealed in forceful terms to the Council in England for aid.[81]

I send this gentleman Mr Burnham humbly to give your Lordships to understand the weak store of all sort of necessary munition that both this town and the castle of Ramekins have. These States I have tried to the uttermost but partly with the opinion it more toucheth her Majesty because it is her pawn, but principally because they have ever present occasion to employ both all they have and indeed much more upon the places nearest to the enemy, we in this town and as I think Brill shall still demand and still go without. Therefore, I cannot but most humbly say it before your Lordships, by the grace of God my trust is in him that my life shall discharge me of blame, but I, nor all that can be here, can perform the service we owe to her Majesty without such merely necessary things. I will neither speak of the consequence of the place, nor of any quantity, your Lordships can better judge; I do only protest to your Honours that I think it very likely we shall have some occasion to use it, and till then it may be kept by some officer appointed by her Majesty, never one grain of it to be used for no service till it be for the last point of extremity. There is nothing will keep these people in better order then that they see we are strong. I beseech your Lordships to consider it according to the weight of the cause.

His other letters of this period show a similar concern; to Burghley he complained that 'the garrison is weak, the people by these cross fortunes crossly disposed,'[82] and in two letters to Walsingham[83] written on the same day, he expressed his dissatisfaction with the military tactics being employed in the Netherlands and noted that his soldiers' pay was once again seriously in arrears causing a genuine possibility of mutiny. 'I often craved the Treasurer might be commanded to pay this place; I assure you, Sir, this nigh we were at a fair plunge to have lost all for want of it. We are now four months behind, a thing unsupportable in this place. To complain of my Lord of Leicester, you know I may not, but this is the case: if once the soldiers fall to a thorough mutiny, this town is lost in all likelihood. I did never think our nation so apt to go to the enemy as I find them.'[84]

The enemy, meanwhile, under the command of Parma, had been far from idle. After reducing Neuss, Parma moved to lay siege to Berck. Leicester massed his forces near Arnhem to meet him, and then suddenly changed his mind, deciding they were not strong enough to take on Parma in the field. Instead, he began a series of diversionary assaults in an attempt to draw Parma away from the siege of Berck. The first assault was made on Doesburg, a weakly fortified town, and after heavy bombardment breaches were made in the walls and the spot successfully stormed. The only dark part of the encounter was the ruthless plundering of the town carried out against the express orders of Leicester. It was just one more demonstration of the almost total lack of discipline that prevailed in the English forces. Sidney played an honourable though relatively minor role in the attack.

The attempt to lure Parma away from Berck had, however, failed. He had decided to attempt the relief of Doesburg too late and had rapidly fallen back on Berck. Leicester and his forces now proceeded to Zutphen, about ten miles from Doesburg and a much more formidable target. Zutphen's defences straddled the River Yssel; on the east side of the river lay the town itself, while on the west bank were two strong forts which were reckoned to be impregnable. Two years earlier they had successfully withstood a ten-month siege by fourteen thousand men. Leicester decided to attack both town and forts and split his force on the two sides of the river, preserving communications by a string of boats. Norris established his forces in a churchyard on the town side and Sidney joined him there, while Leicester established his troops on the meadow side to concentrate on the forts.

Leicester and Sidney were almost at once called away from the scene in order to go to Deventer where there had been disturbances. Before they returned Parma had made a quick survey of the situation, had reinforced the garrison within Zutphen, and, having noted that the road to the town was still open, had resolved to rush a convoy of supplies into the garrison there. On Wednesday, 21 September, the English force completed their trenches around Zutphen. Late in the day a Spanish soldier was captured while trying to make his way into the besieged town, and under questioning he revealed Parma's plan of sending a convoy to Zutphen early the next morning. Norris was ordered to intercept it a mile and a half from the town; so haphazard was Leicester's scouting system that he grossly underestimated the probable size of the Spanish force and decided that three hundred horse and two hundred foot would be sufficient to deal with it. On the night before the battle Sidney penned a letter to Walsingham; though its contents are trivial, it is so much in keeping with Sidney's character that it is worth quoting at length.[85]

This bearer Richard Smyth, her Majesty's old servant, hath my Lord of Leicester his letters directed unto you, in his favour, for a suit to her Majesty, and therewithal requesteth mine, hoping your Honour will the rather help him. I beseech you, therefore, the rather at my request to help him, and be the good mean for the poor man's preferment, having so long served and now being aged and weak, hath such need of this or such other good mean for his relief, as without it he may rest, as I hear, in more misery than the desert of so long service requireth. I commend him and his cause to your Honour, good favour and help and so I humbly take my leave.

Even in the small hours before battle Sidney's thoughts were not of himself but of others. The act of kindness, undertaken when most would have been thinking ahead to the morning's encounter, in its quiet way indicates much of what it was in Sidney that drew to him the love and admiration of his comrades.

Shortly before sunrise Leicester, along with Sidney and some fifty others, crossed the river to Norris's side. A heavy mist shrouded the landscape making identifications difficult. When the Spanish were heard approaching through the mist the camp stood to arms, and as the fog suddenly lifted, the approaching convoy and the English attackers found themselves almost within firing distance. To the surprise of the English, the Spanish convoy was revealed to be no small force; 550 Englishmen found themselves facing a force of 3000 foot and 1500 horse in their fore, while behind them lay the garrison of Zutphen. Bravado and chivalric gesture appear to have been the response of the English camp. Norris and Sir William Stanley, long at enmity, made a formal reconciliation. Norris, overtaking Stanley, cried out: 'There hath been some words of displeasure between you and me, but let all pass, for this day we both are employed to serve her Majesty. Let us be friends, and let us die together in her Majesty's cause.' To which Stanley responded: 'If you see me not this day by God's grace serve my prince with a valiant and faithful courage, account me forever a coward, and if need be I will die by you in friendship'.[86] The most notable of the chivalric gestures belonged, however, to Sidney. 'Remembering that upon just grounds the ancient Sages describe the worthiest person to be ever best armed, he had completely put on his, but meeting the Marshall of the Camp lightly armed . . . the unspotted emulation of his heart, to venture without any inequality, made him cast off his cuisses, and so, by the secret influence of destiny,

to disarm that part where God (it seems) had resolved to strike him.'[87]
The 'battle' was little more than a prolonged skirmish.[88] The
Spaniards fired on the English forces which had been suddenly revealed
by the rising mist; before they could reload, the English cavalry
charged into their midst, driving the Spanish horse back on their own
supporting pikemen before being forced themselves to withdraw under
a hail of shot. The English re-formed and charged twice again with
the same result. For an hour and a half the fighting raged, characterised
by many acts of daring bravery. The young Earl of Essex shattered his
lance on the first Spaniard he met and yet rode on at the head of his
troop, hacking away with an axe. Sir William Stanley's horse was shot
eight times, but Stanley himself fought on. Sir William Russell
charged 'so terribly' that he was accounted by the enemy 'to be a devil
not a man'.[89] While the battle raged, the bulk of Leicester's forces
remained on the other side of the river; Leicester himself half thought
of bringing them into play but was overruled by his advisers, who
feared that Parma was lurking nearby with his full force. The convoy
slowly pushed ahead through the English, until it drew near enough
to the town gates for two thousand men to sally forth from Zutphen
to escort it home, and then the English withdrew.

And what of Sidney? He had battled with a courage equal to the rest.
On the second charge against the Spaniards he had his horse shot out
from underneath him, but he remounted and was soon again in the
thick of the battle. In the third charge he forced his way straight
through the Spanish ranks; turning to rejoin his men, he was struck
by a musket ball just above his unprotected knee and the leg bone
shattered in pieces. With difficulty he steered his animal back towards
his lines. A trooper came forward to help him manage the horse, but
Sidney waved him aside lest the Spanish enemy see that he was too
sorely wounded to ride. The last scene on the battlefield has been
recorded with memorable words by Greville.[90]

The horse he rode upon was rather furiously choleric than bravely proud
and so forced him to forsake the field, but not his back as the noblest and
fittest bier to carry a martial commander to his grave. In which sad progress,
passing along by the rest of the army where his uncle the general was and
being thirsty with excess of bleeding, he called for drink, which was presently
brought him, but as he was putting the bottle to his mouth, he saw a poor
soldier carried along who had eaten his last at the same feast, ghastly casting

up his eyes at the bottle. Which Sir Philip perceiving, took it from his head before he drank and delivered it to the poor man with these words, Thy necessity is yet greater than mine. And when he had pledged this poor soldier, he was presently carried to Arnhem.

It was the most famous scene in Sidney's whole life. Greville's account is the only authority for it, and he was not an eyewitness, but the magnanimity displayed by the wounded knight was so in keeping with his character and what the twentieth century would call his image that it would be rash to reject it outright as a fabrication.

The wound to Sidney cast a gloom over what the English had done. Five hundred and fifty men had bravely and stoutly tangled with a far superior force and had not been disgraced, but what was uppermost in the minds of all was that the most dashing and chivalric of the leaders was wounded. Russell, one of the heroes of the battle himself, burst into tears on meeting his wounded comrade. 'O noble Sir Philip, there was never man attained hurt more honourably than ye have done, nor any served like unto you.'[91]

Chapter 10

THE PASSING OF A HERO

He doth in bed of honour rest
And evermore of him shall live the best.
James VI & I

All things in my former life have been vain,
vain, vain.   Philip Sidney

The wound received by Philip Sidney indeed submerged whatever joy there was to be found in the outcome of the battle, and speculation as to his recovery dominated the discussions of the key figures in the following weeks. Sidney was taken from the scene of the battle to the town of Arnhem, about twenty miles away, and there lodged in the house of Mme Gruitthueissens in the hope that a recovery would be possible.[1] But the wound was a serious one, and the medical technique of the time was hardly sufficient to deal with damage of the extent involved. At first there was considerable fear that Sidney might die almost at once. On the day after the battle Leicester indicated his worry in a letter to Heneage. The wound was, he noted, 'the most grievous that ever I saw with such a bullet', and he commented: 'Albeit I must say it was too much loss for me, for this young man was my greatest comfort, next her Majesty, of all the world, and if I could buy his life with all I have to my shirt, I would give it. How God will dispose of him, I know not, but fear I must needs greatly the worst, the blow in so dangerous a place and so great.'[2] Although the news of the catastrophe was slow in reaching England, once there it produced a consternation and regret akin to that expressed by Leicester. Messages assured the Queen that 'there is no danger or doubt of his leg, much less of his life', but the news of the wound did 'appear much to trouble her'.[3]

In the two weeks that followed the battle the hopes of those close to Sidney were raised by his apparent recovery. The hopeful feelings are revealed clearly in Leicester's letters. In September, shortly after the battle, he wrote to Burghley: 'He is of good comfort, and the surgeons are in good hope of his life if no ill accident come. As yet there is not: he slept this last night four hours together and did eat with good appetite afterward. I pray God save his life, and I care not how lame he be.'[4] Slightly later Leicester wrote that he had received letters from the surgeons that they had high hopes for Sidney: 'They find his wound as well and with all the good signs they could wish. I thank God for it and will hope the best.'[5] At the beginning of October he wrote to Walsingham: 'I trust now that you will have further enjoying of your son, for all the worst days be past, as both surgeons and physicians have informed me, and he amends as well as is possible in this time.'[6]

Sidney had borne his wound and subsequent suffering with great equanimity. After receiving the blow he had been brought back to a tent where he is reported to have lifted his eyes to heaven, not imputing the wound to chance but affirming instead that God had sent the bullet and had intended it to strike him. He returned thanks to God 'that he did not strike him to death at once, but gave him space to seek repentance and reconciliation'.[7] And to the doctors who attended him— 'some mercenarily out of gain, others out of honour to their art, but the most of them with a true zeal . . . to do him good and . . . many nations in him'[8]—Sidney expressed a desire that 'while his strength was yet entire, his body free from fever, and his mind able to endure, they might freely use their art, cut, and search to the bottom'.[9] Beneath the calmness and fortitude with which he endured the barbarous medical practices of the time, Sidney, almost alone among those about him, began to realise that he was approaching death. The doctors radiated hope for his recovery, and their enthusiasm was mirrored in the comments of Leicester, Burghley, Walsingham, and the Queen. Only one of the doctors knew better, 'one owl among all the birds which, looking with no less zealous eyes than the rest, yet saw and presaged much despair'.[10] This doctor was the surgeon of Count Hohenlo, and even though the Count himself at the very moment lay wounded by a musket shot in his neck, he had sent the surgeon to attend Sidney. On returning to dress his master's wound, the surgeon was asked how Sidney fared, and he answered 'with a heavy countenance' that Sidney was in serious condition. 'At these words the worthy Prince (as having more sense of his friend's wound than his own) cries out, "Away villain, never see my face again till thou bring better news of that man's recovery, for whose redemption many such as I were happily lost".'[11]

Philip himself became increasingly aware that he had received a mortal wound. On the eighth day after Zutphen he made his will, a document which Greville felt would ever remain 'a witness to the world that those sweet and large, even dying affections in him could no more be contracted with the narrowness of pain, grief, or sickness than any sparkle of our immortality can be privately buried in the shadow of death'.[12] The details of the will need not be entered into here, although one should note the care with which Sidney remembered his lesser companions as well as the great names of his family. To Dr James 'for his Pains taken with me in this my Hurt'[13] £30 was left, and to the five surgeons in attendance £20. Servants and yeomen were remembered, many by name, and to Lady Sidney was directed the admonition: 'I pray mine Executrix to be good, and to give so much money, as to her Discretion shall seem good, to those mine old Servants, to whom by Name particularly I have given nothing to; referring it to her as she shall think good.'[14]

On the same day in which he made his will Sidney summoned preachers to him 'who were all excellent men of divers nations' and in their presence 'made such a confession of Christian faith as no book but the heart can truly and feelingly deliver'.[15] Following this, he asked them to accompany him in prayer, although in this 'he besought leave to lead the assembly, in respect (as he said) that the secret sins of his own heart were best known to himself'.[16] After prayer he discussed with the assembled divines the question of the immortality of the soul.[17]

He entreated this choir of divine philosophers about him to deliver the opinion of the ancient heathen touching the immortality of the soul; first, to see what true knowledge she retains of her own essence out of the light of herself; then to parallel with it the most pregnant authorities of the Old and New Testament as supernatural revelations, sealed up from our flesh for the divine light of faith to reveal and work by. Not that he wanted instruction or assurance, but because this fixing of a lover's thoughts upon those eternal beauties was not only a cheering up of his decaying spirits, but as it were a taking possession of that immortal inheritance which was given unto him by his brotherhood in Christ.

Among the preachers called to Sidney at this time was George Giffard, and he composed a detailed, though heavily emotional, account of Sidney's last days.[18] Through its pages we can follow the thoughts and concerns of Sidney in his final weeks of life. To Giffard, Sidney confessed 'fear and astonishment in his mind' at the present spectacle of death, but Giffard was able to comfort him on this point by demonstration out of doctrine and scripture that the greatest servants of God were moved in similar fashion in their grievous afflictions.[19] After much serious conversation on this point, 'with great cheerfulness he did often lift up his eyes and hands, giving thanks to God that he did chastise him with a loving and fatherly coercion, and to his singular profit, whether the soul live or die'.[20] To Giffard, too, Sidney often in these days spoke with a firm resolution that if he were to live he would lead his life in a reformed manner, for till now, he thought, 'he had walked in a vague course'. 'These words he spake with great vehemence both of speech and gesture, and doubled it, to the intent that it might be manifest how unfeignedly he meant to turn more thoughts unto God than ever before.'[21] In keeping with thoughts of this kind, he requested from Giffard some godly book, 'which might, as he said, increase mortification and confirm his mind',[22] and he complained on more than one occasion that he found his mind 'dull in prayer'.[23] At other times he conversed with Giffard on related subjects; he spoke of the wretchedness of man—'a poor worm'—of the mercies of God, of the dispensation of providence, and all this he did, according to Giffard, 'with vehement gestures and great joy, even ravished with the consideration of God's omnipotence, providence, and goodness'.[24] As Sidney grew weaker in body he confided to Giffard that he had no fear of death, but only a fear that the pains of death would be such that he would lose his understanding. 'I have vowed my life unto God', he told Giffard, 'and if the Lord cut me off and suffer me to live no longer, then I shall glorify him and give up myself to his service.'[25]

Sidney was offering to those who hovered about him a model in the way of death. Not all that he did partook of the seriousness of his conversation with the divines on the immortality of the soul nor of his discussions with Giffard on the nature of God's mysteries. Comments of those about him remark on his cheerfulness; as Leicester reported to Walsingham in October, 'he feeleth no grief now but his long lying'.[26] He is known to have called for music shortly before his death, 'especially that song which himself had entitled *La Cuisse rompue*',[27] and this has given rise to the story that it was a poem which he had composed and that 'there he most sweetly sung the prophecy/Of his own death in doleful elegy'.[28] The story is part of the legend of Sidney, not part of the fact. He did, however, at this time compose a long letter to the translator of Philo, Bellier, and later, when a copy was shown to Elizabeth, it was praised 'for the excellence of the phrase and fittingness of the matter'.[29]

By the sixteenth day Sidney was well aware that his wound was fatal; by then his shoulder bones had worn through his skin 'with constant and obedient posturing of his body to [the doctors'] art'. And Philip, 'judiciously observing the pangs his wound stang him with by fits, together with many other symptoms of decay, few or none of recovery,' began, as Greville continues, 'rather to submit his body to these artists than any farther to believe in them'.[30] It was at this point that Sidney 'one morning lifting up the clothes for change and ease of his body smelt some extraordinary noisome savour about him, differing from oils and salves as he conceived, and either out of natural delicacy or at least care not to offend others, grew a little troubled with it; which they that sat by perceiving besought him to let them know what sudden indisposition he felt? Sir Philip ingenuously told it and desired them as ingenuously to confess whether they felt any such noisome thing or no? They all protested against it upon their credits. Whence Sir Philip presently gave this severe doom upon himself, that it was inward mortification and a welcome messenger of death.'[31] The doctors in attendance still refused to believe, or at least pretended not to do so; they 'opposed by authority of books, paralleling of accidents, and other artificial probabilities' the conclusion already reached by one 'who judged too truly of his own estate and from more certain grounds'.[32]

On the night of 16 October Sidney wrote his last letter, a short and pleading note to John Weier, a noted physician, begging him to come to his side. 'My dear friend Weier, come, come. I am in peril of my life and long for you. Neither living nor dead shall I be ungrateful. I cannot write more, but beg you urgently to hurry. Farewell, your Philip Sidney.'[33] The letter itself was given to a nephew of Weier's, Gisbert Enerwitz, to be delivered, and Enerwitz wrote urging his uncle to come. 'In the course of the last three days the good gentleman has been attacked by fever and is become on that account a little weaker. He [the General] has therefore urgently besought me, as have also the other gentlemen, that I would write to you, my uncle, and make it my own request that you would be pleased to visit him in his illness, and thereby impart to him all that consolation which you have been wont to afford, and which may prove serviceable to him in his weak state.'[34] Whether the appeal to Weier indicated some revival of hope on Sidney's part that he might recover is not provable, but if it were so, the hope was shown to be false within a day. The following day Sidney took farewell of his brother, 'the weaker showing infinite strength in suppressing sorrow, and the stronger infinite weakness in expressing it'.[35] While Sidney faced death with a stern fortitude, his brother Robert displayed 'an abundance of childish tears'. To spare the feelings of both, Sidney spoke directly to his brother. 'Love my memory, cherish my friends; their faith to me may assure you they are honest. But above all, govern your will and affection by the will and word of your creator, in me beholding the end of this world with all her vanities',[36] and so saying, he asked the gentlemen about him to lead Robert away.

At this time, too, he had another long conversation with Giffard. He had not slept, he had been deeply troubled in his mind, but to him, as before, Giffard brought spiritual solace. Several hours later it was apparent that death was approaching, and Giffard urged him to prepare for it. He faced it, as he had faced the three long, painful weeks, with a serenity. Assured by Giffard that his faith would not fail him, 'he did with a cheerful and smiling countenance put forth his hand and slapped me softly on the cheeks. Not long after, he lifted up his eyes and hands, uttering these words, "I would not change my joy for the empire of the world", for the nearer he saw death approach, the more his comfort seemed to increase.'[37] In these last hours only one regret seems to have escaped his lips; he cried out once that life would indeed be welcome to him for the sake of begetting a son and assisting the commonwealth. As his speech failed, he made signs with his hands that he still wished to be spoken to, and Giffard was at his side to the end: 'even as one that runneth a race, when he approacheth unto the end, doth strain himself most vehemently, he would have the help that might be to carry him forward, now in the very end of his race, to the goal'.[38] At the last he required Giffard to lift up his hands to God, since he could neither speak nor open his eyes. Showing his friends that his heart still prayed, he raised both his hands and set them together on his chest; about two o'clock in the afternoon he died.

The death of the young Protestant hero left Europe, both Protestant and Catholic, stunned. It was a measure of the impact of Sidney on his world that the loss was felt so keenly both by his friends and his enemies. It is also an indication of the extent to which the Sidney myth had been created in his own lifetime. He was already before he died the Protestant knight in gleaming armour, the hero of those who sought the victory of what they considered the true religion over the political machinations of individual states; he was already Philisides, the shepherd knight. The expressions of sorrow that came from his Protestant associates are to be expected, yet they are eloquent in their very intensity. The Master of Gray saw in Sidney's passing not only the loss of a friend but the destruction of any reasons for going to the Netherlands as well.[39]

I must regret with you [Archibald Douglas] my hard fortune in the loss of my dear friend and brother Sir Philip Sidney, the most sorrowful death that ever I heard of in my time; for besides a friend whom I loved well, I lose all my expectation together with the great charge that I have borne, only for desire to have his company which I craved indeed by all means possible. And now I must confess the truth that he and I had that friendship, that moved me to desire so much my voyage to the Low Countries. But now, I mind not to go, although I might have great advancement by it and greater than ever I did see by it. Therefore, now, since it has pleased God to call on that man, I content myself to live at home. But it is not unknown to you how far that matter has run me under seas.

Fulke Greville, needless to say, was shattered by the death of his lifelong friend; he, also writing to Archibald Douglas, stated, 'My Lord, I go no whither, therefore I beseech you pardon me that I visit you not. The only question I now study is whether weeping sorrow or speaking sorrow may most honour his memory, that I think death is sorry for. What he was to God, his friends and country, fame hath told, though his expectation went beyond her good. My Lord, give me leave to join with you in praising and lamenting him, the name of whose friendship carried me above my own worth and I fear hath left me to play the ill poet in my own part.'[40] Lord Buckhurst, writing to Leicester, indicated that grief was nation-wide, not just a mourning for personal loss. By Sidney's death, he stated, 'not only your Lordship and all other his friends and kinsfolk, but even her Majesty and the whole realm besides do suffer no small loss and detriment . . . he hath both lived and died in fame of honour and reputation to his name, in the worthy service of his prince and country, and with as great love in his life and with as many tears for his death as ever any had'.[41] Buckhurst's statement that mourning was not confined to intimates of Sidney but was widespread receives confirmation in other sources; one comments: 'It was accounted a sin for any gentleman of quality for many months after to appear at Court or City in any light or gaudy apparel.'[42]

Abroad, the reaction was much the same. Du Plessis Mornay wrote to Walsingham expressing his grief, and Ortel, the Dutch envoy in London, did the same.[43] Louise de Coligny, writing to Leicester, compared the loss of Sidney to that of a brother.[44] Jean Hotman wrote in a similar vein to Lipsius.[45] Dominicus Baudius, a Dutch poet, referred to Sidney's death as the carrying off of a 'light of intellect, breeding, and nobility'.[46] Even Mendoza, devoted servant of Spain and Catholicism, was reported to have commented sorrowfully on the loss: 'he could not but lament to see Christendom deprived of so rare a light in these cloudy times, and bewail poor widow England (so he termed her) that, having been many years in breeding one eminent spirit, was in a moment bereaved of him by the hands of a villain'.[47] And we have noticed Philip II writing across the Spanish despatch announcing Sidney's death the brief but revealing comment, 'He was my godson.'[48]

The body of Sidney was, a week after his death, taken from Arnhem by water to Flushing, where it lay in state for eight days. The town government of Flushing, too, wrote to Walsingham expressing their sympathy, and the States of Zealand made formal application to Leicester for permission to bury Sidney at their own expense and to erect a costly monument to the memory of the Englishman who had died in fighting their battles. This was not to be; on 1 November Sidney's body was 'brought from his house in Flushing to the sea-side by the English garrison, which were 1200 marching three by three, the shot hanging down their pieces, the halberts, pikes, and ensigns trailing along the ground, drums and fifes playing very softly; the body was covered with a pall of velvet: the burghers of the town followed mourning, and so soon as he was imbarked, the several shot gave him a triple volley, then all the great ordnance about the walls were discharged twice, and so took their leave of their well beloved governor'.[49] From Flushing, Sidney's body was conveyed in his own pinnace back to England, the ship itself fully decked in mourning, its sails, tackling, and other equipment all coloured black, and black cloths covering her sides, on them escutcheons of Sidney's arms. The black pinnace docked at Tower Hill, London, on the fifth; from there Sidney's body was conveyed to the Minories and later to his final resting place.

Not all would cherish the memory of England's shepherd knight with equal affection. The Queen lamented publicly, but it is apparent that she had never totally trusted nor understood one of her finest servants. Not that she ever suspected him of disloyalty; even in his outspoken criticism of the French marriage his intense loyalty to England and his Queen had been most marked. But his policy ran counter to her inclinations, and his growing popularity at home and abroad had done little to bring support for her crafty dealings. Perhaps in one sense she was correct: Sidney was not, despite the faith of Languet, picked out for the subtle world of diplomacy. He was too open, too committed, to indulge successfully in either the seamy or the simply decorative side of diplomacy. And when the Queen later complained about Sidney's death, that he had wasted the life of a gentleman with a common soldier's fate, she indicated only too clearly the gap between her conception of England's duty and that held by Sir Philip.[50] Others, however, saw the appropriateness of his death. Arthur Golding, who completed Sidney's translation of Mornay, expressed this as well as anyone.[51]

He died not languishing in idlenesse, riot, and excess nor as overcome with nice pleasures and fond vanities, but of manly wounds received in service of his Prince, in defence of persons oppressed, in maintenance of the only true Catholic and Christian religion, among the noble, valiant, and wise, in the open field, in martial manner, the honourablest death that could be desired and best beseeming a Christian knight, whereby he hath worthily won to himself immortal fame among the godly and left example worthy of imitation to others of his calling.

It was not just his political and religious role that was remembered. While his fame as a writer was only to gain wide currency in the decade after his death, many looked back on him as a great patron of learning and literature. It was true, as Greville alleged, that Sidney was accounted 'a general Maecenas of learning', and Nashe was to give this feeling a more extended expression when he wrote:[52]

Gentle Sir Philip Sidney! thou knewest what belonged to a scholar, thou knewest what pains, what toils, what travail conduct to perfection. Well couldst thou give every virtue his encouragement, every wit his due, every writer his desert, 'cause none more virtuous, witty or learned than myself. But thou art dead in thy grave, and hast left too few successors of thy glory, too few to cherish the sons of the muses, or water with their plenty those budding hopes which thy bounty erst planted.

Little did it matter that Sidney's self-picked heir as Protestant hero-knight, the Earl of Essex, was to prove to be otherwise in the long run. Sidney's reputation itself remained intact, indeed grew and magnified. Few have been the dissenters from this view since. Over and over again biographers at the end of their task have confessed that the seeming perfection of Philisides is the reality of Philip Sidney. The charm seems almost unbelievable, but on occasion after occasion they have found that they really agree with Hotman's fine tribute to his friend: 'I have noted one thing above all others in his life, that although he had in him the highest virtues he was untouched by any man's envy or detraction, so that he might deservedly be called the darling of the human race'.[53]

It is to this same decision that we have come in the end. There is fact as well as fancy in the picture of the shepherd knight. Not everything in Sidney's character was admirable; he could display flashes of violent temper, his ideas on foreign policy were not all-wise and ignored the hard financial realities his sovereign knew too well, he could display the social disdain for the lower classes which was characteristic of his aristocratic background. He may not have been wholly a handsome, dashing figure, but he was not, as one modern critic has suggested, 'an immoral savage'.[54] That, in a democratic world, we no longer defer automatically to the aristocracy is not cause in itself for repudiating what there was of virtue and heroic quality among their ranks in former times. True that many of Sidney's social views would make him in our own world a despicable rather than an admirable character, but to point this out is as meaningless as it is silly. To the world of

Elizabethan England there was both virtue and heroism in the manner of Sidney's life and death. Elizabeth's England, small and weak on the edges of European power, needed a hero-figure, and in Sidney it found what it needed. The very futility of his career—a great but never realised promise in the affairs of men—has taken its part in the survival of the myth. As one writer notes, 'wasted youth had made the end romantic, while the cause made it heroic, and religious endurance virtuous'.[55] Sidney, represented as embodying all the virtues of the Christian knight, was to become for his nation the myth figure similar to that William of Orange was for the nation in whose service Sidney died. There is more than a measure of justice in this. Sidney was not a typical Elizabethan, though in the outward events of his life there is little that sets him apart from his fellow-men. It was in his inward qualities, his dreams, and the myths that were built around them that he became unique. It has been truly said that the man was greater than the achievement;[56] it might be added that the myth was somewhat greater than both. The very intensity of his vision had set him apart from other men, and the glorification of that vision has widened the gap yet more. 'He only like himself, was second unto none.'[57]

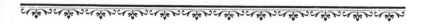

References

BM	British Museum
Bod.	Bodleian Library
ELH	*English Literary History*
HLQ	*Huntington Library Quarterly*
HMC	*Reports*, Historical Manuscripts Commission
JEGP	*Journal of English and Germanic Philology*
JWCI	*Journal of the Warburg and Courtauld Institutes*
MLN	*Modern Language Notes*
MLQ	*Modern Language Quarterly*
MLR	*Modern Language Review*
Mod. Phil.	*Modern Philology*
Phil. Q.	*Philological Quarterly*
PMLA	*Publications of the Modern Language Association*
RES	*Review of English Studies*
Sidney, *Works*	A. Feuillerat, ed., *The Prose Works of Sir Philip Sidney* (Cambridge, 1963), 4 vols.
SP	*Studies in Philology*
TRHS	*Transactions of the Royal Historical Society*

REFERENCES

PROLOGUE

1. T. Lant, *Funeral of Sir Philip Sidney* (London, 1587), plate 30.

2. ibid.

3. The account which follows is based on Lant and on Bod. MS. Ashmole 818.9, fols. 40–41. See also the notes by W. G. Benham, M. H. Dodds, and B. H. Newdigate on 'Mourners at Sir Philip Sidney's Funeral', *Notes and Queries*, vol. 180 (1941), pp. 444–5, 464; vol. 181 (1941), pp. 398–401.

4. For a list of such verses see B. Siebeck, *Das Bild Sir Philip Sidneys in der Englischen Renaissance* (Weimar, 1939), pp. 184 ff. This should be supplemented by the material discussed in J. A. Van Dorsten, *Poets, Patrons and Professors* (Leiden and London, 1962), chap. 5.

5. L. Brysket, *The Mourning Muse of Thestylis*, in E. Spenser, *Poetical Works*, ed. F. J. Child (Boston, 1881), 3: 549.

6. An Epitaph upon Sir Philip Sidney, printed ibid., 3: 577.

7. Van Dorsten, *Poets, Patrons and Professors*, pp. 157–9, 189–91; J. A. Van Dorsten, 'Gruterus and Sidney's *Arcadia*', *RES*, NS 16 (1965), pp. 174–7.

8. Sidney, *Works*, 1: 284–5.

9. Spenser, *Ruins of Time*, in *Works*, 3: 35; L. Bryskett, *A Pastoral Aeglogue*, ibid., 3: 562. cf. F. A. Yates, 'Elizabethan Chivalry: The Romance of the Accession Day Tilts', *JWCI*, vol. 20 (1957), p. 5.

10. D. Coulman, 'Spotted to be Known', *JWCI*, vol. 20 (1957), pp. 179–80.

11. The identification of Sidney as Astrophel and Penelope Rich as Stella is discussed in Chapter 7.

12. Sidney, *Works*, 1: 283. On the Accession Day celebrations see also R. C. Strong, 'The Popular Celebration of the Accession Day of Queen Elizabeth I', *JWCI*, vol. 21 (1958), pp. 86–103.

13. Ditchley MSS. (BM Add. MSS. 41499 A), fol. 7v, printed in Sir E. K. Chambers, *Sir Henry Lee, An Elizabethan Portrait* (Oxford, 1936), p. 272.

14. ibid., p. 268.

15. As for example at the Accession Day Tilt, 1587. See Yates, 'Elizabethan Chivalry', p. 18.

16. Sidney, *Works*, 3: 316.

17. G. Peele, *Polyhymnia* in *Works*, ed. A. H. Bullen (London, 1888), 2: 292.

18. She was specifically represented as an imperial Vestal Virgin in the Accession Day Tilt of 1590. Yates, 'Elizabethan Chivalry', p. 23. See also F. A. Yates, 'Queen Elizabeth as Astrea', *JWCI*, vol. 10 (1947), pp. 27–82.

19. Spenser, *The Shepheardes Calender* in *Works*, 3: 377.

20. A. Collins, *Letters and Memorials of State* (London, 1746), 1: 246.

21. Sir F. Greville, *The Life of the Renowned Sir Philip Sidney*, ed., N. Smith (Oxford, 1907), p. 3.

PART ONE

INTRODUCTION

1. On the significance of the term *empire* see G. R. Elton, *England under the Tudors* (London, 1955), pp. 160–2; G. R. Elton, 'The Political Creed of Thomas Cromwell', *TRHS*, 5th S., vol. 6 (1956), esp. pp. 86–7; G. R. Elton, 'King or Minister: The Man Behind the Henrician Reformation', *History*, NS vol. 39 (1954), esp. pp. 229, 231; G. R. Elton, 'The Tudor Revolution: A Reply', *Past and Present*, no 29 (1964), esp. pp. 28–36. Elton's views are criticised by G. L. Harriss, 'Medieval Government and Statecraft', *Past and Present*, no. 25 (1963), esp. pp. 9–12.

2. For an excellent discussion of the evolution of English foreign relations in this period, see R. B. Wernham, *Before the Armada: The Growth of English Foreign Policy 1485–1588* (London, 1966), esp. pp. 179–92.

3. Sidney, *Works*, 3: 65–6.

4. His birth was recorded in the family Psalter by Sir Henry Sidney. M. W. Wallace, *The Life of Sir Philip Sidney* (Cambridge, 1915), p. 1.

5. On Dudley see D. M. Brodie, 'Edmund Dudley,' *TRHS*, 4th S., vol. 15 (1932), pp. 133–61; G. R. Elton, 'Henry VII: Rapacity and Remorse', *Historical Journal*, 1958, and the subsequent reply by J. Cooper and restatement by Elton, ibid., 1959, 1961.

6. There is no adequate biography of Northumberland. P. Lindsay, *The Queenmaker: A Portrait of John Dudley* (London, 1951) does not fill the gap.

7. See F. Rose-Troupe, *The Western Rebellion of 1549* (London, 1913); N. Pocock, ed., *Troubles Connected with the Prayer Book of 1549* (Westminster, 1885), Camden Society, NS vol. 37; A. L. Rowse, *Tudor Cornwall* (London, 1941); A. G. Dickens, 'Some Popular Reactions to the Edwardian Reformation in Yorkshire', *Yorks Archaeological Journal*, vol. 34 (1939), pp. 151–69.

8. The following discussion of the faked pedigree is based on the introduction by C. L. Kingsford to *HMC Penshurst*, 1: vi–ix.

9. *HMC Penshurst*, 1: 409.

10. See M. Wilson, *Sir Philip Sidney* (London, 1931), p. 18.

11. On her see H. Clifford, *The Life of Jane Dormer Duchess of Feria* (London, 1887).

12. Greville, *Life*, pp. 32–3.

13. *Cal. S. P. Spanish 1580–1586*, p. 650 n.

14. The point is made in A. H. Bill, *Astrophel or the Life and Death of the Renowned Sir Philip Sidney* (London, 1938), p. 18.

15. Sir Henry Sidney to Walsingham, quoted Wilson, *Sidney*, p. 24.

16. An appreciation of the religious difficulties can be gained from a study of the drafting of the actual settlement, brilliantly analysed in Sir J. Neale, *Elizabeth I and Her Parliaments 1559–1581* (London, 1953), pp. 51–84.

17. On Sidney's contact with Languet, see below Chapter 5 and J. A. Van Dorsten, 'Sidney and Languet', *HLQ*, vol. 29 (1966), pp. 215–22.

CHAPTER I

1. J. Buxton, *Sir Philip Sidney and the English Renaissance* (London, 1954), p. 79.

2. Sidney, *Works*, 3: 103.

3. *Huberti Langueti Epistolae Ad Philippum Sydneium* (Edinburgh, 1776), p. 104. Hereafter cited as *Epistolae*.

4. BM Cotton MSS. Titus B II, fol. 304, printed Wallace, *Sidney*, p. 151.

5. ibid., p. 149. It is little wonder it seemed a thankless charge. The expenses incurred by Sir Henry were ruinous. In 1566 he mentioned in a letter to Cecil that he was likely to come home a beggar. Collins, *Letters and Memorials of State*, 1: 10. Three years later he told Cecil, 'I am forced to borrow, yea almost to beg for my dinner.' ibid., 1: 43.

6. S. A. Pears, ed., *The Correspondence of Sir Philip Sidney and Hubert Languet* (London, 1845), p. 97. cf. also his comment in an earlier letter that 'a court is by no means a frugal economist of time'. ibid., p. 95.

7. For accounts see J. Nichols, *The Progresses and Public Processions of Queen Elizabeth* (London, 1823), 1: 426–523.

8. ibid., 1: 492.

9. Warton, *History of English Poetry*, quoted ibid., 2: 123 n. 3.

10. ibid., 1: 497.

11. *Epistolae*, p. 139.

12. Pears, *Sidney–Languet Correspondence*, p. 102.

13. On the Queen's policy see R. B. Wernham, 'English Policy and the Revolt of the Netherlands', in J. S. Bromley and E. H. Kossmann, *Britain and the Netherlands* (London, 1960), pp. 29–40.

14. *Somers Tracts*, ed. W. Scott (London, 1809), 1: 169 quoted ibid., p. 29.

15. ibid., pp. 30–1.

16. Essex referred to Sidney as his son by adoption. Wallace, *Sidney*, p. 165.

17. ibid., p. 166.

18. Whetstone, *Sidney*, cited ibid., p. 168.

19. The suggestion is made by Wallace, *Sidney*, p. 168.

20. Sir Henry Sidney to Walsingham, quoted ibid., p. 168.

21. Collins, *Letters and Memorials of State*, 1: 147.

22. ibid.

23. See D. E. Baughan, 'Sir Philip Sidney and the Matchmakers'. *MLR*, vol. 33 (1938), pp. 512–13. On this occasion the matchmakers were dubious about the advantages; Sir Henry was openly cordial to Essex but privately considered him an enemy. Collins, *Letters and Memorials of State*, 1: 88.

24. *Epistolae*, p. 160.

25. Collins, *Letters and Memorials of State*, 1: 89.

26. ibid., 1: 163–4.

27. BM Harl. MSS., vol. xxxvi, p. 295.

28. BM Cotton MSS. Galba B xi, fol. 412.

29. The inscription is printed in Collins, *Letters and Memorials of State*, 1: 100. E. M. Tenison, *Elizabethan England* (Leamington, 1933–61), 3: 71 notes that it was customary for a diplomat, envoy, or anyone connected with the court to denote his whereabouts by a coat of arms hung over his lodgings. Wallace, *Sidney*, p. 174 n. 4 points out that Sir Henry Wotton used to set up a similar tablet whenever he travelled on the continent.

30. Greville, *Life*, p. 32; see also *Cal. S. P. For. 1575–1577*, pp. 541, 543.

31. Sidney, *Works*, 3: 105–8.

32. Greville, *Life*, pp. 41–2.

33. Sidney, *Works*, 3: 106.

34. ibid., 3: 107. On Casimir's and the Landgrave's interest in the proposed league cf. *Cal. S. P. For. 1575–1577*, pp. 575, 580, 599–600.

35. Notably H. R. Fox Bourne, *Sir Philip Sidney* (New York and London, 1893), p. 120 and S. Lee, *Great Englishmen of the Sixteenth Century* (London, 1907), p. 117.

36. Sidney, *Works*, 3: 109.

37. ibid., 3: 110.

38. ibid., 3: 111.

39. ibid.

40. ibid.

41. Greville, *Life*, pp. 42–4.

42. ibid., p. 42.

43. ibid., pp. 42–3.

44. Wallace, *Sidney*, pp. 177–8.

45. C. H. Warren, *Sir Philip Sidney, A Study in Conflict* (London, n.d.), pp. 78–81.

46. R. Simpson, *Edmund Campion A Biography* (London, 1867), p. 87.

47. Wallace, *Sidney*, p. 178.

48. Sidney, *Works*, 3: 113.

49. ibid., 3: 114.

50. S. P. For., Elizabeth, 20 May 1577 cited Wallace, *Sidney*, p. 180.

51. Pears, *Sidney-Languet Correspondence*, p. 107.

52. Languet reported that a letter reached Sidney in Brussels asking him to go to Orange and attend the baptism of his daughter in her name. *Huberti Langueti ad Camerarium Epistolae* (Groningen, 1646), pp. 234–5. Actually Sidney was to stand godfather on behalf of Leicester. See Van Dorsten, *Poets, Patrons and Professors*, pp. 51–2.

53. Greville, *Life*, pp. 35–6.

54. ibid., pp. 26–7; on Sidney undertaking a diplomatic mission for Orange see *Cal. S. P. For. 1575–1577*, pp. 587, 598.

55. Collins, *Letters and Memorials of State*, 1: 193. cf. also the letter of Edward Waterhouse to Sir Henry, ibid., 1: 193–4, which is very similar in tone.

56. A Gentili, *De Legationibus Libri Tres*, trans G. J. Laing (New York, 1924), p. 111.

57. ibid., p. 201.

58. *Cal. S. P. Span. 1568–1579*, pp. 575–6.

59. Pears, *Sidney–Languet Correspondence*, p. 102.

60. ibid.

61. Wilson, *Sidney*, p. 80.

62. Pears, *Sidney–Languet Correspondence*, p. 108.

63. *Epistolae*, p. 164.

64. ibid.

65. ibid., p. 169.

66. ibid., p. 171.

67. ibid.

68. Pears, *Sidney–Languet Correspondence*, p. 133.

69. ibid., p. 143.

70. ibid., p. 144.

71. ibid., p. 146.

72. ibid., p. 134.

CHAPTER 2

1. Wallace, *Sidney*, p. 191.

2. ibid.

3. Collins, *Letters and Memorials of State*, 1: 227.

4. ibid., 1: 228.

5. Sidney, *Works*, 3: 46.

6. Sidney did have a reputation of concern for the poor. cf. the comment of John Phillips, 'to the poor he was merciful'. S. Lichfield, ed., *Sidneiana* (London, 1837), p. 19.

7. Sidney, *Works*, 3: 49–50.

8. ibid., 3: 50.

9. ibid.

10. Wallace, *Sidney*, p. 193.

11. Sir Henry Sidney to Walsingham, quoted ibid., p. 193.

12. *Cal. S. P. Colonial East Indies 1513–1616*, p. 11.

13. Pears, *Sidney–Languet Correspondence*, pp. 118–20.

14. ibid., p. 120.

15. ibid., p. 124.

16. ibid.

17. ibid., p. 126.

18. *Cal. S. P. Colonial East Indies 1513–1616*, p. 55.

19. Pears, *Sidney–Languet Correspondence*, p. 127.

20. Sidney, *Works*, 3: 119. It is possible that the letter is not to Leicester. The address is torn off and the recipient might have been the Earl of Sussex who had married Sir Henry Sidney's sister. ibid., 3: 336.

21. *Mémoires et Correspondance de Duplessis-Mornay* (Paris, 1824), 1: 117.

22. Pears, *Sidney–Languet Correspondence*, p. 131.

23. Wallace, *Sidney*, p. 198 n. 4.

24. ibid., p. 198.

25. *Cal. S. P. Span. 1568–1579*, p. 595.

26. ibid.

27. Sir H. Nicholas, *Memoirs of the Life and Times of Sir Christopher Hatton* (London, 1847), p. 69. cf. the comments of Casimir in letters to D. Rogers and Sidney strongly requesting Philip's presence in the Netherlands. *Cal. S. P. For. 1577–1578*, pp. 638, 731.

28. *Cal. S. P. For. 1578–1579*, p. 122.

29. ibid.

30. BM Cotton MSS. Titus B xiii, fol. 257, quoted Wallace, *Sidney*, p. 200. For Sir Henry's comments to Philip on this see Collins, *Letters and Memorials of State*, 1: 392.

31. Sidney, *Works*, 3: 124.

32. Collins, *Letters and Memorials of State*, 1: 256.

33. cf. ibid., 1: 293–4 where Molyneux refers to Sidney's 'loving favour'.

34. cf. *Epistolae*, pp. 213–14.

35. Nichols, *Progresses*, 2: 277.

36. Wallace, *Sidney*, p. 205.

37. W. A. Ringler, ed., *The Poems of Sir Philip Sidney* (Oxford, 1962), pp. 260–1.

38. Pears, *Sidney–Languet Correspondence*, p. 157.

39. ibid.

40. Collins, *Letters and Memorials of State*, 1: 285.

41. Sidney, *Works*, 3: 133.

42. Collins, *Letters and Memorials of State*, 1: 285.

43. Pears, *Sidney–Languet Correspondence*, p. 159. In a letter of 4 June 1580 Languet urged Hubner to assist Robert in learning to speak German. ibid.

44. ibid., p. 161. Languet noted slightly later that Robert did not know any languages well enough to converse easily with foreigners and that he tended to avoid their company. ibid., p. 164.

45. ibid., p. 167.

46. C. Read, *Mr Secretary Walsingham and the Policy of Queen Elizabeth* (Oxford, 1925), 2: 3.

47. ibid.

48. Nicholas, *Memoirs of Hatton*, p. 94.

49. *Cal. S. P. For. 1578–1579*, pp. 185, 195.

50. W. Camden, *Annals* (London, 1635), p. 200.

51. Quoted Read, *Walsingham*, 2: 13.
52. ibid., 2: 14–15.
53. ibid., 2: 16.
54. ibid., 2: 18.
55. Froude, *History of England*, 10: 487, cited Wallace, *Sidney*, p. 211.
56. BM Lansdowne MSS. vol. xxviii, no. 70, cited ibid., p. 211.
57. *Cal. S. P. Span. 1568–1579*, pp. 681–2.
58. Greville, *Life*, p. 60.
59. *Cal. S. P. Span. 1568–1579*, p. 693.
60. ibid.
61. Spenser, *Shepheards Calander* in *Works*, 3: 377.
62. Pears, *Sidney–Languet Correspondence*, p. 187.
63. Greville, *Life*, pp. 63–6. It was rumoured two years later that Oxford intended to murder Sidney. *Cal. S. P. Dom. 1584–1590*, pp. 38, 40.
64. cf. W. Segar, *The Booke of Honor and Armes* (London, 1590), p. 2. Segar asserts that all injuries are either by words or deeds. In every injury by words, the injurer ought to be the challenger. The challenge, then, should have come from Oxford. The question of social rank is irrelevant. Segar also maintains that gentlemen descended from the most noble houses, unless in martial or jurisdictional command, may be challenged by any private or particular gentleman. ibid., p. 36.
65. Pears, *Sidney–Languet Correspondence*, p. 165.
66. ibid.
67. Sidney, *Works*, 3: 128.
68. ibid., 3: 51.
69. ibid., 3: 52.
70. ibid., 3: 53.
71. ibid.
72. ibid., 3: 53–4.
73. ibid., 3: 58.
74. ibid., 3: 60.
75. J. Stubbs, *The Discoverie of a Gaping Gulf* (London, 1579) sig. A 2.
76. ibid., sig. A 3v.
77. ibid., sig. C 2.
78. ibid., sig. A 7v–8.
79. *Cal. S. P. Venetian 1558–1580*, p. 621.
80. *Cal. S. P. Span. 1568–1579*, p. 704.
81. Quoted in Wallace, *Sidney*, p. 220. See also Sir J. Harington, *Nugae Antiquae* (London, 1804), 1: 154 ff. and Camden, *Annals*, p. 239.
82. Pears, *Sidney–Languet Correspondence*, p. 185. cf. also Languet's comments in October 1580 that Sidney had come forth from his hiding place to the open day. ibid., p. 187.
83. ibid., p. 170.
84. Greville, *Life*, p. 61.

278 *References*

CHAPTER 3

1. Neale, *Elizabeth and Her Parliaments 1559–1581*, p. 369.

2. ibid., p. 374.

3. ibid., p. 384.

4. ibid., p. 385.

5. Sir S. D'Ewes, *The Journals of All the Parliaments during the Reign of Queen Elizabeth* (London, 1682), p. 288.

6. Sidney, *Works*, 3: 134.

7. 23 Eliz. Cap. 1, printed in G. W. Prothero, *Select Statutes and Other Constitutional Documents Illustrative of the Reigns of Elizabeth and James I* (Oxford, 1913), p. 75.

8. A. D. Meyer, *England and the Catholic Church under Elizabeth* (London, 1916), p. 178.

9. *Journal of the House of Commons*, 1: 121.

10. Neale, *Elizabeth and Her Parliaments 1559–1581*, pp. 393 ff.

11. Stubbs was, in fact, punished under the terms of this act.

12. Neale, *Elizabeth and Her Parliaments 1559–1581*, p. 415.

13. cf. *HMC Hatfield*, 3: 302.

14. Sir J. Neale, *Elizabeth and Her Parliaments 1584–1601* (London, 1957), p. 29.

15. ibid.

16. ibid., p. 31.

17. D'Ewes, *Journals*, p. 352.

18. ibid., pp. 337, 339, 346, 356, 370.

19. It is, however, worthy of note that Sidney on occasion expressed approval of bishops. cf. P. Sidney, *An Apology for Poetry*, ed. G. Shepherd (Edinburgh, 1965), p. 124, where he refers to the 'reverend title of a bishop'. He was certainly opposed to the extreme left wing in religion. cf. his comments on the Anabaptists in *Works*, 3: 174. See also M. Poirier, *Sir Philip Sidney Le Chevalier Poète Elizabéthain* (Lille, 1948), p. 144. On the other hand, Sidney was connected with men who attacked bishops; his associate Robert Beale (who was Walsingham's brother-in-law) attacked the bishops in Parliament and drew on himself the wrath of the Queen. *DNB*.

20. Sidney, *Works*, 3: 136–7.

21. ibid., 3: 137–8.

22. ibid., 3: 140.

23. See Wallace, *Sidney*, p. 272, n. 3; cf. *Cal. S. P. Dom. 1581–1590*, p. 147.

24. Collins, *Letters and Memorials of State*, 1: 295.

25. Sidney, *Works*, 3: 137.

26. Wallace, *Sidney*, p. 282.

27. Sidney, *Works*, 3: 141.

28. ibid., 3: 145.

29. ibid., 3: 142–5.

30. J. P. Collier, ed., *The Egerton Papers* (London, 1840), Camden Soc., no. 12, p. 92.

31. Sidney, *Works*, 3: 143.

32. *Cal. S. P. Dom. 1581–1590*, pp. 220–1.

33. ibid., p. 254.

34. ibid., p. 180.

35. ibid., p. 189.

36. Sidney, *Works*, 3: 146.

37. *Cal. S. P. Dom. 1581–1590*, pp. 255, 263.

38. Segar, *Book of Honor*, p. 101.

39. ibid., p. 95.

40. Bod. MS. Ashmole 845, fol. 165.

41. ibid., fol. 168.

42. H. Goldwell, *A Briefe Declaration of the Shews* (London, 1581). All quotations in the following, unless otherwise indicated, are taken from this pamphlet. See also E. M. Denkinger, 'Some Renaissance References to *Sic Vos non Vobis*', *Phil. Q.*, vol. 10 (1931), pp. 151–162.

43. Ringler, *Sidney's Poems*, p. 345.

44. ibid., p. 346.

45. Camden, *Annals*, p. 235.

46. R. C. Strong and J. A. Van Dorsten, *Leicester's Triumph* (Leiden and London, 1964), p. 15.

47. *Cal. S. P. For. 1581–1582*, p. 517.

48. ibid., p. 514. See Strong and Van Dorsten, *Leicester's Triumph*, pp. 15–16.

49. S. P. Scotland, xxxv, no. 48, quoted Read, *Walsingham*, 2: 116.

50. BM Cotton MSS Galba E vi, fol. 241.

51. Scottish Correspondence, vol. xxxv, quoted Wallace, *Sidney*, pp. 309–310.

52. Wallace, *Sidney*, p. 288.

53. Sidney, *Works*, 3: 139.

54. *Cal. S. P. Dom. 1581–1590*, p. 95.

55. This occurred sometime before July 1581. Camden tells how Sidney on the next tilt day had as his device 'SPERAVI, dashed through to show his hope therein was dashed'. W. Camden, *Remaines Concerning Britaine* (London, 1637), p. 357.

56. *HMC Penshurst*, 1: 272–3.

57. Quoted Wallace, *Sidney*, p. 292.

58. Nicholas, *Memoirs of Hatton*, pp. 327–8.

59. *HMC Rutland*, 1: 149.

60. ibid., 1: 150.

61. Lambeth MSS., no. 647, quoted Wallace, *Sidney*, p. 294.

62. *HMC Hatfield*, 3: 126.

63. Lichfield, *Sidneiana*, p. 26.

64. On the confusion of Stella with Frances Walsingham, see H. H. Hudson, 'Penelope Devereux as Sidney's Stella', *Huntington Library Bulletin*, no 7 (1935), pp. 116 ff.

65. Spenser, *Works*, 3: 537.

CHAPTER 4

1. *Cal. S. P. Span. 1580–1586*, p. 64; cf. Read, *Walsingham*, 2: 51.

2. Read, *Walsingham*, 2: 51.

3. ibid., 2: 51 ff. See the comments of Mendoza which suggest there may have been a third plan under discussion. *Cal. S. P. Span. 1580–1586*, pp. 70–1.

4. Collins, *Letters and Memorials of State*, 1: 294. A further indication of Sidney's connection with Portuguese interests is indicated by indirect contact with da Sousa. *Cal. S. P. Dom. 1580–1586*, p. 23.

5. *Cal. S. P. Span. 1581–1590*, p. 139; Read, *Walsingham*, 2: 55.

6. Read, *Walsingham*, 2: 55.

7. *Cal. S. P. Span. 1580–1586*, p. 144.

8. Read, *Walsingham*, 2: 83.

9. *Cal. S. P. Span. 1580–1586*, pp. 172, 178.

10. Sidney, *Works*, 3: 135–6.

11. Read, *Walsingham*, 2: 84–5.

12. *HMC Hatfield*, 3: 8.

13. G. Donaldson, *Scotland James V to James VII* (Edinburgh, 1965), p. 181.

14. ibid.

15. cf. Read, *Walsingham*, 2: 223 ff.

16. Especially by Fox Bourne, *Sidney*, pp. 308 ff., but see also Wallace, *Sidney*, p. 321.

17. Hamilton Papers II, quoted Wallace, *Sidney*, p. 321.

18. ibid., pp. 321–2.

19. ibid., p. 322; on Sidney and the Scottish pension see also *Cal. S. P. Scot. 1509–1603*, 1: 495.

20. Fox Bourne, *Sidney*, p. 309 n.

21. ibid., p. 308.

22. Wallace, *Sidney*, p. 323.

23. Read, *Walsingham*, 2: 238.

24. ibid., 2: 231.

25. On Bruno see F. A. Yates, *Giordano Bruno and the Hermetic Tradition* (London, 1964); F. A. Yates, 'The Religious Policy of Giordano Bruno', *JWCI*, vol. 3 (1939–40), pp. 181–207; D. W. Singer, *Giordano Bruno His Life and Thought* (New York, 1950).

26. Singer, *Bruno*, p. 10.

27. *Cal. S. P. For. 1583 and Addenda*, p. 214.

28. Quoted Yates, *Bruno*, p. 206.

29. Quoted ibid., p. 207. See in addition A. M. Pellegrini, 'Giordano Bruno and Oxford', *HLQ*, vol. 5 (1941–2), pp. 303–16; R. McNulty, 'Bruno at Oxford', *Renaissance News*, vol. 13 (1960), pp. 300–5.

30. H. R. Trevor-Roper, 'The Last Magician', *New Statesman*, 5 June 1964, p. 879.

31. Quoted Yates, *Bruno*, p. 208.

32. Yates, *Bruno*, p. 208.

33. G. Bruno, *Spaccio de la Bestia Trionfante* (London, 1585), dedication, pp. 1–2.

34. F. A. Yates, *John Florio: The Life of an Italian in Shakespeare's England* (Cambridge, 1934), pp. 104–7 assumes a knowledge of the Stella affair because of Bruno's use of the word *le stelle* in the dedication. Ringler, *Sidney's Poems* p. 435, n. 1 casts doubt on this.

35. Quoted in Yates, *Florio*, pp. 104–5.

36. See Yates, *Bruno*, pp. 235 ff.; Singer, *Bruno*, pp. 93 ff.

37. Singer, *Bruno*, p. 37.

38. Spampanato, *Documenti della vita di Giordano Bruno*, cited ibid., p. 37.

39. On the relations of Bruno and Sidney see in addition to the sources previously cited: A. M. Pellegrini, 'Bruno, Sidney, and Spenser', *SP*, vol. 40 (1943), pp. 128–44; F. B. Newman, 'Sir Fulke Greville and Giordano Bruno: A Possible Echo', *Phil. Q.*, vol. 29 (1950), pp. 367–74; O. Elton, *Modern Studies* (London, 1907).

40. M. S. Goldman, 'Sidney and Harington as Opponents of Superstition', *JEGP*, vol. 54 (1955), pp. 526–48.

41. See J. E. Phillips, 'Daniel Rogers: A Neo-Latin Link between the Pléiade and Sidney's Areopagus', in *Neo-Latin Poetry of the Sixteenth and Seventeenth Centuries*, William Andrews Clark Memorial Library Pubs. (Los Angeles, 1965), p. 25; Yates, *Bruno, passim*; Yates, 'Religious Policy of Bruno'.

42. Sidney, *Works*, 3: 232.

43. Moffett, *Nobilis*, p. 75.

44. See the introduction to Shepherd's edition of *Apology for Poetry*. There has been considerable discussion of the relative influence of Platonic and Aristotelian themes in the work. See F. M. Krouse, 'Plato and Sidney's *Defence of Poesie*', *Comparative Literature*, vol. 6 (1954), pp. 138–47; I. Samuel, 'The Influence of Plato on Sir Philip Sidney's *Defense of Poesy*', *MLQ*, vol. I (1940), pp. 383–91.

45. *The Book of the Ordre of Chyualry*, ed. A. T. P. Byles (London, 1926), pp. 56–7. See also Yates, 'Elizabethan Chivalry', p. 22. The Aristotelian and chivalric fusion is also noted in passing in M. Greaves, *The Blazon of Honour: Studies in Medieval and Renaissance Magnanimity* (London, 1964), p. 50.

46. M. H. Curtis, 'Library Catalogues and Tudor Oxford and Cambridge', *Studies in the Renaissance*, vol. 5 (1958), pp. 111–20; the best treatment of Ramism in England is W. S. Howell, *Logic and Rhetoric in England 1500–1700* (Princeton, 1956).

47. T. Banosius, *Petri Rami Commentariorum de Religione Christiana Libri IV* (Frankfort, 1577), dedication.

48. Sidney, *Works*, 3: 145.

49. See J. P. Thorne, 'A Ramistical Commentary on Sidney's *An Apologie for Poetrie*', *Mod. Phil.*, vol. 54 (1956), pp. 158–64.

50. *Tyros Roring Megge*, quoted in G. Watson, 'Ramus, Miss Tuve, and the New Petromachia', *Mod. Phil.*, vol. 55 (1958), pp. 259–62.

51. Thorne, 'Ramistical Commentary', p. 164.

52. On Bright see Sir G. Keynes, *Dr Timothie Bright* (London, 1962); J. E. C. Hill, *Intellectual Origins of the English Revolution* (Oxford, 1965), p. 133.

53. BM Harl. MSS. 6995. fol. 35.

54. Quoted Buxton, *Sidney*, p. 147.

55. *The Beehive of the Romishe Churche* (London, 1579), sig. A 5–5v.

56. A list of dedications to Sidney is printed in Siebeck, *Das Bild Sir Philip Sidneys*, pp. 182–3; it should be supplemented by the note in Van Dorsten, *Poets, Patrons, and Professors*, p. 93, n. 3.

57. Buxton, *Sidney*, p. 150.

58. Quoted, ibid., p. 151.

59. P. Mornay, *A Worke Concerning the Trewnesse of the Christian Religion* (London, 1587); the part of the work assumed to represent the effort of Sidney is printed in Sidney, *Works*, 3: 189–307. On Golding see L. T. Golding, *An Elizabethan Puritan: Arthur Golding* (New York, 1937).

60. The change in style at the end of chapter 6 has been questioned by D. P. Walker, 'Ways of Dealing with Atheists: A Background to Pamela's Refutation of Cecropia', *Bibliothèque d'Humanisme et Renaissance*, vol. 17 (1955), p. 253. Walker suggests that however much Sidney translated, Golding revised the whole text. On the alleged change in style see Sidney, *Works*, 3: viii–ix; Tenison, *Elizabethan England*, 7: 151 ff, which argues Sidney translated more than usually allowed.

61. Sidney, *Works*, 3: viii.

62. Quoted Wallace, *Sidney*, p. 327.

63. On du Bartas and his translators, see V. T. Holmes, Jr., J. C. Lyons, R. W. Linker, *The Works of Guillaume De Salluste Sieur Du Bartas* (Chapel Hill, 1935–40); J. Carscallen, 'English Translators and Admirers of Du Bartas 1578–1625', (Oxford Univ., B. Litt. thesis, 1958, unpublished); A. W. Osborn, *Sir Philip Sidney en France* (Paris, 1932).

64. J. Florio, trans., *Essayes of Montaigne* (London, 1613), dedication to second book.

65. On translation of the Psalms see L. B. Campbell, *Divine Poetry and Drama in Sixteenth Century England* (Cambridge, 1959); H. Smith, 'English Metrical Psalms in the Sixteenth Century and Their Literary Significance', *HLQ*, vol. 9 (1945–6), pp. 249–71.

66. Sidney, *Apology for Poetry*, p. 99.

67. Much of the following is drawn from Ringler, *Sidney's Poems*, pp. 500–509.

68. On the merits of the translation see I. Baroway, 'Tremellius, Sidney, and Biblical Verse', *MLN*, vol. 49 (1934), pp. 145–9; J. C. A. Rathmell, 'Hopkins, Ruskin, and the Sidney Psalter', *London Magazine*, vol. 6, no. 9 (1959), pp. 51–66.

69. Sidney, *Works*, 3: 61–71.

70. ibid., 3: 71.

71. ibid.

72. W. I. Trattner, 'God and Expansion in Elizabethan England: John Dee', *Journal of the History of Ideas*, vol. 25 (1964), pp. 17–34. Philip's father, too, was interested at any early date in overseas voyages. cf. *HMC Penshurst*, 1: 243, 254.

73. On this scheme, see R. B. Merriman, 'Some Notes on the Treatment of the English Catholics in the Reign of Elizabeth', *American Historical Review*, vol.13

(1907–8), pp. 480–500; D. B. Quinn, ed., *The Voyages and Colonising Enterprises of Sir Humphrey Gilbert* (London, 1940). On Gilbert, see W. G. Gosling, *The Life of Sir Humphrey Gilbert* (London, 1911). Sir Henry Sidney had been connected with Gilbert since at least 1567. cf. *HMC Penshurst*, 1: 243.

74. Quoted in Merriman, 'Some Notes', pp. 496–7.

75. *Cal. S. P. Span. 1580–1586*, p. 384; cf. also *Cal. S. P. Dom. 1581–1590*, p. 146.

76. *Cal. S. P. Colonial Addenda 1574–1674*, p. 22; on the transfer to Peckham see *Cal. S. P. Dom. 1581–1590*, p. 116.

77. Quinn, *Voyages of Gilbert*, p. 329.

78. Sidney, *Works*, 3: 145.

PART TWO

CHAPTER 5

1. B. Jonson, *Poems*, ed. B. H. Newdigate (Oxford, 1936), pp. 57–8.

2. Sidney, *Works*, 1: 15.

3. T. Moffett, *Nobilis or A View of the Life and Death of a Sidney*, ed. and trans. V. B. Heltzel and H. H. Hudson (San Marino, 1940), p. 70.

4. ibid., pp. 70–1.

5. ibid., p. 71.

6. ibid.

7. Greville, *Life*, p. 6.

8. Pears, *Sidney–Languet Correspondence*, p. 29.

9. Collins, *Letters and Memorials of State*, 1: 9.

10. Moffett, *Nobilis*, p. 72.

11. A. Rimmer, *A History of Shrewsbury School* (Shrewsbury and London 1889), p. 51.

12. Wallace, *Sidney*, p. 408.

13. ibid., p. 422.

14. ibid., p. 410.

15. ibid., p. 408.

16. Sidney, *Works*, 3: 133.

17. The phrase was used by Sidney's mother in a letter to him, quoted Wallace, *Sidney*, p. 70.

18. Moffett, *Nobilis*, p. 73.

19. S. Jayne, *Library Catalogues of the English Renaissance* (Berkeley and Los Angeles, 1956), p. 51, states categorically that there was a 'contrast between conservative, scholastic Oxford and reforming, humanist Cambridge'. But see M. H. Curtis, *Oxford and Cambridge in Transition 1558–1642* (Oxford, 1959) and L. Stone, 'The Educational Revolution in England 1560–1640', *Past and Present*, no. 28 (1964), pp. 41–80 which provides some statistics on the expansion of the universities.

20. R. Carew, *The Survey of Cornwall* (London, 1602), p. 102. Perhaps Sidney gained some skill in debate before entering Oxford. It appears that he may have spent a short time at Gray's Inn before going up to Oxford. See Poirier, *Sidney*, p. 25.

21. See Curtis, *Oxford and Cambridge in Transition*, chaps. 3–6; M. H. Curtis, 'Education and Apprenticeship', in *Shakespeare in His Own Age*, ed. A. Nicoll (Cambridge, 1964), p. 64.

22. The phrase is from Curtis, 'Education and Apprenticeship', p. 65. Curtis's views have been challenged by a number of writers, but the fact that tutors at Oxford were aware of the work of men like Ramus is convincingly demonstrated in Curtis, 'Library Catalogues and Tudor Oxford and Cambridge', pp. 111–20.

23. Buxton, *Sidney*, p. 39. A transcription of the Latin epitaph is printed on p. 261.

24. Sidney, *Works*, 3: 76–7.

25. Wood, *Athenae Oxonienses*, 1: 608, cited Wallace, *Sidney*, p. 102.

26. *The Merry Devil of Edmonton*, act 1, scene 2, quoted Wilson, *Sidney*, p. 38.

27. N. Baxter, *Sir Philip Sidneys Ourania* (London, 1653), sig. N lv.

28. Moffett, *Nobilis*, p. 77.

29. Wallace wrongly asserts that Greville was at Broadgate Hall. *Sidney*, p. 107. This error is repeated in Bill, *Astrophel*, p. 83; Warren, *Sidney*, p. 30; and E. M. Denkinger, *Philip Sidney* (London, 1932), p. 40. See G. Bullough, ed., *Poems and Dramas of Fulke Greville First Lord Brooke* (New York, 1945), 1: 2.

30. This is conjectured by Wallace, *Sidney*, p. 108. Some biographers have assumed his friendship with Edward Dyer dated from his Oxford years. This, however, is unlikely. Dyer was about ten years older than Sidney, had left the university without taking a degree, and was at court by 1566. Sargent dates their acquaintance from 1575–6. R. M. Sargent, *At the Court of Queen Elizabeth: The Life and Lyrics of Sir Edward Dyer* (London, 1935), p. 39.

31. Sidney, *Works*, 3: 130.

32. Moffett, *Nobilis*, p. 76.

33. ibid.

34. See Baughan,'Sydney and the Matchmakers', pp. 506 ff.; Wallace, *Sidney* pp. 89–91; *HMC Hatfield*, 1: 415–6, 439; Collins, *Letters and Memorials of State*, 1: 44.

35. Sidney, *Works*, 3: 75. Translation from Wallace, *Sidney*, p. 94.

36. Buxton, *Sidney*, p. 43 asserts categorically that 'After leaving Oxford Sidney spent some time (how long we do not know) at Cambridge'. He adds one bit of evidence (p. 261) from Harvey's *Gratulationes Valdinenses* to the material assembled by Wallace, *Sidney*, pp. 105–7. Wallace concludes that there is 'no reasonable doubt' but that Sidney studied at Cambridge. F. S. Boas, *Sir Philip Sidney Representative Elizabethan* (London, 1955), pp. 21–2, is sceptical

37. *HMC Hatfield*, 1: 439.

38. Pears, *Sidney–Languet Correspondence*, p. 29.

39. Sidney, *Works*, 3: 132.

40. Moffett, *Nobilis*, p. 77.

41. ibid., p. 75.

42. ibid.

43. ibid., p. 78.

44. Sidney, *Works*, 3: 124.

45. ibid., 3: 126.

46. ibid., 3: 127.

47. ibid.

48. Collins, *Letters and Memorials of State*, 1: 98.

49. *HMC Penshurst*, 1: 271–2.

50. T. Zouch, *Memoirs of the Life and Writings of Sir Philip Sidney* (York, 1809), p. 39.

51. L. Bryskett, *A Discourse of Civill Life* (London, 1606), pp. 160–1.

52. Banosius, *Petri Rami Commentariorum*. Translation from Buxton, *Sidney*, p. 45.

53. *HMC Penshurst*, 1: 271.

54. Greville, *Life*, p. 31.

55. Buxton, *Sidney*, p. 50, asserts that they met in Paris, as does Wallace, *Sidney*, p. 119. This is questioned by R. W. Zandvoort, 'Sidney in Austria', *Wiener Beiträge zur Englischen Philologie*, vol. 66 (1958), p. 230, and by Van Dorsten, *Poets, Patrons, and Professors*, p. 30, who asserts they first met at Frankfort or more likely in Vienna.

56. cf. Buxton, *Sidney*, pp. 47–8, who is sceptical. A discussion of Sidney's French acquaintances is contained in Osborn, *Sidney en France*. For a good discussion of the work of the Pléiade, see G. Castor, *Pléiade Poetics* (Cambridge, 1964). I am grateful to W. G. Moore for drawing my attention to this work.

57. J. Sylvester, *Bartas His Deuine Weekes and Works Translated* (London, 1605), p. 433.

58. J. Hall, *Virgidemiarum*, VI: 255–6, quoted Buxton, *Sidney*, p. 49. For a discussion of the compound epithet, see Wilson, *Sidney*, p. 309.

59. Digges, *Compleat Ambassador*, p. 250, quoted Wallace, *Sidney*, p. 122.

60. Sidney, *Works*, 3: 77–9.

61. H. Stephanus, *Novum Testamentum Graece* (Paris, 1576), dedication.

62. Buxton, *Sidney*, p. 59.

63. *Zurich Letters*, 2nd S., p. 217, cited Wallace, *Sidney*, p. 127. On Sidney's friendships in this period, see also A. Koszul, 'Les Sidney et Strasbourg', *Bulletin de la Faculté des Lettres de Strasbourg*, vol. 17 (1938), pp. 37–44.

64. On the visit to Basle see BM Add. MSS. 15914, cited Buxton, *Sidney*, p. 263. The best discussion of Sidney's stay in Vienna is Zandvoort, 'Sidney in Austria'.

65. *Epistolae*, pp. 1–2. Translation from Buxton, *Sidney*, pp. 61–2.

66. Buxton, *Sidney*, p. 60.

67. The correspondence is in BM Add. MSS. 15914, fols. 21, 27, 28; 17520, fol. 8; 18675, fols. 4, 6, 7, 8.

68. *Epistolae*, p. 35.

69. cf. R. Ascham, *The Scholemaster*, ed. E. Arber (London, 1870), pp. 74–8.

70. Quoted in J. L. Lievsay, *The Elizabethan Image of Italy* (Ithaca, 1964), p. 1. For a general discussion of England and Italy in the sixteenth century see also L. D. Einstein, *The Italian Renaissance in England* (New York, 1902); J. R. Hale, *England and the Italian Renaissance* (London, 1954); G. B. Parks, 'The First Italianate Englishmen', *Studies in the Renaissance*, vol. 8 (1961), pp. 197–216.

71. Bryskett, *Pastorall Aeglogue* in Spenser, *Works*, 3: 561.

72. Pears, *Sidney–Languet Correspondence*, p. 8.

73. ibid.

74. ibid., p. 12.

75. ibid., p. 87.

76. ibid., p. 51.

77. ibid.

78. Buxton, *Sidney*, pp. 68–9.

79. Pears, *Sidney–Languet Correspondence*, p. 28.

80. Although Sidney at this time rated the *Politics* the most worthy of Aristotle's works (ibid.) he later told his brother that the *Ethics* were 'the begyning and foundacion of all his workes'. Sidney, *Works*, 3: 124. On Zabarella, see Buxton *Sidney*, p. 72.

81. See on his reading Sidney, *Works*, 3: 81. On Venice and the English see Z. Fink, *The Classical Republicans* (Evanston, 1962), chap. 2.

82. Pears, *Sidney–Languet Correspondence*, p. 20.

83. ibid.

84. ibid., p. 26.

85. ibid., p. 25. See also p. 28. His interest in astronomy is perhaps also reflected in his gift to his father of 'an instrument for an astronomy of silver gilt'. *HMC Penshurst*, 1: 277.

86. Pears, *Sidney–Languet Correspondence*, p. 28.

87. ibid., p. 43.

88. ibid., p. 53. It is apparent that Languet's interest in Sidney was in part a matter of policy. cf. his comments in a letter to Dr Johannes Glauburg recommending Sidney to him. 'His friendship may be useful to you and your friends in the future, since he will surely be given great authority in his own country, if God grants him long life.' W. H. Bond, 'A Letter of Languet about Sidney,' *Harvard Library Bulletin*, vol. 9 (1955), p. 107.

89. Pears, *Sidney–Languet Correspondence*, p. 56.

90. Sidney, *Works*, 3: 100.

91. ibid., 3: 98–102.

92. Sidney, *Apology for Poetry*, p. 95.

93. See Wallace, *Sidney*, p. 143 n. 1.

94. Ringler, *Sidney's Poems*, p. 99.

CHAPTER 6

1. Pears, *Sidney–Languet Correspondence*, pp. 169–70, 176–7.

2. Wallace, *Sidney*, p. 221.

3. Greville, *Life*, p. 33.

4. Holinshed, *Chronicles* (1587 uncensored version), p. 1554, cited Ringler, *Sidney's Poems*, p. 365.

5. Sidney, *Works*, 2: 208–17.

6. ibid., 2: 209.

7. See Ringler, *Sidney's Poems*, p. 362.

8. Sidney, *Works*, 2: 216.

9. Ringler, *Sidney's Poems*, p. 362.

10. S. K. Orgel, 'Sidney's Experiment in Pastoral: *The Lady of May*', *JWCI*, vol. 26 (1963), pp. 198–203.

11. For a discussion of Sidney's literary associates at this time see Ringler, *Sidney's Poems*, pp. xxviii–xxxiv.

12. On Drant's rules, see W. R. Ringler, 'Maister Drant's Rules', *Phil. Q.*, vol. 29 (1950), pp. 70–4, and on the general subject of the use of classical metres, see G. D. Willcock, 'Passing Pitefull Hexameters', *MLR*, vol. 29 (1934), pp. 1–19.

13. Ringler, *Sidney's Poems*, p. xxix.

14. Greville was in the Netherlands from 15 June till 7 October 1578. In February 1579 he left for an extended continental tour, and in March 1580 he was preparing to sail with the Irish fleet. It is significant that the Spenser–Harvey correspondence does not refer to him. ibid., p. xxx.

15. Greville, *Works*, ed. Bullough, 1: 25.

16. Ringler, *Sidney's Poems*, p. 263.

17. G. Bullough in his edition of Greville's poems and dramas lists similarities in the notes. See also J. M. Purcell, 'Sidney's *Astrophel and Stella* and Greville's *Caelica*', *PMLA*, vol. 50 (1935), pp. 413–22.

18. On Dyer, see Sargent, *At the Court of Queen Elizabeth*.

19. Ringler, *Sidney's Poems*, p. xxxi.

20. See ibid., p. xxxi, n. 2. The poem for which he is best known ('My mind to me a kingdom is') is almost certainly not his work.

21. On this see Ringler, *Sidney's Poems*, pp. xxxi–xxxiv; T. P. Harrison, Jr., 'The Relations of Spenser and Sidney', *PMLA*, vol. 45 (1930), pp. 712–31; J. M. Purcell, 'The Relations of Spenser and Sidney', *PMLA*, vol. 46 (1931), p. 940; M. Behler, 'Die Beziehungen zwischen Sidney und Spenser', *Archiv für das Studium der neureren Sprachen und Literaturen*, vols. 146–7 (1923–4), pp. 53–9; P. W. Long, 'Spenser and Sidney', *Anglia*, vol. 38 (1914), pp. 173–93.

22. Sidney, *Apology for Poetry*, p. 95.

23. ibid., p. 133.

24. Ringler, *Sidney's Poems*, p. xxxiv.

25. Spenser, *Faerie Queene*, dedicatory poem to the Countess of Pembroke, in *Works*, 1: 28.

26. W. L., commendatory poem to *Faerie Queene*, ibid., 1: 15.

27. On Rogers, see Van Dorsten, *Poets, Patrons, and Professors*, and Phillips, 'Daniel Rogers'.

28. He told Burghley later he arrived to study in France toward the end of 1561. *Cal. S. P. Dom. Addenda 1566–1579*, p. 382. cf. Phillips, 'Daniel Rogers', p. 11.

29. At this time he produced his only published work, *De Laudibus Antverpiae* (Antwerp, 1565). Phillips, 'Daniel Rogers', p. 11.

30. Rogers wrote some half-dozen poems in his honour. Hertford MSS., cited

Phillips, 'Daniel Rogers', p. 14. On Ramus, see R. Hookyass, *Humanisme, science et réforme: Pierre de la Ramée* (Leiden, 1958).

31. See the discussion in F. A. Yates, *The French Academies of the Sixteenth Century* (London, 1947).

32. Sidney, *Works*, 3: 121.

33. Leiden Univ. Library MS. BPL 885, printed in Van Dorsten, *Poets, Patrons and Professors*, p. 94.

34. See J. B. Fletcher, 'Areopagus and Pléiade', *JEGP*, vol. 2 (1898–9), pp. 429–453; H. Maynadier, 'Areopagus of Sidney and Spenser', *MLR*, vol. 4 (1908–9), pp. 289–301; F. E. Faverty, 'A Note on the Areopagus', *Phil. Q.*, vol. 5 (1926), pp. 278–80.

35. Fletcher, 'Areopagus and Pléaide', p. 430.

36. Faverty, 'Note on the Areopagus', p. 280.

37. Van Dorsten, *Poets, Patrons and Professors*, pp. 66–7. Phillips, 'Daniel Rogers', p. 21, has 'and that you allow me' rather than 'if you were to allow me'.

38. Spenser, *Works*, 3: 585–92.

39. See Ringler, 'Maister Drant's Rules'.

40. See J. E. Phillips, 'George Buchanan and the Sidney Circle', *HLQ*, vol. 12 (1948–9), pp. 23–35; L. B. Campbell, 'The Christian Muse', *Huntington Library Bulletin*, no. 8 (1935), pp. 29–70; Campbell, *Divine Poetry and Drama*.

41. Sidney had an evident interest in music. cf. Lichfield, *Sidneiana*, p. 81; Buxton, *Sidney*, pp. 113 ff. See also E. Doughtie, 'Sidney, Tessier, Batchelar, and *A Musicall Banquet*', *Renaissance News*, vol. 18 (1965), pp. 123–6; B. Pattison, 'Sir Philip Sidney and Music', *Music and Letters*, vol. 15 (1934), pp. 75–81.

42. Sidney, *Works*, 1: 3.

43. *Aubrey's Brief Lives*, ed. O. L. Dick (Harmondsworth, 1962), p. 337.

44. Sidney, *Works*, 1: 3.

45. Wallace, *Sidney*, p. 233. Yates, *Florio*, p. 205, suggests John Florio rather than Greville was the overseer.

46. For the identification of Sanford, see Yates, *Florio*, pp. 208–9.

47. Sidney, *Works*, 2: 218.

48. ibid.

49. Quoted in J. Buxton, *Elizabethan Taste* (London, 1963), p. 249.

50. See B. Dobell, 'New Light upon Sir Philip Sidney's *Arcadia*', *Quarterly Review*, vol. 211 (1909), pp. 74–100.

51. T. Powell, *Tom of All Trades* (London, 1631), p. 47.

52. Some indication of its popularity is given by the fact that it was published in nearly twenty editions in 120 years and was translated into numerous foreign languages. It was probably the first literary work of any kind to be translated from English to either French or Italian. By 1668 there were more than thirty foreign editions. See Buxton, *Sidney*, pp. 134–5; M. Eccles, 'A Survey of Elizabethan Reading', *HLQ*, vol. 5 (1941–2), pp. 180–2.

53. For example, he took the plot of Gloucester and his sons from one of the episodes. See in addition: A. D., 'Possible Echoes from Sidney's *Arcadia* in Shakespeare, Milton, and Others', *Notes and Queries*, vol. 194 (1949), p. 551; H. W. Hill, 'Sidney's *Arcadia* and the Elizabethan Drama', *Univ. of Nevada*

Studies, vol. 1 (1908), pp. 1–59; D. M. McKeithan, 'King Lear and Sidney's *Arcadia*', *Univ. of Texas Studies in English*, vol. 14 (1934), pp. 45–9; M. Poirier, 'Sidney's Influence on *A Midsummer Night's Dream*', *SP*, vol. 44 (1947), pp. 483–9. Beaumont and Fletcher also borrowed from Sidney. J. E. Savage, 'Beaumont and Fletcher's *Philaster* and Sidney's *Arcadia*', *ELH*, vol. 14 (1947), pp. 194–206.

54. Charles quoted Pamela's prayer. Sidney, *Works*, 1: 382–3.

55. E. E. Duncan-Jones, 'Henry Oxinden and Sidney's *Arcadia*', *Notes and Queries*, vol. 198 (1953), pp. 322–3.

56. E. G. Fogel, 'Milton and Sir Philip Sidney's *Arcadia*', *Notes and Queries*, vol. 196 (1951), pp. 115–17.

57. See K. O. Myrick, *Sir Philip Sidney as a Literary Craftsman* (Cambridge, Mass., 1935).

58. J. Hoskins, 'Directions for Speech and Style', quoted Wallace, *Sidney*, p. 235.

59. Hoskins missed some of the ingredients such as *Amadis of Gaul* and possibly Malory's *Morte d'Arthur*. On the latter see M. S. Goldman, *Sir Philip Sidney and the Arcadia* (Urbana, 1934). cf. the comment in R. F. Patterson, ed., *Ben Jonson's Conversations with William Drummond of Hawthornden* (London, 1924), p. 14, that 'S. P. Sidney had an intention to have transformed all his *Arcadia* to the stories of King Arthur'.

60. Buxton, *Elizabethan Taste*, p. 255.

61. Quoted ibid., p. 256.

62. Greville, *Life*, pp. 15–16.

63. It was at one time fashionable to argue that the *Old Arcadia* was superior. See Dobell, 'New Light on *Arcadia*', and M. Praz, 'Sidney's Original *Arcadia*', *London Mercury*, vol. 15 (1926–7), pp. 507–14. This view was effectively refuted by R. W. Zandvoort, *Sidney's Arcadia: A Comparison between the Two Versions* (Amsterdam, 1929).

64. cf. Moffett, *Nobilis*, p. 74. The earliest printed allusion to Sidney's request to destroy his works is J. Owen, *Epigrammatum Libri Tres* (London, 1607), 2: 67.

65. Greville, *Life*, p. 16.

66. On the question of her editorship see Praz, 'Sidney's Original *Arcadia*'; K. T. Rowe, 'The Countess of Pembroke's Editorship of the *Arcadia*', *PMLA*, vol. 54 (1939), pp. 122–38; K. T. Rowe, 'Elizabethan Morality and the Folio Revisions of Sidney's *Arcadia*', *Mod. Phil.*, vol. 37 (1939–40), pp. 151–72.

67. Sidney, *Works*, 4: 2.

68. It is also interesting to note the change in the proportion of noble to rustic characters from 9: 6 in *Old Arcadia* to 22: 6 in the revised version. D. E. Baughan, 'Sidney's *Defence of the Earl of Leicester* and the Revised *Arcadia*', *JEGP*, vol. 51 (1952), p. 40.

69. Wilson, *Sidney*, p. 140.

70. In addition to the works already cited, the following may be consulted with profit: F. Brie, *Sidney's Arcadia: Eine Studie zur Englischen Renaissance* (Strassburg, 1918); K. Brunhuber, *Sir Philip Sidneys Arcadia und ihre Nachläufer* (Nürnberg, 1903); J. F. Danby, *Poets on Fortune's Hill* (London, 1952); W. R. Davis and R. A. Lanham, *Sidney's Arcadia* (New Haven, 1956); K. T. Rowe,

Romantic Love and Parental Authority in Sidney's Arcadia (Ann Arbor, 1947); P. A. Duhamel, 'Sidney's *Arcadia* and Elizabethan Rhetoric', *SP*, vol. 45 (1948), pp. 134–50.

71. On this see J. H. Hanford and S. R. Watson, 'Personal Allegory in the *Arcadia*: Philisides and Lelius', *Mod. Phil.*, vol. 32 (1934), pp. 1–10.

72. J. Aubrey, *Brief Lives*, ed. A. Clark (Oxford, 1898), 2: 250–2.

73. See E. Greenlaw, 'Sidney's *Arcadia* as an Example of Elizabethan Allegory', *Kittredge Anniversary Papers* (Boston, 1913), pp. 327–337; E. Greenlaw, 'The Captivity Episode in Sidney's *Arcadia*', *Manly Anniversary Studies* (Chicago, 1923), pp. 54–63; D. M. Anderson, 'The Trial of the Princes in the *Arcadia*', *RES*, vol. 33 (1957), pp. 409–12.

74. Wallace, *Sidney*, p. 237.

75. Sidney, *Apology for Poetry*, p. 3.

76. The following is drawn substantially from W. Ringler, *Stephen Gosson: A Biographical and Critical Study* (Princeton, 1942).

77. S. Gosson, *The School of Abuse* (London, 1841), p. 4.

78. cf. W. Ringler, 'The First Phase of the Elizabethan Attack on the Stage 1558–1579', *HLQ*, vol. 5 (1941–2), pp. 391–418; Ringler, *Gosson*, pp. 37, 61.

79. Sidney, *Apology for Poetry*, pp. 133, 137.

80. Spenser, *Works*, 3: 586.

81. Gosson, *School of Abuse*, pp. 10–11.

82. Another possible factor in Sidney's not answering the pamphlet was that Gosson had the patronage of Walsingham. Tenison, *Elizabethan England*, 5: 51. It is possible that Sidney either quickly forgave Gosson or that the rebuke did not have much impact, for Gosson dedicated his next work, *The Ephemerides of Phialo* (London, 1579) to Sidney. Gosson commented in the dedication: 'Sith it hath been my fortune to bear sail in a storm since my first publishing *The School of Abuse* and to be tossed by such as some without reason and threaten me with death without a cause, feeling not yet my finger ache, I cannot but acknowledge my safety in your worship's patronage and offer you Phialo . . . as a manifest pledge of my thankful heart.'

83. Ringler, *Gosson, passim* and Sidney, *Apology for Poetry*, p. 3, n. 1.

84. See Myrick, *Sidney as a Literary Craftsman*; Sidney, *Apology for Poetry*, pp. 11–17.

85. Sidney, *Apology for Poetry*, p. 16.

86. ibid., p. 101. cf. also C. M. Dowlin, 'Sidney's Two Definitions of Poetry', *MLQ*, vol. 3 (1942), pp. 573–81; A. C. Hamilton, 'Sidney's Idea of the "Right Poet"', *Comparative Literature*, vol. 9 (1957), pp. 51–9.

87. Sidney, *Apology for Poetry*, p. 120.

88. ibid., p. 123.

89. ibid., pp. 123–4.

90. ibid., pp. 125–6.

91. ibid., pp. 129–30.

92. ibid., p. 132.

93. ibid., pp. 141–2.

94. ibid., p. 142.

CHAPTER 7

1. On this see J. W. Saunders, 'The Stigma of Print: A Note on the Social Bases of Tudor Poetry', *Essays in Criticism*, vol. 1 (1951), pp. 139–64.

2. Buxton, *Elizabethan Taste*, p. 269.

3. *Accounts of the Wardens of the Stationer's Company*, ed. Arber, 1: 555, cited ibid.

4. ibid. See also J. Buxton, 'On the Date of Syr P. S. his Astrophel and Stella', *Bodleian Library Record*, vol. 6 (1960), pp. 614–16.

5. These two sonnets were accepted, for example, by Denkinger, Bill, and Wilson in their biographies. See K. M. Murphy, 'The 109th and 110th Sonnets of *Astrophel and Stella*', *Phil. Q.*, vol. 34 (1955), pp. 349–52. See also J. B. Fletcher, 'Did Astrophel Love Stella?' *Mod. Phil.*, vol. 5 (1907–8), pp. 253–264; P. N. Siegel, 'The Petrarchan Sonneteers and Neo-Platonic Love', *SP*, vol. 42 (1945), pp. 164–82; E. C. Pettet, 'Sidney and the Cult of Romantic Love', *English*, vol. 6 (1947), pp. 232–40.

6. The version as originally contained in A. Feuillerat's edition of Sidney's *Works*.

7. Ringler, *Sidney's Poems*; J. Carey, review of Ringler, *Oxford Magazine*, 21 November, 1963, p. 86.

8. J. M. Purcell, *Sidney's Stella* (London, 1934), pp. 13–14.

9. This has been the subject of much writing. In addition to sources already cited see: T. H. Banks, 'Sidney's *Astrophel and Stella* Reconsidered', *PMLA*, vol. 50 (1935), pp. 403–12; W. G. Friedrich, 'The Stella of Astrophel', *ELH*, vol. 3 (1936), pp. 114–39; J. Stillinger, 'The Biographical Problem of *Astrophel and Stella*', *JEGP*, vol. 59 (1960), pp. 617–39; M. S. Rawson, *Penelope Rich and Her Circle* (London, 1911).

10. Purcell, *Sidney's Stella*, p. 42.

11. Ringler, *Sidney's Poems*, pp. 171, 180, 198.

12. ibid., pp. 176–7, 183; cf. also the line in sonnet 35: 'Fame/Doth ever grow rich, naming my Stella's name'.

13. ibid., p. 436.

14. ibid.

15. See Hudson, 'Penelope Devereux', p. 93.

16. J. Robertson, 'Sir Philip Sidney and Lady Penelope Rich', *RES*, NS vol. 15 (1964), pp. 296–7.

17. Printed in Hudson, 'Penelope Devereux,' pp. 90–1.

18. Ringler, *Sidney's Poems*, pp. 436–7.

19. ibid., p. 437, n. 2.

20. ibid., p. 437.

21. ibid.

22. BM Lansdowne MSS. 31, fol. 105, printed ibid., p. 438.

23. *HMC Rutland*, 1: 128. See L. C. John, 'The Date of the Marriage of Penelope Devereux', *PMLA*, vol. 49 (1934), pp. 961–2.

24. J. M. Purcell, 'A Cup for My Lady Penelope', *MLN*, vol. 45 (1930), p. 310.

25. Ringler, *Sidney's Poems*, p. 439.

26. ibid., pp. 179–80.

27. ibid., pp. 439–40.

28. Quoted in Buxton, *Elizabethan Taste*, p. 272.

29. As noted by Hudson, 'Penelope Devereux', p. 90, n. 1.

30. cf. Ringler, *Sidney's Poems*, p. 447.

31. C. Lamb, 'Some Sonnets of Sir Philip Sidney', *Last Essays* (London, 1833), cited ibid.

32. I take this suggestion from Buxton, *Elizabethan Taste*, pp. 265–94.

33. C. S. Lewis, *English Literature in the Sixteenth Century* (Oxford, 1954), p. 328.

34. Nichols, *Progresses*, 2: 301.

35. Ringler's *Sidney's Poems*, p. 165.

36. ibid., p. 181.

37. Tenison, *Elizabethan England*, 5: 70.

38. Sidney, *Works*, 3: 139.

39. *HMC Hatfield*, 3: 435.

40. G. Goodman, *The Court of King James I*, ed. Brewer (London, 1837), 1: 17 quoted in Ringler, *Sidney's Poems*, p. 443.

41. ibid., p. 445.

42. ibid., p. 446, n. 3.

43. C. Cross, *The Puritan Earl* (London, 1966), appeared too late to be used for information on Huntingdon.

44. Much of the following is drawn from Buxton, *Elizabethan Taste*, pp. 269–94.

45. Ringler, *Sidney's Poems*, p. 166.

46. ibid., p. 167.

47. ibid., p. 168.

48. ibid., p. 171.

49. ibid., pp. 180–1.

50. ibid., p. 175.

51. ibid.

52. ibid., pp. 171–2.

53. ibid., p. 180.

54. ibid., p. 181.

55. ibid., pp. 181–2.

56. ibid., pp. 184–5.

57. ibid., p. 185.

58. ibid., p. 188.

59. ibid.

60. ibid., pp. 191–2.

61. ibid., p. 196

62. ibid., p. 199.

63. ibid., p. 200.

64. ibid.

65. ibid., p. 201.

66. ibid., pp. 202–3.

67. ibid., p. 204.

68. ibid., p. 206.

69. ibid., p. 211.

70. ibid., p. 218.

71. ibid., p. 219.

72. ibid., p. 220

73. Buxton, *Elizabethan Taste*, p. 292.

74. Ringler, *Sidney's Poems*, p. 233.

75. ibid., p. 237.

76. ibid., pp. 161–2.

77. ibid., p. 423.

78. In addition to works previously cited, see: R. L. Montgomery, Jr., *Symmetry and Sense: The Poetry of Sir Philip Sidney* (Austin, 1961); R. B. Young, *Englishe Petrarke: A Study of Sidney's Astrophel and Stella* in *Three Studies in the Renaissance*, ed. B. C. Nangle (New Haven, 1958); D. Kalstone, *Sidney's Poetry* (Cambridge, Mass., 1965); J. Scott, *Les Sonnets Elizabéthains* (Paris, 1929); L. C. John, *The Elizabethan Sonnet Sequences* (New York, 1939); H. Smith, *Elizabethan Poetry* (Cambridge, Mass., 1952); J. W. Lever, *The Elizabethan Love Sonnet* (London, 1956); J. Robertson, 'Sir Philip Sidney and His Poetry', in *Elizabethan Poetry*, Stratford upon Avon Studies 2 (London, 1960), pp. 110–29; T. Spenser, 'The Poetry of Sir Philip Sidney', *ELH*, vol. 12 (1945), 251–78; R. G. Whigham and O. F. Emerson, 'Sonnet Structure in Sidney's *Astrophel and Stella*', *SP*, vol. 18 (1921), pp. 347–52.

79. See for example J. Thompson, 'Sir Philip Sidney and the Forsaken Iamb', *Kenyon Review*, vol. 20 (1958), pp. 90–115.

80. cf. Robertson, 'Sidney and His Poetry', p. 129.

81. ibid.

82. Ringler, *Sidney's Poems*, p. 201. For an analysis of the sonnet see Kalstone, *Sidney's Poetry*, pp. 117–24.

83. Ringler, *Sidney's Poems*, p. 180. On this sonnet see the notes by C. S. Burhans, Jr., C. R. B. Cornbellack, and E. H. Essig in *The Explicator*, vol. 18, no. 4 (1960), and vol 20, no. 3 (1961).

84. Ringler, *Sidney's Poems*, p. 224.

CHAPTER 8

1. The question of Sidney's indebtedness to other writers for his poetic theory has been extensively investigated. Myrick, *Sidney as a Literary Craftsman*, p. 216, concluded: 'He is not so much a thinker as a persuasive advocate of other men's thoughts.' See also C. M. Dowlin, 'Sidney and Other Men's Thought', *RES*, vol. 20 (1944), pp. 257–71; A. C. Hamilton, 'Sidney and Agrippa', *RES*, vol. 32 (1956), pp. 151–7; F. M. Padelford, 'Sidney's Indebtedness to Sibilet', *JEGP*, vol. 7 (1908), pp. 81–4; F. L. Townshend, 'Sidney and Ariosto', *PMLA*, vol. 61 (1946), pp. 97–108. He borrowed equally heavily in his social and political thought.

2. Greville, *Life*, pp. 77–8.

3. ibid., p. 79. Not all felt Sidney was so bellicose. See Poirier, *Sidney*, p. 104. Sidney's tutor Thornton felt that he was as much a child of peace as he was of war. '*In plus quam Martis, pacis, alumnus eras*.' T. Thornton in *Exequiae Illustrissimi Equitis D. Philippi Sidnaei* (Oxford, 1587), quoted in Wallace, *Sidney*, p. 101, n. 2. But T. Digges felt Sidney was one of the followers of Mars; he proposed to write an apology for the military profession in lieu of the one he felt Sidney should have written and did not. L. B. Campbell, 'Sidney as the Learned Soldier', *HLQ*, vol. 7 (1943–4), pp. 175–8.

4. Greville, *Life*, pp. 79–80.

5. ibid., p. 80.

6. ibid., p. 81.

7. ibid., pp. 86–7.

8. ibid., p. 87.

9. ibid., p. 88.

10. ibid.

11. ibid., p. 89.

12. ibid., p. 90.

13. ibid.

14. ibid.

15. ibid., p. 92.

16. ibid., pp. 94–5.

17. ibid., p. 95.

18. ibid., p. 102.

19. ibid., p. 104.

20. ibid., p. 105.

21. ibid., p. 109.

22. ibid. Sidney appears to have sought out relevant books in connection with this sort of plan. cf. his letter to Christopher Plantin. Sidney, *Works*, 3: 134. The letter should be dated 1586, not 1581 as printed, nor even 1585 as suggested by C. F. Bühler, 'On the Date of the Letter Written by Sir Philip Sidney to Christopher Plantin', *RES*, vol. 12 (1936), pp. 67–71. See W. H. Bond, 'A Letter from Sir Philip Sidney to Christopher Plantin', *Harvard Library Bulletin*, vol. 8 (1954), pp. 233–5.

23. Greville, *Life*, p. 110.

24. ibid., p. 112.

25. ibid.

26. ibid., p. 116.

27. ibid., pp. 116–17.

28. One should, however, note that Sidney's pronouncements on the law of nature were vague. cf. Sidney, *Works*, 2: 45. 'For in trueth so it is, nature gives not to us her degenerate children, any more general precepte, then one to helpe the other, one to feele a true compassion of the others mishappe.'

29. Greville, *Life*, pp. 118–19.

30. ibid., p. 119.

31. ibid.

32. ibid.

33. The basic discussion of Sidney's political thought are by W. D. Briggs: 'Political Ideas in Sidney's *Arcadia*', *SP*, vol. 28 (1931), pp. 137–61, and 'Sidney's Political Ideas', *SP*, vol. 29 (1932), pp. 534–42. They have been questioned by I. Ribner, 'Sir Philip Sidney on Civil Insurrection', *Journal of the History of Ideas*, vol. 13 (1952), pp. 257–65. I find his argument unconvincing. See also Hill, *Intellectual Origins of the English Revolution*, pp. 136–7, and J. H. M. Salmon *The French Religious Wars in English Political Thought* (Oxford, 1959), pp. 181–5.

34. Briggs, 'Political Ideas in *Arcadia*', *passim*.

35. Sidney, *Works*, 3: 187.

36. Ringler, *Sidney*'s Poems, p. 100. This idea is attributed to Languet. cf. Briggs, 'Political Ideas in *Arcadia*', pp. 152, 159.

37. I. Ribner, 'Machiavelli and Sidney's *Arcadia* of 1590', *SP*, vol. 47 (1950), pp. 152–72; I. Ribner, 'Machiavelli and Sidney's *Discourse to the Queene's Majestie*', *Italica*, vol. 26 (1949), pp. 177–87.

38. W. G. Zeeveld, 'The Uprising of the Commons in Sidney's *Arcadia*', *MLN*, vol. 48 (1933), pp. 209–17.

39. Ribner, 'Sidney on Civil Insurrection', p. 261.

40. Sidney, *Works*, 1: 317.

41. S. R. Watson, '*Gorbuduc* and the Theory of Tyrannicide', *MLR*, vol. 34 (1939), p. 359.

42. See Phillips, 'Buchanan and the Sidney Circle', p. 29.

43. Quoted ibid., p. 30.

44. Watson, '*Gorboduc* and the Theory of Tyrannicide', p. 359.

45. A. I. Cameron, ed., *The Warrender Papers* (Edinburgh, 1931), Scottish History Society, 3rd. S., vol. 18, 1: 146.

46. Phillips, 'Buchanan and the Sidney Circle', p. 34.

47. Mornay, *Opera Omnia*, 2: 740, quoted ibid., p. 37, n. 55.

48. ibid., p. 45.

49. Read, *Walsingham*, 2: 219; Phillips, 'Buchanan and the Sidney Circle', p. 44.

50. Phillips, 'Buchanan and the Sidney Circle', p. 45.

51. ibid., p. 52.

52. On Sidney and history see Sidney, *Apology for Poetry*, pp. 36–42; F. J. Levy, 'Sir Philip Sidney and the Idea of History', *Bibliothèque d'Humanisme et Renaissance*, vol. 26 (1964), pp. 608–17.

53. Sidney, *Works*, 3: 130–3.

54. Levy, 'Sidney and History', p. 617.

55. The basic discussion (on which I have drawn heavily) is Goldman, 'Sidney and Harington as opponents of Superstition'.

56. See Walker, 'Ways of Dealing with Atheists', and L. Whitney, 'Concerning Nature in *The Countesse of Pembrokes Arcadia*', *SP*, vol. 24 (1927), pp. 207–22. A major theme of *Arcadia* is that man's passion must be ruled by reason. cf. Sidney, *Works*, 1: 77, and the comments in M. Rose, 'Sidney's Womanish Man', *RES*, NS 15 (1964), pp. 353–63.

57. Goldman, 'Sidney and Harington as Opponents of Superstition', p. 528.

58. Moffett, *Nobilis*, p. 75.

59. Ringler, *Sidney's Poems*, pp. 177–8.

60. Bod. MS. Ashmole 356, no. 5, cited ibid., p. 470.

61. ibid., p. 469.

62. Sidney, *Works*, 1: 188.

63. Sidney, *Apology for Poetry*, p. 98.

64. Moffett, *Nobilis*, p. 75.

65. ibid.

66. ibid., p. 76.

67. See Trattner, 'God and Expansion in Elizabethan England'.

PART THREE

CHAPTER 9

1. See Strong and Van Dorsten, *Leicester's Triumph*, pp. 20 ff.

2. ibid., p. 21.

3. *HMC Rutland*, 1: 177.

4. See Strong and Van Dorsten, *Leicester's Triumph*, pp. 23–4.

5. ibid., p. 24.

6. Wallace, *Sidney*, p. 330.

7. ibid., p. 332, n. 4.

8. S. P. Dom., Elizabeth, quoted ibid., p. 331.

9. Greville, *Life*, p. 70.

10. ibid.

11. ibid.

12. Quoted in Wilson, *Sidney*, p. 229.

13. Greville commented that Sidney left the Court without suspicion and overshot 'his father-in-law in his own bow'. Greville, *Life*, p. 73. Mendoza at first reported Sidney had left to meet Don Antonio, though within a week he knew the real reason. *Cal. S. P. Span. 1580–1586*, pp. 548, 550.

14. Greville, *Life*, p. 73.

15. ibid., p. 74.

16. ibid.

17. ibid.

18. ibid., p. 75.

19. *HMC Rutland*, 1: 178.

20. Greville, *Life*, pp. 75.

21. ibid., p. 75–6.

22. *HMC Rutland*, 1: 178.

23. ibid.

24. Greville, *Life*, p. 76.

25. ibid., pp. 76–7.

26. The fleet had to put in at the Bayona Islands to complete the organisation and distribution of supplies. Wilson, *Sidney*, p. 233.

27. Greville, *Life*, p. 77.

28. Wilson, *Sidney*, p. 233.

29. The date of her birth has been assumed, erroneously, to be January 1584. Her baptism was recorded, however, in the parish register of St Olave's Hart Street as 15 November 1585, and since Scipio Gentili wrote a Latin ode on her birth also in 1585, it is certain she was born in that year. See Wallace, *Sidney*, pp. 333–4; Tenison, *Elizabethan England*, 6: 35.

30. Sidney, *Works*, 3: 147.

31. ibid.

32. Holland Correspondence, vol. 5, quoted Wallace, *Sidney*, p. 342.

33. Sidney, *Works*, 3: 148.

34. Holland Correspondence, vol. 6, quoted Wallace, *Sidney*, p. 345.

35. ibid.

36. Sidney, *Works*, 3: 148.

37. Holland Correspondence, vol. 5, quoted Wallace, *Sidney*, p. 345.

38. Sidney, *Works*, 3: 149.

39. ibid., 3: 153.

40. ibid., 3: 152–3.

41. ibid., 3: 148.

42. ibid., 3: 152.

43. ibid., 3: 148.

44. Wallace, *Sidney*, p. 347.

45. Quoted ibid.

46. Sidney, *Works*, 3: 149.

47. I have drawn extensively on Strong and Van Dorsten, *Leicester's Triumph*, for the following.

48. J. Bruce, ed., *Correspondence of Robert Dudley, Earl of Leycester* (London, 1844), Camden Soc., no. 27, p. 47.

49. ibid., p. 110.

50. ibid., p. 168.

51. ibid.

52. ibid., p. 169.

53. Ibid., p. 118.

54. Sidney, *Works*, 3: 162.

55. ibid., 3: 165.

56. ibid.

57. ibid., 3: 168.

58. ibid., 3: 169–70.

59. ibid., 3: 166–7.

60. Holland Correspondence, quoted in Wallace, *Sidney*, p. 354.

61. Sidney, *Works*, 3: 162–3.

62. Greville, *Life*, p. 125.

63. ibid., p. 29.

64. *Cal. S. P. Span. 1580–1586*, pp. 582, 585.

65. Sidney, *Works*, 3: 160.

66. ibid., 3: 161–2.

67. T. Lant, *Funeral of Sir Philip Sidney* (London, 1587), plate 1.

68. Wilson, *Sidney*, pp. 255–6.

69. Sidney, *Works*, 3: 172.

70. ibid., 3: 174.

71. Holland Correspondence, vol. 9, fol. 102, quoted Wallace, *Sidney*, p. 369.

72. Quoted ibid., pp. 366–7.

73. Bruce, *Correspondence of Robert Dudley*, pp. 284–5.

74. Stow. *Annals*, quoted Wallace, *Sidney*, p. 370.

75. Quoted ibid.

76. Bruce, *Correspondence of Robert Dudley*, p. 346.

77. Greville, *Life*, p. 121.

78. ibid., pp. 123–4.

79. ibid., pp. 124–5.

80. Sidney, *Works*, 3: 177.

81. ibid., 3: 178–9.

82. ibid., 3: 181.

83. ibid., 3: 179–80.

84. ibid., 3: 180.

85. ibid., 3: 182–3.

86. Stow, *Annals* (London, 1615), p. 736 quoted Wallace, *Sidney*, p. 377.

87. Greville, *Life*, p. 128. Moffett, *Nobilis*, p. 102, has a different story. He asserts that Sidney, hearing the news that Willoughby was surrounded by the Spaniards, went off in so great a hurry that he did not trouble with the armour for his left thigh.

88. cf. *HMC Hatfield*, 3: 189–90, where a description of the battle refers to it as a skirmish.

89. Stow, *Annals*, p. 736, quoted Wallace, *Sidney*, p. 379.

90. Greville, *Life*, pp. 129–30.

91. Quoted Wallace, *Sidney*, p. 379.

CHAPTER 10

1. G. F. Beltz, 'Memorials of the Last Achievement, Illness, and Death of Sir Philip Sidney', *Archaeologia*, vol. 28 (1840), p. 35.

2. Quoted Wallace, *Sidney*, p. 380.

3. Quoted ibid., p. 388.

4. Quoted ibid., p. 381.

5. ibid.

6. Bruce, *Correspondence of Robert Dudley*, p. 422.

7. Narrative of George Giffard in Zouch, *Sidney*, p. 269.

8. Greville, *Life*, p. 130.

9. ibid.

10. ibid., p. 131.

11. ibid., p. 132.

12. ibid., p. 138.

13. Sidney, *Works*, 3: 314.

14. ibid., 3: 315.

15. Greville, *Life*, p. 135.

16. ibid.

17. ibid., p. 137.

18. Printed in Zouch, *Sidney*, pp. 267 ff.

19. ibid., p. 269.

20. ibid., p. 270.

21. ibid.

22. ibid., p. 271.

23. ibid.

24. ibid.

25. ibid., p. 272.

26. Bruce, *Correspondence of Robert Dudley*, p. 429.

27. Greville, *Life*, p. 138.

28. Quoted Wilson, *Sidney*, p. 272. On this poem see Ringler, *Sidney's Poems*, p. 351.

29. Quoted Wilson, *Sidney*, p. 272.

30. Greville, *Life*, p. 133.

31. ibid., pp. 133-4.

32. ibid., p. 134.

33. Sidney, *Works*, 3: 183.

34. Beltz, 'Memorials of Sidney', p. 36.

35. Greville, *Life*, p. 139.

36. ibid., pp. 139-40.

37. Zouch, *Sidney*, p. 274.

38. ibid., p. 276.

39. *HMC Hatfield*, 3: 190-1; see also his letter to Walsingham, *Cal. S. P. Scot. 1509-1603*, 1: 536.

40. *HMC Hatfield*, 3: 189.

41. Collins, *Letters and Memorials of State*, 1: 393.

42. 'The Life and Death of Sir Philip Sidney', in *Countess of Pembroke's Arcadia* (London, 1655), sig. C 1.

43. *Mémoires et Correspondance de Duplessis-Mornay*, 3: 488-9; Holland Correspondence, vol. xi, fol. 5, printed Wallace, *Sidney*, p. 391.

44. P. Marchegay, ed., *Correspondance de Louise de Coligny* (Paris, 1887), p. 36,

45. *Francisci et Joannis Hotomanorum epistolae* (Amsterdam, 1700), p. 341.

46. BM MS. Burney 371, fol. 125, printed in Van Dorsten, *Poets, Patrons, and Professors*, p. 156.

47. Greville, *Life*, pp. 32-3.

48. *Cal. S. P. Span. 1580-1586*, p. 650 n.

49. Lant, *Funeral of Sidney*, plate 1.

50. Wilson, *Sidney*, p. 283.

51. Mornay, *Trewnesse of the Christian Religion*, dedication.

52. Quoted in Wallace, *Sidney*, p. 399.

53. *Hotomanorum epistolae*, p. 341.

54. John Carey in *Oxford Magazine*, 21 November 1963, p. 86.

55. Van Dorsten, *Poets, Patrons, and Professors*, p. 153.

56. A. L. Rowse and G. B. Harrison, *Queen Elizabeth and Her Subjects* (London, 1935), p. 46.

57. *Epitaph upon Sidney* in Spenser, *Works*, 3: 578.

INDEX